Actress
of a
Certain
Age

*My Twenty-Year Trail to
Overnight Success*

Jeff Hiller

Simon & Schuster

New York   Amsterdam/Antwerp   London
Toronto   Sydney/Melbourne   New Delhi

Simon & Schuster
1230 Avenue of the Americas
New York, NY 10020

Interior design by Ruth Lee-Mui

Manufactured in the United States of America

1   3   5   7   9   10   8   6   4   2

Library of Congress Cataloging-in-Publication Data is available.

ISBN 978-1-6680-3185-8
ISBN 978-1-6680-3187-2 (ebook)

For good parents everywhere. I'm so glad I had mine.

Contents

Actress
of a
Certain
Age

Girl Walks into a Bar

by RACHEL DRATCH[*]

Hello. Welcome to my memoir. My essay collection? My celebrity autobiography with a really loose definition of the word *celebrity*? Which one sounds the least pretentious and navel-gaze-y? Let's call it that.

You might be concerned that you are going to invest time in reading this book and it won't give you what you want. I want you to know that I have your back, because I am also a voracious reader of these types of books. I have read literally hundreds of books by actors about their lives.

For real. This is not an exaggeration. *Hundreds.*

Most of the books I have read are by actresses of a certain age. I am a middle-aged homosexual, after all, it's what we do. There is only so much fighting it before you just have to lean in and admit that you can't get enough of Candice Bergen talking about her life. And trust me, I cannot get enough. I have read not one but *two* full-length memoirs

---

*Rachel Dratch was thirty-three years old when she was cast on *Saturday Night Live*.

by Ms. Bergen. And she isn't the only actor whose multiple volumes I have consumed. I've also conquered two volumes each from Anjelica Huston, Brooke Shields, and Alan Cumming. I listened to Barbra Streisand's book—which is technically just one volume, but at forty-eight hours and fifteen minutes, it does a lot to illustrate my commitment to the genre.

I possess all sorts of intimate knowledge about these celebrities. For instance, did you know that Blanche made love to Benson? Yes! Rue McClanahan, who played Blanche on *The Golden Girls*, had an affair with Robert Guillaume, who played Benson on *Benson* (and on *Soap*, 'cause *Benson* was a spin-off). She rated his lovemaking skill a 10 and referred to him as "Mr. Guillaume"! This fact has absolutely nothing to do with my life or this book. Please don't expect me to have stories about sex with other actors on sitcoms. I'm just telling you this because I need to mention this sexy real-life crossover episode to as many people as possible.

You want to hear some other fun facts I have gleaned? Rosie Perez was fired from *Soul Train* for throwing a piece of chicken at Don Cornelius; Rita Moreno was on the cover of *Time* magazine before any movie role made her famous because she looked like a Latina Liz Taylor; and Blake Edwards referred to the genitalia of his wife, Julie Andrews, as a lilac bush.

I have read so many books that I know the tricks and pitfalls. I assure you that I am aware of the clichés in celebrity memoirs. Which is not to say I am necessarily going to *avoid* these clichés. I like some of them. One of my favorites is the Buried Importance cliché, where the celebrity mentions something as if it's an innocuous fact and then gives you the full details in a tone that suggests *Can you even believe that was what I was talking about? Yeah*. Here are a couple of extreme (and fictional) examples:

I received a script in the mail and read it. It was garbage, but what could I do? I needed the money and they were willing to pay. And so I agreed to be in a movie called . . . Titanic!

And:

I loved the play and knew it would be a huge hit once we opened on Broadway on March 12, 2020!

See? You think the movie is crap, but then it's one of the highest-grossing films of all time! You think the play will be a hit, but then it turns out it opened during a global pandemic. It's a fun cliché that I hope to employ at least once in this book.

Another one I love is the Body Electric cliché, which is when a celebrity addresses a random part of their body for which they are very well known. Jennifer Grey opens her book discussing her ever-changing nose. Kathleen Turner spends an entire chapter on her voice. Not her metaphorical voice—her literal vocal cords. And Linda Gray—wait, *what?* You don't know who Linda Gray is? Linda Gray played Sue Ellen on the hit prime-time soap *Dallas* in the 1980s. I guess that *is* the extent of her résumé. See? I told you I've read a *lot* of these books. Anyway, Linda Gray devotes a full chapter to her sexy legs and how they got her lots of jobs in commercials. So maybe I will devote a chapter to something on my body, like the space between my bottom teeth or how I don't have eyebrows.

Oh! A cliché I *will* use in almost every chapter is the You Have to Remember cliché. This is when you have to give the context of the time a story occurred in order to explain your actions in said story. It can be as innocuous as "You have to remember that in the nineties, there was no GPS system in anyone's car" or as dark as "You have to remember that in the nineties, sexual harassment was a normal part of life in Hollywood."

Now, let me tell you a cliché I will *not* employ. I promise not to do the Good Ol' Days cliché. There will be no romanticizing about how great my life was before I was popular enough to get a book deal. It is exceptionally common in celebrity memoirs for an actor to describe their big break after "years" of struggling. They describe the play that was a Broadway sensation, the film role that won them their first Oscar, or the TV show that made them a household name. "That was when it all changed," they say, meaning they were no longer a regular person but instead a celebrity plagued by the misery that is fame, riches, and career satisfaction. When I read these sentences, I get out my calculator to find out exactly how old they were when they got this break and compare it to the age I am when reading their book. The math equation is never consoling. *Years* in memoir time usually translates to *months* in actual human time. I feel no sympathy for the person describing how it was a "decade-long slog to success" when the decade they're talking about was from ages fifteen to twenty-five.

I will not spend time referring to my life before I was a full-time actor as "the good ol' days" because the good ol' days of struggling are romantic only when they are actually days rather than decades. Waiting tables while hustling for an acting job is not fun unless it's a *novelty*. I will never say I miss that time because (and I cannot stress this enough) I *do not* miss that time.

It is one thing to rest on your laurels as you age, but it is a very different thing to be searching for laurels when you are on the wrong side of forty. I will not spin a folksy yarn about my pre-TV-show days walking around New York City, eating at greasy spoons, and stuffing the daily papers in my shoes. (For the record, I never had to put newspapers in my shoes. In fact, print media was dying by the time I arrived in New York. I just really love Sondheim lyrics.)

I've heard only one star refuse to glamorize their pre-fame days and that star is Edie Falco. Edie gets it. Edie's my sister. (To be clear: I have never met Edie Falco, and she does not think of me as *her* sister. Or at all.) She was on *Ellen* once and spoke about being a waitress for a long time and how happy she was that she could describe herself as an actor rather than a struggling actor. I loved her for saying this. For putting it out there that it *sucks* to be someone with a dream who isn't living that dream. Ellen said something like "But isn't it great that you were a waiter? So that you know how hard it is to be a waiter?" but Edie wasn't having it. She said that awards were nice but not being a waiter anymore was better. When she said that, I hooted and pumped my fists! Probably because I was watching that episode of *The Ellen DeGeneres Show* while putting on a marinara-stained white shirt to wait tables at Olive Garden. I feel the same way today, though. Don't get me wrong, I really want to win an award (I'd place it on top of the toilet to keep me humble), but the truth is, I am just happy to be an actor who gets to act and who doesn't have to grate mounds of Parmesan onto someone's pasta in hopes of a large tip.

Also, I have health insurance now! Did you know that you have to earn a certain amount of money from acting to get health insurance from SAG-AFTRA, the TV and film actors' union? So if (when) you are out of work, you are not only stressed about not getting paid and not getting to do the thing you know you are meant to do but also petrified that you will get a sinus infection and CityMD will haunt you for ten years because you can't pay the bill for that Z-Pak they prescribed. And that isn't even pointing out the greatest irony—you get mental-health benefits only if you are working, but it's the not working that makes you depressed, so that's when you need the mental-health benefits! I feel like the proper thing for me to do would be to turn this book into a screed about the need for universal health care, but I have lots of humiliating stories about farting in auditions that need to be told, so that other book will have to wait.

I refuse to sigh wistfully about life before I got a TV show on HBO. Not to say that my life was horrible, but life is a lot easier when you have money and health insurance and don't live with roommates. This is a book about what it is like to be an actor who isn't famous. An actor who clawed, scraped, and fought their way to the lower-middle rung of the ladder. I will tell you stories about the humiliations of auditioning for jobs, the humiliations of networking for jobs, and the humiliations of the jobs I actually got. I will try to describe the dream I had (and have) of being a professional performer even though I started off as a way-too-gay little boy in 1980s Texas with zero connections to Hollywood and looks that can kindly be described as "unconventional." I will tell you about the hustle to live a dream even when the world tells you (repeatedly) that you are not destined for that dream. And I will also tell you three stories about assholes.

These are not stories about metaphorical assholes, like rude people. No. These are stories about anatomical assholes. The bussy. The stink wrinkle. The leather Cheerio. I have three stories about literal human buttholes and not one of them leads to sex, which is both impressive and a little embarrassing. These stories are my gift to you, dear reader. Three assholes are a traditional gift for honored guests in gay male culture, and I want to honor you.

I have read so many celebrity memoirs that I think I know the difference between the good stuff (famous people they knew before they were famous) and the boring stuff (stories about how their great-grandparents met). I will try to give you a Buried Importance cliché and a Body Electric cliché, and I will be saying "You have to remember" hundreds of times because a lot of my life happened before the internet existed.

I will not be giving you wistful memories of the great times I had temping before people felt the need to treat me with dignity. I mean, I will absolutely be sharing those pitiful stories because they are a fun read. I just won't wax nostalgic about them.

I hope the clichés are fun and even enlightening, because, after all, *cliché* is really just another word for *truth*. Thank you for reading this book; I hope you enjoy it and also the asshole stories.

Finding Me

by VIOLA DAVIS*

I would like to be vulnerable with you. Brené Brown told me that I should be. She did not tell me personally. What, you think I'm hanging out with self-help royalty? She told me via her books and podcasts. So let me be vulnerable and share something I have great shame about: I was born in 1975. It should be noted that it was December of 1975, so please consider that as you start doing the math in your head about my current age. Depending on the time of year, I am usually younger than you would expect. The problem is that no matter when you are reading this, 1975 was several decades ago, which means, like Roxie Hart in *Chicago*, I am older than I ever intended to be.

I know that aging is natural. I believe that we should respect the lines on people's faces and the experience and knowledge that comes with those lines. I know that aging is better than the alternative (though I have always thought that line about dying young and

---

*Viola Davis won a Tony award for *King Hedley II* when she was thirty-six years old. She was forty-three when *Doubt* was released.

leaving a good-looking corpse was offensive to those of us who were ugly teens). The fear of aging comes from our fear of mortality. Pema Chödrön told me that. Obviously not to my face, because, again, I am not hanging out with self-help royalty. I do not know the world's most famous Buddhist nun, but I've read her many books because I am very deep. Okay. I read *one* of her books and she said that thing about how the fear of aging is a fear of mortality and now I quote it all the time so I *sound* deep.

What Pema doesn't realize is that I do not *fear* aging. I am embarrassed by it. It is embarrassing for me to admit that I am the age that I am (though, again, December birthday, so subtract a year, please) because I have so few accomplishments to show for all those decades lived.

This feeling was especially pronounced when I turned forty. I thought I would have accomplished more in my life by that time. I imagined fame and riches, a huge family with adoring children running through my six-thousand-square-foot home and knocking over all the honorary degrees and awards I had accumulated. Instead, I was crossing my fingers that the improv class I was teaching wouldn't conflict with my audition to play Annoying Employee in a FedEx commercial. For the record, it did not, so I was able to go to the audition and not get the job. Whew!

I did not handle turning forty well. I had a straight-up, hack midlife crisis. I mean, I didn't buy a Corvette (not enough money), get a tattoo (not enough confidence), or have sex with a twenty-two-year-old (not enough patience), but I did look into getting a toupee. Guess what— a really good toupee costs ten to fifteen thousand dollars and requires maintenance every two to three weeks! Who knew? It was painful to realize I hadn't earned enough money in forty years to buy a wig to cover my rapidly thinning hair.

Now, some folks might be saying, "Hey, Jeff, forty isn't middle-aged! You can't have a midlife crisis at forty!" I have heard this before, and I appreciate this thought. Also, I am pretty sure I can predict that your age is over forty. I wish I could protect your feelings. I wish I could agree with you that forty isn't middle age, but I've done the math, and the facts are on my side.

When one doubles forty, the number is eighty. If you woke up one morning, groggily padded into your kitchen, and heard from your roommate or partner that an eighty-year-old celebrity had died, would you tilt your head to the heavens and scream, *"Why, God, why? They had so much more to live for!"* No. You would not. You would say, "Awwww, that's sad. Did you make coffee yet or . . ." And that is because eighty is considered a pretty good age to live to in our society, and half of eighty is forty, which is middle age.

I'm not telling you this to depress you; this was just the information swirling in my head on my fortieth birthday. If it makes you feel any better, there was a Japanese nun whose middle age was fifty-nine, but frankly, the idea of living to a hundred eighteen seems more like a punishment than a gift.

Anyway, back to my midlife crisis. I was halfway through life, and I had nothing to show for it. I kept googling *Actors who got a TV series after forty years old*. For the record: Lucille Ball, Estelle Getty, and Kathryn Joosten, President Bartlet's secretary on *The West Wing*. But of course, these comparisons aren't perfect. Lucy was a movie star before TV, Estelle did *Torch Song Trilogy* on Broadway before *Golden Girls*, and Kathryn Joosten was a psychiatric nurse who'd raised two sons as a single mother. At the time, I didn't even have pets. I owed money on my credit cards, and my greatest role to that point was in a parody musical based on *Silence of the Lambs*, playing the guy who throws cum on Clarice. I was tired of hustling every day and embarrassed that I didn't have any money, security, or respect in my industry.

I guess I should mention that there were other rough things happening in my life at that time. I had just returned to New York from Los Angeles. I moved out West thinking it was just location that was preventing me from landing a regular role on a TV show, but after four years in the TV-show-making capital of the world, I still hadn't secured a high-paying television gig. I had burned up my life savings living a bicoastal life (a life savings earned primarily from a series of Snickers commercials in which I played a hungry Pilgrim). I had spent the past four years in a long-distance relationship with the man who is now my husband, so I moved back full-time to be with him. I had to figure out how to live with him again, which was surprisingly difficult because the apartment felt like his instead of ours. I had to find friends in New York again since at that point, all my close friendships were with people in LA.

Oh, and also my mother was dying from pulmonary fibrosis and my father could no longer walk and had to go to an assisted-living facility, so I guess maybe that had something to do with my depression at the time, but honestly, who can say?

I had metaphorical pain in my heart and literal pain in my lower back. I began to self-medicate. My drug of choice was baked goods. Cookies, mainly, but I dabbled in cake sometimes and I had a harrowing few months when I discovered a shop less than two blocks from my apartment that sold banana pudding.

Why are rock stars with drug habits considered badass but people with an addiction to food are considered pitiful? Drugs are associated with "cool" people, like Keith Richards, Sid Vicious, and Jimi Hendrix. Who do those of us with food issues have to admire? Valerie Bertinelli? I think this double standard is because drug addictions are associated with men, and food addictions are associated with women. Yeah. I dropped the misogyny bomb. See? I told you I'm deep.

I know I present as male, but I can't imagine any of you are having a hard time comprehending that I know my way around a pecan pie. There is one story that encapsulates the totality of my food issues. My husband and I were flying home from Puerto Rico, where we had just spent a lovely week celebrating getting married. I guess you could call it a honeymoon, but our wedding wasn't a big deal, and it had happened a year before this trip. Plus we had been together for seven years before we tied the knot. In fact, the only reason we got married at all was that it had recently become legal, and I wanted half his money if he left me. But to raise the stakes of this story, my new husband, Neil, and I were flying back from our storybook romantic honeymoon in Puerto Rico.

Everything seemed normal until we hit a slight patch of turbulence. Then the cabin filled with smoke. You could only smell it at first, but soon a cloud was visible above us in the coach cabin. The woman in the row behind us shouted, *"Are we going to die? We are going to die!"* You know, the way you do when you want to keep people calm. Other than her shrieks, the plane was completely silent. A flight attendant sprinted down the aisle so fast that my hair blew in her backdraft. Not a great sign. We were setting up the tragic ending for the biopic of some famous person I assumed was sitting in first class. In the petrified stillness, Neil took my hand and looked into my eyes. He tenderly said to me, "Girl, if we are going down, I am so glad I am going down with you." It was the most romantic thing I had ever heard. I responded without even thinking—the words fell from my mouth: "I'm just glad I ate whatever I wanted to this week!"

It turned out the smoke was just from food burning, and we landed safely. Neil laughed about what I said, but I was personally devastated to discover that my true nature in a crisis is a *Cathy* cartoon. Ack, ack, ack!

That airplane story is bad, but it isn't my rock bottom. That happened one spring day in 2017. After teaching an improv class in Midtown, I went to a deli and bought a bag of Tate's chocolate chip cookies. Not the small pack with two cookies—the family-size bag. Two sleeves of eight cookies each. I consumed the entire bag in the subway on my commute home to the Lower East Side. I got out of the subway, went to a bodega, and bought a bag of Tate's Chipless Wonder cookies (a full-size bag again, and this felt like a coup because you don't find the Chipless Wonder cookies in bodegas that often). I consumed this entire bag on the way back to my apartment. Once I got to my apartment, I pressed the up button on the elevator but did not wait to get on it. Instead, I exited the back door of the building, went to yet another bodega (Never buy two bags from the same bodega. It's about dignity), and bought a bag of Tate's white chocolate and macadamia nut cookies (I know, a lot of folks don't like macadamia nuts, but for me, it's fun to guess if you are getting a nut or a piece of white chocolate just before you bite). I was able to get back to my building without consuming these cookies, but I'd be lying if I said I didn't open the bag in the elevator.

That was rock bottom. Quick tangent (I heard this amazing factoid from a friend of mine in a recovery program): When someone in AA has a not-particularly-dramatic rock-bottom story, they say they hit a . . . wait for it . . . *soft bottom!* I mean, isn't that a great term? Oh! I should have named this book *Soft Bottom!* What a missed opportunity.

Ironically, my three-bags-of-cookies rock bottom gave me a soft bottom. I felt sick for a week after that binge, and I decided I had to make a change in my life, a change that would help not only my food addiction but also my midlife depression in general. I knew exactly what I needed to do to become happy: I just had to lose a shit-ton of weight. That was it. This was not a subconscious thought. I said it out loud and defended it like it was my college thesis: "I'll be happy if I'm skinny!"

I know what you are thinking: *You should love your body, Jeff! Sam Smith does that now.* My millennial and Gen Z friends say this to me all the time: "Love your body, Jeff! It's the only one you've got!" I want to love my body. Trust me—I want to worship it and rub it with fine oils and take sexy Lizzo selfies where I'm drinking champagne directly from the bottle in a hot tub. I *want* to feel that way, but I do not. Millennials and Zoomers shout the importance of body positivity, but I am solidly Gen X, and we stick to old-fashioned body hating. I think it's because younger people had that Dove Real Beauty campaign at a formative age. All we had was *The Truth About Cats and Dogs.* That movie was great, but Janeane Garofalo was supposed to be the ugly one? No wonder we hate ourselves!

So all I had to do was lose somewhere between thirty and a hundred and eighty pounds and I would be happy. I wanted to lose enough weight that people would think I was sick or had a drug problem, then I would finally be lovable to the masses and that would allow me to love myself.

I had these two friends, a gay couple, who were quite thin but had become thinner and more muscular over the past year. When I ran into them on the street one day, I did that thing you do when you see someone who has had a body transformation that conforms to society's agreed-upon ideal: I felt hot hate toward them. Then I said out loud, "You two look great! Whatcha doin' to get those hot bodies?"

They told me they were doing a program that— the specifics didn't matter because I was already in before hearing any details whatsoever.

Basically, the program was like having a life coach, only instead of focusing on your career or mental-health goals, you focused on eating and exercise. It cost a lot of money and at the time I didn't have much, but I was sure it was the key to my happiness. They told me it was a yearlong commitment that began in June and ran to the following May. This was in March. I had three months to eat my face off, and then, come June, I would start this program and become thin (and therefore happy) forever.

June arrived. I downloaded the video tutorials. Some of them were led by a hot middle-aged guy who had a shockingly bushy soul patch under his bottom lip, others by a woman with the worst haircut I had ever seen. It looked like she'd taken a Halloween wig you'd buy to play Kate Gosselin and turned it to the side. No matter. I wasn't in this program to learn about styling. I was in it to get skinny.

They said, "This program is *not* a diet." (Pro tip: Every diet program says that.) He said this program was about finding a new relationship to food. (Pro tip: All diet programs say this too.) She said this program was not about losing weight; it was about living differently. (Do I need to give you the pro tip on this one? They all say this, but then they show you pictures of people living differently, and these people are all a lot skinnier than they were before they were in the program.)

The program gave you habits to focus on for two weeks at a time.

The first habit was ridiculous: It was simply to eat slowly. That was it. I could eat whatever I wanted, I just had to take an hour to do it. I remember thinking, *What a ridiculous thing to work on. How hard can it be?*

I couldn't do it! I tried to eat like a sloth. I would slowly raise the food to my mouth, chew it for several minutes, and dab my lips with a napkin between each bite, only to look up after finishing my meal and find it had taken me ninety seconds to eat.

As the year went on, the habits they introduced made more sense. Eat lean proteins. Incorporate more fruits and vegetables into your meals. But then somewhere near November, they started poking around in your brain trying to find out *why* you eat instead of telling you what to eat. The program taught me the word *Kummerspeck*, a German term that can be translated as "grief fat" or sometimes "grief bacon" and that refers to the weight acquired from emotional overeating. Germans also have *Frustessen,* which translates to "stressed eating" or "frustrated eating." These crazy Germans. They have a word for everything and also pornography with poop in it. What a culture!

The definition of *grief bacon* came with a drawing of an animated animal eating a slice of pizza while crying. I say *animal* rather than the specific creature, because it was more of a representational figure than a realistic one. I wanna say it was a kangaroo, maybe? It was just a big circle with tiny arms and really big ears. Anyway, the circle critter was eating pizza and crying and I knew right away that the artist was a skinny person who knew absolutely zilch about emotional overeating. Pizza *stops* the tears, ya idiot!

The concept of emotional overeating froze me in my tracks. I wasn't unhappy because I was fat—I was fat because I was unhappy.

I know. I know! This is not rocket science. This is a lesson from a middling episode of *Oprah*. I have no excuse for not recognizing this basic fact other than to say I knew it but I didn't feel it. ·

It should be noted that this is my personal story. There are lots of fat people out there who are very happy, so don't go twisting my words around and saying all big folks are physically and mentally unhealthy!

I saw *Lizzo's Watch Out for the Big Grrrls* and listened to *Maintenance Phase*. I read Roxane Gay, Lindy West, and Jes M. Baker, and I suggest you do too. I am learning to like myself regardless of my body's size, but at this specific depressing time in my life, I was leaning hard on food in a way that wasn't emotionally or physically healthy for me, so let's stop hating on fat people, please.

You would think that once I realized that I was emotionally over-eating, I would stop doing it, but I didn't. In fact, I still occasionally shove down feelings with a pint of chocolate chip cookie dough ice cream. Sometimes we do things we shouldn't do even though we know we shouldn't do them. It's just like my obsession with celebrity memoirs. Take Brooke Shields. She was engaged to Liam Neeson. He proposed to her and then told her he had to go to LA for a little bit and then—*he never spoke to her again!*

When I read that in her (second) book, I *gasped*! Brooke learned that she shouldn't be with Neeson, who was a heavy drinker and unable to commit. Men with addictions were bad for her—that was the takeaway—and yet she ended up marrying Andre Agassi, who was smoking meth in their powder room! She eventually married Chris Henchy, so it all worked out, but there was a steep learning curve there for Brooke. I am no different from America's Sweetheart.

It's hard for us to learn, right?

No, I'm sorry, that wasn't rhetorical—I'm actually asking. Is it hard for everyone else to learn? It was clear I needed to do a lot more than lose weight to be happy. I decided to stop chasing physical beauty and instead chase mental health.

I started with religion.

Every. Single. Sunday. I would go to my phone and download the *Super Soul Sunday* podcast. I know some people don't like Oprah, but . . . why? Often, the same people who say things like "Sure, this director rapes people, but he makes classic movies!" turn to Oprah and say, "Who the hell does she think she is, trying to make people's lives better?" Oprah could have pulled a Jerry Springer and done shows about ladies who lie in vats of tuna while they sleep with their brother, but she decided to help people find their spirit. And, yes, I know— Dr. Oz and Dr. Phil. Fair. I will give you that they suck, but I would say that someone who makes a mistake while trying to do good doesn't deserve the hate she gets. So, please, don't yell at me about Oprah. I promise not to come after your religion if you don't come after mine.

The *Super Soul Sunday* podcast often has interviews with people who have written self-help books. So I started buying *a lot* of self-help books. In addition to Brené Brown and Pema Chödrön, I have read Gary Zukav, Cheryl Strayed, and Michael Pollan, and I even did a ten-week podcast course with Eckhart Tolle and Oprah herself. I might not hang out with self-help royalty, but it doesn't stop me from dropping their names like I do.

These books instruct you to do certain things to find happiness in your life. The advice is often similar. First, they tell you to meditate. They *all* tell you to meditate. They are *hot* for meditation. So I downloaded six different meditation apps (and this is not an exaggeration; I went back and looked) so I could do the free one-week trial and not have to pay the monthly fee. They all said basically the same thing: "Focus on the breath." Though sometimes they said it with a British accent.

Somewhere around when I was creating a fake email for a second weeklong trial of *Ten Percent Happier*, I realized I had to make a more serious commitment to my meditation practice. I researched what type of meditation Oprah did. It turned out she was a fan of Transcendental Meditation.

I balked at first. Transcendental Meditation sounded like something that would be made fun of on *Laugh-In*, a sort of 1960s fad where some cult leader who wore too much paisley tricked you into giving him money in exchange for a meaningless mantra. I continued my online research, however, and discovered that both David Lynch and Jerry Seinfeld practiced TM. That was a bonkers combination of celebrities, like if *Watch What Happens Live* had a baby with *The Graham Norton*

Show. I decided to take in-person classes to learn about Transcendental Meditation. If it was good enough for the makers of *Eraserhead* and *Bee Movie,* surely it was good enough for me.

I paid a *lot* of money to learn how to properly meditate in a transcendental way. There was a weeklong training session where they give you a personal mantra. Between the first and second day, I forgot my mantra. I thought that was hilarious and told my husband the story, practically begging him to tell me how unique and interesting I was. He said, "That was a plot point in a Woody Allen movie." I went back to class and my teacher said, "Everyone forgets their mantra." Perhaps meditation could help me work through the realization that I was basic?

I began a twice-daily practice in 2017. It was difficult to find a place in the city to do my afternoon meditations. I tried doing it on a bench in Central Park, but with my eyes closed, I kept worrying that someone would steal my bag or a rat would crawl up my leg. I once did it in a storage room at the Upright Citizens Brigade training center. An intern walked in and acted as if he'd caught me masturbating. "I'm so sorry!" he shouted. "I didn't know you were here! Keep doing whatever you were doing!" And then he scurried away, covering his eyes, as I yelled, "It isn't what it looks like!"

When I told the story to my nebbishy Transcendental Meditation instructor, he said, "The next time that happens, put up your hand and authoritatively declare, 'I'm meditating,' so he will leave." Honestly, that just seems like the worst thing to do. Not only is it aggro, but it's patronizing—you're implying that you are more enlightened than the other person 'cause you close your eyes in a dark room for twenty minutes twice a day. I ended up meditating in the morning before I left and then right before bed. Best to keep it close to home.

These self-help books also tell you to get out and walk. "Move your body to change a thought." One article in the *New York Times* stated that if you sit too long, you could get "dead butt syndrome." Obviously I took a screenshot of that title, but the article also said that despite its silly name, it was a serious condition that could cause chronic pain and was as bad for you as smoking. It seemed dramatic, but I love drama, so I got a Fitbit and began a daily obsession with getting as many steps in as possible. I would go to Whole Foods on Fourteenth Street even though I had to pass a Whole Foods on Houston to get there. I entered competitions with people who had Fitbits. I scoffed at their measly fifty-five thousand steps a week! Not out loud, of course—I am afraid of conflict—but internally, I knew I was superior because I got twenty thousand steps a *day*. Fifty-five thousand steps a week? Poor bastards.

Another thing all the self-help books tell you to do is to make a gratitude journal. Boo! I hated this one. I found it so grating to do, especially when I was depressed. *I'm sad! I am not grateful for anything!* I always ended up writing something like *I'm grateful for air . . . but not when it stinks.* My mom made up a song about gratitude that she used to sing to my nephew. It didn't really have a tune, but it rhymed. The lyrics were "An attitude of gratitude will get you through the day!" I hated that song. Just let the kid feel the way he wants to feel, for crap's sake. I stopped doing the gratitude journal after less than a week.

Once I had meditation and walking down, I decided to take my self-help journey a step further. The books didn't really talk much about this, but I knew the best thing to do for myself was to get into one-on-one talk therapy. I started seeing a therapist named Sandy. I loved her. We worked at identifying the issues that caused me to repeat unhealthy behaviors and on self-esteem, impostor syndrome, and allowing myself to take up space. Those were all worthy things to focus on, and Sandy was incredibly helpful, but that's not what I want to tell you about her. She lived for a very long time in New Jersey, and for several years after the hurricane, she passed a large sign on her commute home that said HAS YOUR LIFE BEEN RUINED BY SANDY? Can you imagine? I mean, that must be so much more complicated for a therapist to see.

Once I was in therapy, I also started a podcast with my friend Jenn Harris. We wanted a place to discuss how difficult it was to be actors who had been working for twenty years but still occasionally had to take day jobs making spreadsheets. It was called *Touché* because we often said "Touché!" when the other made a good point. Okay, that isn't entirely true. We originally wanted to name the podcast after a term that Broadway dancers use, a phrase that means they are worn out after a two-show day (a day with both a matinee and an evening performance). It felt like the perfect name thematically because we were exhausted after a long career. The only problem was that the phrase was rather untoward. You see, when dancers have had a long day of time-stepping on the boards, they say they have "two-show pussy," a reference to the sweat accumulated in a certain part of the anatomy. It is important to note that the use of this phrase is not limited to cisgendered female performers. In fact, you might be surprised to learn that gay male dancers use it more than female dancers. (Oh, no one is at all surprised?) Jenn and I started recording the podcast with that title, but neither of us had the, you know, vulva to stick with it, so we changed it to *Touché*.

You might be thinking, *How is a podcast a form of self-growth? Doesn't every actor and their dog have a podcast?* Good question. This was a podcast where we talked with other actors about how difficult it is to want to perform when no one will let you. The podcast became a sort of virtual group therapy that we unsuccessfully tried to monetize. The answer to your second question is yes. Every actor and their dog has a podcast.

I was addressing my feelings of powerlessness. Through therapy, meditation, self-help books, and podcasting, I came to the conclusion that losing weight wasn't what I needed to do to be happy. What I needed to do was pack it in and quit acting. I was forty-five years old. An acting career was not in the cards for me. I was too old for it to suddenly happen now. There is no such thing as a middle-aged ingénue. I needed to make money more consistently. I wanted to have control over my schedule—I had taken only two vacations in twelve years for fear an audition might come up while I was gone. Those two vacations were paid for by my parents.

The responsible thing to do was find a new career. I started looking into grad school. Maybe a master's in public health? I'd worked in HIV prevention after college and sort of liked it. Maybe I could do that instead of acting? You get to wear a lab coat and a badge, so I could feel like I was a less sexy version of the doctors on *Grey's Anatomy*.

I also explored teaching. There was a master's program that would pay you while you got your degree if you taught in a New York City school for five years after you graduated. They say that those who can't do, teach. So maybe I could teach acting to kids and sit backward in a chair like Michelle Pfeiffer in *Dangerous Minds*?

I heard you could get twenty-five dollars an hour plus tips taking people on tours around the Broadway theaters if you had ever been in a Broadway show. I had! Once. So I researched what it would take to become a licensed tour guide in the city of New York. If I did that, I could gain a following, and then film director Bennett Miller could make a black-and-white documentary about my whimsical mind!

I had just finished playing a minion to the villain in *Hercules* Off-Broadway. I had made a little over a thousand dollars a week playing a character named Panic. I'd thought, *A thousand a week! That's a ton of money!* But then I realized that if the job lasted for a full year, I would make only $52,000, which didn't feel like enough to live in New York City. And anyway, the job lasted for only four weeks. This felt like the universe telling me to "end the panic" and get a real job. Also, I was *in* a financial panic, as my bank account had just enough to cover two months of rent, assuming I did not buy nonnecessities like clothing and food. That character's name offers a lot of depressing wordplay when you're in the throes of a midlife crisis.

I needed money quick, and now that I no longer had to keep my days free on the off chance an audition might come up, I took a temp job at an international nonprofit with an office in Midtown in the fall of 2019. When I got the job, my supervisor asked me if I knew Excel and I said, "Oh, totally," and then I spent two harrowing weeks constantly googling *How to make numbers add in Excel*. During my second week, I got an email from an acquaintance, cabaret chanteuse Bridget Everett.

She had a pilot at HBO and she thought I might be right for a role in it and would I mind putting myself on tape? She apologized for the fact that the budget was small, so it wouldn't pay a lot. I was currently crapping out spreadsheets for sixteen dollars an hour.

I had checked my personal email as a respite to calm my nerves from this stressful job. The agency dealt with international aid, and I had just been told to get someone a visa to travel to Afghanistan. This felt outside my skill set, and my face must have said that because my supervisor told me she would handle the visa application and then she sighed in a way that conveyed *I have to do everything myself!* In this particular instance, she did.

Her enabling allowed me to start reading the script right there on my temp job's desktop computer. The script had just been sent to me along with instructions to put my audition on video and send it in. The show was about a woman in her forties who felt as if life had passed her by (*Girl! Same.*) The character I was auditioning for—Joel—was active in his church (I had been a theology major), loved music (I sing), and idolized the character Bridget was playing (I idolize Bridget! I've been going to her cabaret shows for years). The character was gay (a prerequisite for any role I play, judging by my IMDb page), middle-aged, and awkward. He was just like me except he loved himself!

The script was hilarious but also nuanced. There was a scene where Joel tries to tell Sam about an emotional essay he read at work, can't get it out, starts crying, realizes how silly it is that he's crying, and laughs at himself while continuing to sob. Nobody writes characters that real and specific, or if they do, they don't let nonfamous people play them. Paul Thureen and Hannah Bos's writing was brilliant, and I knew I could play the hell out of it! I mean, that scene was cut from the pilot that aired, so I guess eventually the writers thought it was not good writing, or maybe I just didn't play the hell out of it.

There was one scene that made me tear up in the middle of my temp job, right under the fluorescent lights and dropped ceiling: Sam and Joel sing together. I realized that if I got this job, I would get to sing a duet with Bridget Everett—*on television* (or streaming, depending on where you watch)! I looked at the lyrics and could practically hear the universe sigh dramatically and roll its eyes because the song was the Peter Gabriel and Kate Bush duet "Don't Give Up." It was almost *too* on the nose, but I'm often dense, so I appreciated the lack of subtlety.

So anyway, I got that job and now I am completely happy, and nothing is wrong in my life.

I'm obviously joking, but I do have a point to make. I told myself I was giving up acting. I half-heartedly googled how to go to grad school (I googled more about how to highlight rows in Excel), but the truth was that I never was going to give up. If I were going to give up, I would have called my agent and told her that I would no longer be auditioning. I would have told my husband we needed to move out of the city to a place we could afford. I would have cleaned out all the nerd drag that I keep in my closet because I only audition for characters who dress poorly. I didn't do any of that. Performing is my greatest joy. If I were going to give it up, I would have done it before I spent twenty years of my life auditioning for obviously uninterested casting directors.

I'd had to do years of therapy and meditation and read multiple books about manifesting your best life to tell myself I had the *option* to give up. I think I needed to feel a little bit of control. I *could* say no to this dream. Not that I ever would, but I *could*.

That's why *Somebody Somewhere* is so special. It is a show about hope. When I told myself that acting was a dead-end street, I didn't take concrete steps toward quitting because deep down, I still had hope that I could make a living doing the thing I loved. I could find success in a way that *I* wanted to define it. I could be like Kathryn Joosten and Estelle Getty, or I could find joy in a day job and still perform for free at night. I was allowed to define my own success.

Knowing I could quit this poker game called acting gave me a sense of control I needed in my life. Even if I hadn't gotten the audition for *Somebody Somewhere*, I would have auditioned for the next thing that came up, because while logic said it was time to let go of the dream, my heart never could. That said, I'm *so* glad the next audition was for *Somebody Somewhere* because it is the best job I've ever had and also because starting this book with a job that you've seen makes for a more dramatic ending to this chapter.

Stories I Only Tell My Friends

by ROB LOWE*

L et's lighten the mood, shall we? Would you like to hear a humiliating story about my acting career? Good! I've got a lot of them.
One of my biggest goals when I moved to Los Angeles in 2011
was to be a regular on a TV show. It had been my dream from childhood, though as a kid, I'd seen myself in a family sitcom where I played
a li'l scamp in a house with only three walls (better for the camera to
see inside). My character would have an uncle or a butler or a neighbor
whom I would terrorize with my impish antics. I had aged out of that
character, but becoming a regular on a TV show was still my biggest
dream.

My second year in Los Angeles, I booked a pilot presentation. You
probably know that a pilot is just the first episode of a television series.

---

*Rob Lowe was fifteen years old when he booked a sitcom on ABC but nineteen years old
when he became famous for *The Outsiders*.

A network will order pilots from maybe a hundred writers and then choose twenty or so to film. For each pilot, a director is hired and actors are cast. Sets are built, costumes are sewn, props are bought, and the episode is filmed, and most of the time the pilot isn't picked up by the network, and all the effort that went into creating an entire world is never seen by anyone.

It is incredibly difficult to become a TV star on a series. First you need an agent to send you out on a pilot audition, then casting must call you back for another audition, aptly termed a *callback*. Then there's often a meeting (which is just a third audition) with the creator of the show and the director of the pilot, and then, if you're really being considered for the role, you make it to the final audition, which is called a *test*. I guess it comes from the term *screen test*, but you've been on camera for all the previous auditions, so it feels more like a test of your will. Before you go into this last audition, you sit in a waiting room *with your competition*! Someone who you hope is the poor man's version of you but who is usually a famous person, which makes you realize that you are the poor man's version of him. While you sit next to your famous competition, you are given a contract. This is not a contract that means you've gotten the job; it is a contract that your agent has spent days negotiating and calling you about frequently. You have learned how much you are going to make *if* you get this job. You sign this contract and dream of making tens of thousands of dollars per episode! And then you have to audition. Again.

The test is usually in a room with several rows of chairs filled with comedy executives from the network. You audition. They do not laugh. You feel like a loser. You leave the audition, and on the way to the parking lot, you get a call from your agent telling you whether or not you got the role. (Usually, I didn't get the role.) On the rare occasions that one does get the part, the process continues! You have an exciting month of fittings and meetings with the writers, and you take publicity stills and have cast dinners, and then you film the actual pilot! You work hard on it and you imagine playing this character for the next seven to ten years. He is part of you. You love him. Then it is over. You wait around for three months, not sure if you should say yes to this audition for an Off-Broadway musical because you will probably soon be in LA ·driving onto the Warner Brothers lot with a Starbucks. You'll be able to afford Starbucks! Finally, the network announces its fall lineup, and nine times out of ten, your show isn't picked. You call your agent to ask if you can still audition for that Off-Broadway musical, but it turns out that role has been filled by the person you beat out for the pilot.

That is what it is like for an actor to book a pilot, but you might have noticed that I didn't say, "My second year in Los Angeles, I booked a pilot." I said, "My second year in Los Angeles, I booked a pilot *presentation*." A pilot presentation is when a network exec looks at a pilot script and says, "I don't know, I *guess* this is okay?" A typical pilot might cost a million dollars to film, but with a pilot presentation, the network spends a small amount of money to make one section of the pilot script. For shooting a pilot on ABC, you might get paid forty thousand dollars. For a pilot presentation, you will get three hundred dollars a day. As you can see, when I booked this pilot presentation, the stakes could not have been lower.

The network producing this pilot was Logo—the LGBTQ network! According to the internet, the network still exists. I honestly thought it had perished. It primarily showed reruns of *Melrose Place*, but a few years earlier, it had found a hit in *Drag Race*. Now Logo wanted to make some original content, presumably to air on the nights that *Drag Race* wasn't on.

Did execs at the queer network go to the many queer writers and creators working in the TV landscape and try to lure them with lucrative contracts and creative freedom? Did they search out new stories from queer voices that had historically been underrepresented? Did they take a chance on a young, original queer voice coming up in stand-up?

No. That is not what they did. At least not on this particular show. They hired two cisgendered straight white men who had a pilot about a beautiful woman and said, "We'll pay you a piece of chicken if you make this show gay." And the dudes said, "Thanks for the chicken!"

The show was originally about a young woman named Samantha who works at a day spa, but they changed it to a young gay man named Sam who works at a day spa. They added an authentic gay voice by erasing -antha. I was cast as Sam! I would be a gay guy who was beautiful but didn't know it. Sam was secretly having an affair with a famous married man.

When the producers called my agent to tell him I got the role, they were very up front. They said, "As part of this role, Jeff will be *required* to kiss another man. Do *not* let him take this role if he won't kiss him. He is *required* to do it! If he won't do it, we will move to the next actor on the list!"

My agent took a deep breath and said, "I'm pretty sure he'll do it."

The night before we shot, I got a call from the assistant director telling me where to go and what time to be there. Then after a pause he said, "And just so you know, you will be kissing another man tomorrow in the first scene. Do *not* show up and expect to get out of it. You are *required* to kiss another man."

I took a deep breath, steeled myself, and declared bravely, "I'll do it."

I showed up on set and was asked to sign a contract. I did, and the producer took it from me and almost yelled, "You *signed* the contract! You have to kiss the guy now!"

"Don't worry," I said. "I'm willing. I've even been practicing the kiss with my boyfriend."

I kissed the guy. I was commended for my bravery. By the way, the other guy was straight, terrified, and smelled of cigarettes and stress. We moved on.

In the next scene, my character was doing laser hair removal on a client and oversharing about his new boyfriend. The joke of the scene was that my character was causing this client pain but was too self-centered to care because he wanted to brag about being in love. It was a fine scene, I guess, but the director wanted to spice it up.

He pulled me aside, chuckled to himself, and said, "We're gonna try something crazy. We think"—*giggle-giggle*—"it would be funny if"—*giggle-giggle*—"you're doing laser hair removal on the guy's"—*full guffaws*—"on the guy's *butthole!*"

Oh, yay! It's already time for asshole story number 1!

I asked the director the only question I could think to ask. "So I'll be just staring at another actor's butthole?"

Suddenly the giggles disappeared, and the director became serious. "He'll be wearing a modesty pouch," he said indignantly.

Allow me to explain. A modesty pouch is a cock sock. It's just a little nylon sack that you put over your, well, sack. And also your shaft. It is useful if an actor has a scene where he wants the audience to see his butt but doesn't want the crew to see his junk. It is less useful if an actor is on all fours on an exam table with his cheeks spread and his hole blinking at the camera lens like it's *I Dream of Jeannie* granting a wish.

The problem was that Logo couldn't show hole. Which was a shame. Maybe we would still be talking about Logo if they could. The director needed something to hide the other actor's hole from the camera.

He used my head.

Perhaps the best way to describe it is with the analogy of a solar eclipse. The other actor's hole was the sun, the camera was the Earth, and my head was the moon, eclipsing the butt sun. My nose was directly in front of the anus. I had to be that close to ensure that I looked like I was performing laser hair removal while also not revealing his most precious flower. I was millimeters away from this young man's butthole, taint, and sheathed balls for the entire time we shot this scene.

We shot this scene for four and a half hours.

The young actor playing the hole was very handsome and very clean (bless). Still, I couldn't help thinking this was asking a lot of an actor who, even if this show went on to become a series and took him with it, would be a guest star on one episode. And—You Have to Remember cliché alert—this was a time before intimacy coordinators were hired to make actors comfortable when performing vulnerable scenes. He could have used one, and frankly, so could I. I wasn't sure where to put my hand to steady myself so I wouldn't bop him with my nose and accidentally toss his salad. I mean, *three* warnings about the gay kiss and nary a whisper of a real live human doo-doo hole?!

You might be thinking, *Hey! I thought gay guys liked hole.* Sure they do, but on their terms.

I walked with the young man back to our *shared* dressing room (see the low-stakes comment earlier), and we spoke as we changed clothes. Or while I changed my clothes and he put his on. We laughed about how strange the day had been. I was worried this was traumatizing for him, but he just sweetly shrugged. I liked him and his indomitable spirit.

Then he said one of the saddest things I had ever heard: "The things you do for fifty bucks!"

If you are a young actor, please learn from this story. If anyone asks you to expose your anus, demand more than fifty dollars. You are worth it.

Little Girl Lost

As you know by now, I read a lot of celebrity memoirs, and I know the part where the celebrity talks about their childhood is often the part you must slog through. Julianna Margulies spent more time talking about her bohemian childhood in France than about her feuds with costars on *The Good Wife*. So I will share only the parts that are formative to my development. I'll make this quick and will respect your decision if you skip ahead.

Here is what you need to know about my childhood. I was bullied. I could tell you a lot about my parents, who were very loving and provided a safe, middle-class home for me. I could tell you about how they laid a foundation of being compassionate and practical and how the former outweighed the latter. I could tell you about my sister and how as a kid she did a couple of mean things to me, like giving me a jalapeño but telling me it was a pickle and then pretending there was no water in

*Drew Barrymore was six years old when she was cast in *E.T.*

our house. I could tell you that those silly pranks didn't affect the close relationship we have today.

I could tell you all these things, which are true, but the only real fact from my childhood that you need to know is that the children of San Antonio, Texas, hated my guts. This wasn't some sort of goofy sitcom kind of bullying where they called me a clever nickname like "Gir-*eff*" because I was tall and as awkward as a giraffe. This was cruel bullying. The only nickname I had growing up was "faggot." Sorry if that word feels too harsh to read in a book. When you are called that every day for the first thirty years of your life, it sort of dulls the senses.

High school was bad, elementary school sucked, but the worst part of not just my childhood but my entire life was junior high. From the ages of eleven to fifteen, I was bullied mercilessly. I was taunted both verbally and physically. I ate lunch alone in the library and held my pee all day because the cafeteria and the boys' room were lawless places where other children delighted in being cruel to me.

I once saw an internet challenge that said to look up your junior-high bully online and compare how your lives had turned out. I was so confused. I didn't have the time to look up every single boy who'd attended my middle school plus a few of the girls. There hadn't been many female bullies, but a few did shatter that glass ceiling. And then they'd held the shards to my throat.

I don't know why so many kids picked on me.

Just kidding! It was because I was an obvious homosexual who didn't conform to the gender roles set by society and strictly adhered to in Texas in the 1980s. This is retrospective knowledge. At the time, I didn't understand why I was singled out.

I had zero friends. This is not an exaggeration. When I walked the halls, I tried to keep my eyes on the ground so no one would hit me, but they often did anyway, which I never saw coming because my eyes were focused on the ground. I don't remember a single teacher defending me, but I do remember a couple of them laughing when other kids called me Lard Ass, Faggot, and Lard-Ass Faggot.

I know it doesn't make intuitive sense that I was very tall and very large and also very picked on. I'm not sure I can explain it either. I was over six feet by the time I was in sixth grade and roughly two hundred pounds. It was not two hundred pounds of muscle, though. I was a fat kid. I was also sloppy and girlish, and this is the part that is difficult to explain—it seemed like other kids just felt I *should* be bullied. It was an attitude. A je ne sais quoi that said *Take this piece of shit down!* I had a gay lisp (an even bigger one than I do now, if you can imagine); I slumped my shoulders; I had a nervous and girlish giggle. Maybe my size was the breaking point because I had been given this natural gift and yet I didn't take advantage of it by playing sports or stealing kids' lunch money? It was a slap in the face to all of those tiny bullies.

I had this one rat-faced bully named Josh. I know I shouldn't make fun of someone's appearance, but in this case, *rat-face* is factual. He had beady little eyes and big nostrils that screamed *I wanna carry a piece of pizza up the subway stairs.* He was vicious even though he was a foot shorter than me. He probably had insecurities about that. Maybe he felt that beating me up would make him equal to his peers. Maybe others made fun of him for being scrawny, and this was his way of proving he was dominant . . . Wait. Am I feeling sympathy for one of my bullies? Damn it.

One day in gym class, I found myself alone with Josh on the tennis court. He started kicking me in the shins, 'cause that's how you hurt someone who is a foot taller than you. I'm not sure if I was subconsciously practicing nonviolence or if I just didn't know where to start when it came to fighting back physically, but I rarely ever did. On this day, however, I finally found the courage to clap back with my words.

"Why do you always do this to me?" I weakly asked. As clapbacks go, it was not all that harsh. What can I tell you? I'm not Cardi B.

Josh looked at me and uttered a haunting sentence: "Because you carry your books like a girl."

At that moment, I had an intense realization of clarity. I *did* carry my books like a girl. I carried them against my chest, clasping them with both hands over the boobs I had developed from eating my eighth-grade feelings. Every other boy, however, carried his books with only one arm on the side of his body, down by his hips.

Why did I carry my books differently than all the other boys? I think I liked having my books up to my chest because Patty Simcox carried her books like that in the movie *Grease*. She held them tight and swung her body so that her ponytail moved like a pendulum as she passed. I realize now that Patty Simcox was an unorthodox choice for a pop-culture hero. She was the preppy, frigid, goody-two-shoes-without-even-a-leather-pants-redemptive-makeover character that most people do not remember from the film. So maybe the way I held my books wasn't the only reason kids were picking on me, but again, this is in retrospect.

The knowledge that I carried my books incorrectly felt empowering. I could change myself and stop the bullying! That afternoon I switched to carrying my books on my hip. It wasn't easy. I had to balance four spiral notebooks, four textbooks, and a generic Trapper Keeper. I kept all my books with me to avoid going to my locker because the guy with the locker above mine would shout "Bruise" and punch me on my arm. It often did produce a bruise. It was especially painful when he punched in the same spot two days in a row, so I tried to visit my locker only before lunch, when I knew he wouldn't be there.

I managed to get everything balanced on my hip as I walked through the halls of Eisenhower Middle School. This would fix it. Now I would find friends and be loved!

I think we all know where this is going. It wasn't just the books. It was the giggles. It was the way I shrieked things like "*Designing Women* is on tonight!" It was the tilting of the head when I saw pets and babies, followed by an "Awwwww, *cuuuuute*." It was all of that and a million other things that made me stand out like a pride flag in Alabama. The bullying continued.

I tried to keep it from my family because it's embarrassing to admit you're a pariah. My mom was onto me, though. Shoot. I know I told you I was only going to talk about how I was bullied, but I guess I have to tell you a little about my mom too. I know, I know. No one wants to read celeb memoirs to find out about the celebrity's mom. Diane Keaton wrote an entire book about her mom, and I kept waiting for some deep *Baby Boom* cuts, but she barely even mentioned *Annie Hall*! So I will keep this brief, but I have to explain some things about my mom, and if you want to skip ahead, I totally understand.

Mary Hiller was a lady who really loved being a parent and grandparent. It was her passion. To give you an idea of how seriously she took it, let me tell you about my birth. At almost thirty-two years old, she was the oldest woman on the maternity floor and had the largest baby. I was nine pounds, eight ounces at birth, but I carried it well. She was the only mother who didn't take drugs during labor and delivery, which is saying a lot because I have a very large head. And this was in 1975 (but it was December)! I'm not telling you this to shade mothers in labor who use drugs—I'd take an epidural right now and I'm not even pregnant (that I know of). I'm just trying to show you that my mom was *so* into being a mother that she researched natural childbirth in the 1970s, long before Ricki Lake was posting videos of her home birth in a hot tub. My mom took the role of keeping her kids safe seriously enough to endure great physical pain.

Back to the bullying—oh, crap. I have to tell you one more thing about my mom. Again, if you want to skip ahead, just shoot right to the next chapter. In addition to being very dedicated to her children, she was also a perfectionist. I'll be honest with you, the perfectionist thing was often a drag. You'd clean your room to what you thought was an acceptable standard and she'd be all "Really?" It was just the way she was. She did *everything* to the best of her ability. It is also the way my sister is and my father is. I'm the only one in the family willing to hand in an essay that is the two-hundred-word equivalent of a shrug emoji.

Let me give you an example of my mother's commitment to getting it right. She grew up quite poor, one of six kids, and she was female, so she didn't go to college until the younger of her two kids (me) was in first grade. She started college when she was thirty-seven years old. She told me that she did it so she could get a good-paying job and bank her earnings for my and my sister's college tuition while our family lived off my dad's earnings. She said, "I looked up the degree most likely to make a good salary and it was accounting, so that's why I chose it, but I don't like it at all. I'm not even good at it."

She graduated summa cum laude from the University of Texas at San Antonio, so I think she was maybe better at it than she let on. In fact, she got only one B and that was because she missed a quiz to see a school show I was in and the professor wouldn't let her make it up. Ooh, that really made her mad! She would spell-cuss him out right in front of us! "He's a real a-s-s!" My mother didn't say curse words, but she did sometimes spell them. She got her bachelor's degree in accounting and later an MBA in finance. By the time she retired, she was the comptroller of a national insurance corporation. I'm digressing into bragging about her but I'm also telling you this so you know exactly how hard she worked when she had a problem to deal with.

In 1987, the problem was me. Or, rather, how unhappy I was. She was a full-time mother, full-time student, and part-time secretary, but now she also became a part-time PR consultant, helping me make over my image so I could stop being sad and start being cool! Phase one was aesthetics.

"What kind of clothes do the popular kids wear?" she said as if she were Columbo investigating a case.

I told her they wore Coca-Cola shirts. This is a specific that you don't see much in movies and TV shows that take place in the 1980s, presumably because of trademark infringement, but trust me, this was the number-one shirt to wear at the time. It was sort of like a rugby shirt with three colored panels and COCA-COLA in the iconic font displayed across the center.

My mother took me to the store and got me a Coca-Cola shirt! She also got me an acid-washed jean jacket. We got both items at Solo Serve, a chain of off-price retail stores that was a precursor to Ross Dress for Less. My sister was with us, but she would have been mortified if her friends had seen her shopping at such a humiliating place during the "greed is good" '80s, so when my mom pulled into the parking lot, she got down on the floorboards and stayed there. I had no image to lose. I went in happily with my mom and we got a mint-green-and-white-striped Coca-Cola shirt. I felt impossibly chic! Unfortunately, on the first day I wore it to school, the shirt somehow had a pizza grease stain on it *before* lunch. Later that day, I left my jean jacket in English class, and when I returned to retrieve it, it was gone. Some little thief would get all the "cool cred" from the discounted clothes that my mom had bought for me.

The next thing we tackled was my hair. At the time I had a lot of it and it grew straight out of the crown of my head into a perfect bowl. It's the kind of hairstyle that booked a kid a role as an adorable moppet on '70s television. You know, the heretofore unmentioned cousin who is conveniently younger than the kids who started out cute on the show but are now in an awkward pubescent phase? The hair worked for that cute kid in the 1970s, but it had fallen out of favor during my own awkward pubescent phase, so my mom helped me. By perming my hair. At home. Herself.

I need you to take a moment to imagine how jarring a change in my physical appearance this was. I left school on a Tuesday with bone-straight hair and came back on Wednesday looking like a low-rent Little Orphan Annie. Within days I was called "Bouffant Betty." Just kidding. It was still "faggot," only somehow louder.

Unfortunately, the hair made things worse. I decided to fake an illness. I told my mom my stomach hurt, so I *had* to stay home from school, but also, could she get us a bucket of fried chicken that night? My mom narrowed her eyes and said, "Why do you want to skip school?" I returned her honesty with my own.

"Gym," I said.

PE was the worst time of the day. There was no end to the misery. There were the run-of-the-mill indignities—playing touch football, where I was somehow *always* on the "skins" side, forced not only to be shirtless in public but to run (and therefore jiggle) *while* I was shirtless in public.

The torture continued in a more personal way for me in the locker room. For some reason, 1980s middle-school physical education had a mandate that everyone had to take a shower after gym class. The coach insisted, and checked, that we all get in the shower completely naked. I had to shower naked with bullies who suspected I wanted to have sex with them. Beyond the obvious body-shame issues (which were completely present), the communal showers were lawless with feral boys. *Lord of the Flies* seems cute in comparison. The coaches seemed to think it was important for young boys to bond by finding the weakest among them and *destroying* him. I was usually the weak kid.

I wasn't the only kid targeted. I wish I had gotten all the boys who were tormented to join forces, unite, and stand up to the bullies. I wish we had created a community, but instead, we looked down at the ground when another kid was being destroyed, hoping that he would take the heat that day and that we could get a respite. I'm ashamed of that now, but I also know I had many days of taking the heat and *giving* others respite, so that's a sort of comfort.

The locker room was ground zero for torture. Most of the time it was taunting, being slapped with wet towels, or being shoved into walls, lockers, and the shower drain. However, for a few months, there was a disturbing trend of trying to stick a finger up the butt of perceived gay kids. I was the only perceived gay kid in my gym class, so there was a lot of heat on me. They never got inside all the way, but the attempts were terrifying. Isn't it ironic that these kids, coaches, and the entire state of Texas were desperately afraid of homosexuality being present in schools and yet they encouraged young boys to get naked and wet so they could finger each other?

I didn't mention these specifics to my mother because . . . I don't think I have to explain why I didn't tell my mother that other boys were trying to shove their fingers up my ass. I told her enough, though, and she initiated phase two: Call the coach.

I'd begged her not to, but she did it anyway. According to my mom, she and the coach had a beautiful conversation in which he confessed that his own son had been taunted by bullies and promised to keep an eye on me. In actuality, he once asked if I wanted to join the football team, since "you're such a big fella." I did not join the team. Maybe it would have helped, but I hate sports and sports culture. Even now when my husband tells me that a bunch of queer folks are playing a friendly game of football in Prospect Park, I do not go. There is no such thing as "friendly" football. Someone will always yell at you for not catching the ball, letting the other team get the ball, or singing the score to *Dreamgirls* while doing what you imagine is the original choreography on the thirty-yard line.

Phase three in solving the problem of my unhappiness was also the most drastic. My mom sent me to a therapist. We weren't a therapy family. Very few families in Texas were, especially at that time, but my mom would do anything for her kids. Even send me to a headshrinker.

I assume the therapist specialized in child psychology because there were brightly colored toys in his office. At thirteen, I was put off by being taken to a place with cardboard bricks in the waiting room instead of old issues of *People* magazine. The therapist and I met for only two or three sessions. We played board games. I could tell he wanted me to be competitive, so I tried to appease. When I won Candy Land, I said something like "Yeah! I won! In your face!" He seemed to think standing up to him would help me stand up to my peers, but I knew he *wanted* me to stand up to him, and I'm a people pleaser. I'm not sure if he told my mom I was cured or if she got tired of taking me downtown during rush hour, but we stopped going to him very quickly. It was less successful than the acid-washed jean jacket but not as destructive as the perm.

Finally, my mom stopped trying to fix the situation and instead focused on providing as much love and safety as possible for me at home. One of my most treasured memories from childhood, or life, really, was one Wednesday when she let me skip school. Her class had been canceled that morning, and she called out of her secretary job that afternoon so that the two of us could go to SeaWorld of Texas.

This was pre-*Blackfish*. At the time, the world thought that killer whales loved putting on shows for tourists sipping forty-ounce sodas. SeaWorld had just opened in San Antonio, and my mom wanted to give me a day of peace. The trip was a reprieve—like oxygen to a drowning orca trainer.

We saw beluga whales, seals, starfish, and, weirdly, six-foot-tall statues of classic books that one could pose with for photo opportunities. We fell into quiet meditation gazing at the twenty-foot-high aquarium inside a darkened, air-conditioned room, a lovely respite from the Texas heat. We laughed a lot. We bought forty-ounce sodas. It was heaven. She did require me to write a report on our trip. I used photos we took of the animals, placed them on black construction paper, and used a white pen to write the captions. It was chic. She gave me an A.

I can't say that the SeaWorld trip helped me avoid being bullied after that. The kids were still mean. Teachers would either turn a blind eye or offer me tips on how to fit in better, which, not for nothing, feels a bit like what the kids today call victim blaming. School continued to suck, but SeaWorld and white ink on black paper provided some comfort.

As I grew up, life got better. I made a few friends in high school and created a beautiful chosen family as an adult. I found people who were kind and supportive, because I had the foundation of love and compassion from my family, especially my mom.

But I need to tell you one more thing, and if you haven't skipped ahead at this point, don't do it now. We're almost done. This is important because it shows how screwed up bullying can make you. To this day, I *still* think about how to carry my books. I mean, I barely even have books to carry (though I do love a nice memoir). If I catch myself carrying anything next to my chest, even my laptop in its case, I immediately put it down by my side because of what that rat-faced little bully said to me thirty-five years ago while kicking my shins. My life was completely shaped by the cruelty of school bullying, and without the privilege of a mother who intervened and supported me, I am not sure I would have survived it.

I know adolescence is difficult for everyone. I wasn't guiltless either, never stepping in when other kids were picked on. I know that a lot of the kids who bullied me had issues in their homes and would have been jealous if they'd known that I had a supportive and safe space in mine. I know that there are many sides to every story, and perhaps the directors of *Blackfish* should make a documentary about that too. That's a million-dollar idea right there! You can have it as thanks for not skipping this chapter!

Scrappy Little Nobody

by ANNA KENDRICK*

I have done quite a bit of work as a guest star on sitcoms. I had a niche on these shows. I played bitchy customer-service representatives. My characters rarely had names; they were just a profession preceded by the word *gay*. My IMDb page read like a hate crime. I played waiters, baristas, and flight attendants. In fact, I have played a flight attendant four times in my career. I'm sure Russell Crowe can say the same thing. It's sort of silly because I am six foot five. No airline in the world would want my huge body weighing down its flights as I crouch and ask passengers, "Is Diet Pepsi okay?"

As an actor, when you are obviously gay but not hot, your roles are very limited. You just play the bitchy gay. If you have abs, you can hit on the main character or be the lead in an indie gay rom-com, but those of us with asymmetrical faces just get to tell the leading lady that she

---

*Anna Kendrick was twelve years old when she was nominated for a Tony for *High Society*. She was twenty-four when she was nominated for an Oscar for *Up in the Air*. She made *Twilight* in between.

doesn't have a reservation. It's not that I want to play straight men. I tried that for the first twenty years of my life and the reviews were not good. I just wish there were more options for queer roles.

I think things are changing, though. I mean, in 2022, I played Joel, a queer Christian who loves himself fully and is the ideal best friend, and I also played Mr. Whitely, a homicidal maniac who kills gay men to create a Frankenstein monster from their corpses to show that killing gay men is wrong. Huh. That character description was so complicated, I'm sort of confused about the point I was trying to make. Oh, yeah: Gay people contain multitudes—so let's show that on-screen.

I have played some questionable roles in the past. One of my first TV jobs was in an FX show called *Starved*. It starred Laura Benanti, Jackie Hoffman, and Sterling K. Brown as members of a support group for people with eating disorders. I only know this from checking IMDb. I didn't watch the show because I couldn't afford cable. It was very exciting to be cast in a real sitcom, though! They had sets and a costume designer and catering. I was used to doing web sketches that were shot in people's studio apartments, where I felt like I was really being taken care of when they offered me a place to sit.

The role on *Starved* was small but it did set the precedent for the customer-service professionals I would portray in my life. I was cast as Gay Hooker! IMDb currently has me listed as "gay man," but I remember being cast as a sex worker before anyone used the term *sex worker*.

I had only one line, in a scene that took place in a men's room. I was on my knees and I was pretending to fellate an extra. This was long before intimacy coordinators, and I was a bit player interacting with a background artist, so there wasn't a lot of concern about whether we were "comfortable." They told me to get on my knees, so I got on my knees. I also had to put my hands on this person's butt. I asked him if he was okay with that and he just stared ahead and didn't respond. In fact, he didn't speak to me the entire day. Even when I asked him questions, like "What's your name?" And before you say something along the lines of "Maybe he didn't speak English," I heard him speaking to the assistant director. In English. With a standard New York accent. Maybe he was just freaked out that I was on my knees looking at his (completely covered) crotch. Imagine if this guy had been in that laser-hair-removal scene? That was later in my life, but I acknowledge that I have many stories involving my face in other actors' private regions.

The scene was primarily focused on the main characters, who were in the next stall. One of them was teaching the other one how to vomit. I never got a full script, and as I said, I didn't watch the show, so this is just context clues, but I think this (*very edgy*) comedy had its characters trying to *become* bulimic? This is another thing about actors who are beginning their careers. Sometimes you are forced to throw your morals out the window. The Mormon girl who loves musical theater will totally play a Times Square sex worker if there is a Broadway revival of *The Life*. Young actors do not have the luxury of rejecting anything. We are trying to build careers. So if your friend's kid is an actor and gets a Valtrex commercial, don't laugh and roll your eyes. Have some compassion and give a nice compliment like *You are so attractive!*, because you have to be hot to be in a commercial aimed at people with herpes.

So, yes, I was in this sitcom about people learning how to vomit in the men's room. My character was in the stall next to the main characters. I placed my hands on the butt of a mute extra while kneeling on a wet floor and pretended to blow him for money. This is what they mean by "Hollywood glamour." I had only one line in the scene. After hearing the main characters retching, I said, "That's just wrong!" Now, the funnier line for a sex worker giving oral would have been *You'll never make it in this town with that gag reflex*, but I was young and didn't have the courage to improvise on set yet.

It turns out they couldn't use any of the footage of me and the extra, but they still needed the line to be heard from off-camera. I went to a studio to record the line, which would be added into the footage later. When I arrived, the sound engineer told me the director wasn't there yet, but since it was just one line, he would direct me himself. His direction? "They want it really flamboyant."

Even though I was a timid youth who was just starting out and didn't have the courage to stand up for myself, this was so egregious that I had to comment on it. I wasn't brave enough to call him out, so I attempted humor. I said, "One gay special coming up! How about this? '*Ohhhhh*, that'sssssss jusssssst *wroooooonnnnggg!*'" And I trilled the word *wrong* so hard that a Chanel purse fell from my lips.

The engineer said, "Perfect. We got it, thanks!"

He used that take! I was shocked and embarrassed! I left the booth feeling like I had set my people back forty years. And also desperately hoping that the Gay Hooker character would recur.

There is an evil audition room in Midtown Manhattan. The room is evil because its bathrooms are in the audition room rather than the waiting room. This means you can use the facilities only when there is a scheduled break in the audition process lest your urination interrupt your fellow auditioners' sixteen bars of an up-tempo contemporary musical-theater song.

Every actor I know hates this audition room. I understand that actors can sometimes be seen as demanding, but an easily accessible bathroom does sort of feel like the least a space could offer.

Once, while I was in this room auditioning for a musical to be directed by Sam Mendes, I had a crisis. The crisis was in my tummy. The crisis was brought on by something I ate. The crisis was diarrhea.

After I sang my audition piece, Mr. Mendes asked if I had any questions for the team. I answered way too quickly, *"Can I use the bathroom?"*

Taken aback, the director of James Bond movies looked at me and nodded.

I went into the bathroom and proceeded to blow the toilet up. Just as I was thinking of an excuse as to why I needed to use the bathroom so quickly, I heard the creative team speaking outside. I was horrified.

It wasn't *what* they said that was so horrific; it was that I could hear *exactly* what they were saying. It was as if there were no wall between us whatsoever. If I could hear them, then that meant that the

Oscar-winning director of *American Beauty* and the Tony-winning director of *Cabaret* had just heard my insides explode.

It is a shocking story with an even more shocking ending: I got that job.

I once auditioned for Stephen Sondheim.

I rarely feel like I have nailed an audition. *Rarely.* This audition, though? *I nailed it.* I also rarely know when someone I am auditioning for likes what I am selling. I usually assume that anyone I am auditioning for does *not* like me. It's a self-preservation technique. That way, if I get the job, it's a delightful surprise! If I do not get the job, I expected that.

At this audition, I could tell without a shadow of a doubt that Mr. Sondheim was into me! I mean, not sexually—he was just, like, into my performance. I was auditioning for Hysterium in a planned revival of *A Funny Thing Happened on the Way to the Forum.* The character sings the song "I'm Calm," in which he pretends to be relaxed but is obviously very, *very* nervous. Let's just say I was able to use the energy in the room and infuse the song with a specific type of nervous energy. Good ol' Steve—I'm sorry; I can't call him that even in jest—*Mr. Sondheim* was tapping his toes and laughing the entire time. After I finished he even said, "Wonderful!" and clapped. The entire room was effusive but especially Sondheim. I felt like a *rock* star! Well, I felt like a *musical-theater* star, which is very different but still feels good.

I was so in love with the way that Stephen Sondheim was clearly in love with *me* that I went home that night and watched tons of interviews of him on YouTube.

In one of them, Mr. Sondheim was asked, "Do you ever pretend to like shows you are watching from the audience since everyone watches *you* watching the show?" He replied, "No, the only thing I fake is that I pretend to love every audition I see because if I didn't, actors would kill themselves." It was the sweetest thing to say and the cruelest thing to hear.

It turns out that the production didn't happen because the lead was supposed to be James Corden but he got *The Late Late Show* on CBS. I could easily tell you I was almost in a Sondheim revival, but I have to be honest: They told me I did not get the role and then announced a month later that the show wouldn't go to Broadway.

If I *had* been cast in this Broadway show that withered on the vine and was never produced, I would have been devastated. But I was *not* cast in this show, so when it didn't go to Broadway, I felt consoled! So I guess that's a surprise happy ending that you didn't see coming!

Are You There, Vodka? It's Me, Chelsea

by CHELSEA HANDLER[*]

My parents set the rule of law that our family went to church every Sunday. We even went when we were on vacation. My mother would get out the phone book and find a Lutheran church to visit. I can count on one hand how many Sundays I missed church before the age of eighteen, and all of them involved me vomiting. I can count on two hands how many Sundays I missed church when I was in college, and all of those absences also involved me vomiting. It was a Christian college, but even the Jesus freaks like to par-tay!

For my sister, church was a duty, something she had to endure because our parents made her attend. Not me. I loved it. I couldn't get enough of it. There was so much drama in the service. The candles, the huge pipe organ, and the ushers handing out playbills! They called

---

*Chelsea Handler was thirty-one when she got *The Chelsea Handler Show*.

them bulletins, but a rose by any other name, you know? I loved when the pastors got dramatic, like when they would say the invocation from the back of the church and then lead a processional with the full adult choir marching up the aisle. It was magical to hear the individual voices as they passed. My favorite Sunday of the year was Easter because the church hired trumpet players. It felt like I was in the opening credits of *Falcon Crest!*

Church was like theater, which was a big draw for me. I've wanted to be a performer since I saw *E.T. the Extra-Terrestrial*. I was six years old. I confessed to my parents that I was worried about Elliott and Gertie, and my mother and father informed me that they were characters played by actors. I knew immediately not only that I wanted to act but that I would be amazing at it. No shade to Henry Thomas, but I genuinely felt I also could have laid out those Reese's Pieces in such a natural way that it would have made Mr. Spielberg weep with pride. The only problem was that I didn't know how to become a child star. It seemed like you needed to have famous parents or live next door to the Disney Channel. I was forced to find other outlets for performance.

Enter the Holy Spirit—aka that ol' razzle-dazzle! I didn't know how to get work in theater, but church *was* theater! There was a built-in performance every week! Admittedly, Sunday morning at eleven was not the most coveted hour, but if you had a big enough congregation, you could squeeze in a matinee at eight thirty a.m. and have a two-show weekend. Church had all the elements of a Las Vegas revue. The pastors put on robes, lit candles, and went from speaking right into singing. There is a very thin line between a Sunday service and a Liberace concert.

I am being flippant. Yes, I did love the drama of church services, but I also sincerely felt the joy of God. When school was awful, I found that God was my friend, holding my hand, making me feel safe. No matter where I went or what I encountered, I always had God inside of me, guiding me. That reminds me of this story that happened at a Christian camp I worked at during college. We sang this song at morning worship that went "Jesus is inside of me and I am awake!" *Clap-clap!* It was a silly little song designed to wake up campers with a high-energy tune. One morning, a fellow counselor was leading morning worship. She was very innocent, even compared to the other white-bread college kids working that summer. If you told me she wasn't exactly sure what a blow job was, I'd believe you. That morning, I could tell she was trying to get the kids excited, so she did a little improvising. She replaced *Jesus* with the name of a fellow counselor who was entering the worship circle, so she sang, "Dan is inside of me and I am awake!" No one is innocent enough not to hear such a *filthy* double entendre. I saw her realize what she had said in real time. In that moment, the innocence faded away and a hard woman who drinks brown liquor appeared in her place.

Getting back to my point, though, I did feel God in my heart and in the world. Embarrassingly, I was sometimes moved to tears thinking of Jesus and the difficult life that He endured on Earth to save us. I had a passion for the Passion! That led to me discerning I had a call to ordained ministry at roughly eight years old.

Perhaps you aren't familiar with the terminology, but you do not say you "want to become a pastor"; you say you are "called by God" to become a pastor. A church does not "hire" a pastor; it "calls" a pastor. You do not "apply" to seminary; you say that you have "discerned God's call to ordained ministry." That language is exclusively for work in the church, though. No one ever says they feel called by God into HVAC repair.

Occasionally, someone would say they were "wrestling with the call." I don't doubt them, I suppose, but in the end, they could just as easily say they don't want to be a pastor, right? I mean, if you really don't want to be a pastor and you hear a call that you should become one, just hang up. God is omnipotent, so why would God strive to create unnecessary conflict like some inexperienced scriptwriter fresh from reading *Save the Cat*?

I didn't wrestle with the call one tiny bit! I felt the call! Did I feel called to preside over church council meetings or create an annual budget? No. Not really. I just felt called to be a singing, dancing, wocka-wocka showman of God. Pastor Charo! "In the name of God, let's cuchi-cuchi!"

I love believing in stuff. Seriously, do not introduce me to a high-ranking Scientologist. I know that after one dinner, they could convince me to take out Leah Remini myself. I saw *The Vow*, the HBO documentary about the NXIVM cult, and thought to myself, *They're making some interesting points.*

Want to hear something wild? I know Allison Mack. She's the actor from *Smallville* who spent time in prison for her role in branding and brainwashing women for NXIVM's leader. I was in a musical with Allison and we had lunch together almost every day for a month. I really liked her. She was warm and funny, and while she didn't eat much, I assumed that was just standard Hollywood brainwashing rather than cult brainwashing. After the documentary about NXIVM came out, my former castmates from that show texted one another about how wild it was that Allison was in this dangerous cult. I was shocked by it, for sure, but what was more shocking was that they all said, "She asked me to join the cult!" All of them!

She did not ask me to join the cult. Why am I so offended by that? I've never been in a cult, but I do love believing in things. I haven't spoken to her since 2010, but I understand what it's like to trust things blindly. I hope she's doing well.

Perhaps some of you are saying, "Never been in a cult? Jeff, you said you grew up as a Christian, which means you *were* in a cult!" Well, touché, you cynical bish. Aren't you just Dorothy Parker? You aren't wrong, though, because when it came to church, I drank the Kool-Aid. Literally! Every Sunday, they served it at fellowship hour along with coffee for the adults. The Kool-Aid didn't have cyanide in it, but it did have sugar, which I understand is considered just as poisonous in Los Angeles.

There was a time when I attended church every single day of the week.

Saturday—Youth group

Sunday—Services and Sunday school

Monday—After-school tutoring

Tuesday—Handbell choir

Wednesday—Senior choir

Thursday—Alleluia children's choir (I was the teen assistant)

And Friday—well, I guess it wasn't every day of the week because there wasn't any activity on Friday that I *could* volunteer for, but I would have if there had been one. Trust me that I had no other plans. Outside of my immediate family, the only people who were nice to me were people who went to my church. That might sound pitiful on the surface, but if you dig a little deeper . . . nope, it's still pitiful.

Even kids who were mean to me at school had to be nice to me at church. Or at least not as mean as they were at school. The church was the central part of my family's social life. Most of my parents' friends were from our church, and we built our lives around belonging to that tight-knit community.

It helps that we went to a church that was slightly left of center. I mean, we weren't Unitarians, but we were in the (slightly more) progressive arm of the Lutheran Church, the Evangelical Lutheran Church in America. The word *evangelical* sounds pretty right wing, but actually our church let women be pastors and hold other leadership roles. My mom wouldn't have been able to stomach a church that said women were inferior baby-making machines. Don't misunderstand me, we were still in Texas in the 1980s, so nobody was calling to defund the police, but it wasn't nearly as conservative as many other local churches. There was a focus on serving others and on grace instead of fire and brimstone.

Here is an interesting point about Protestant theology. (I bet you didn't expect to read that sentence in this book.) Protestants don't talk a lot about the afterlife. Other churches use heaven as the carrot and hell as the shock collar, but Protestants rarely discuss the specifics of life after death other than that they believe in it. We treat heaven and hell sort of like how you treat your great-aunt Bernice and her best friend and roommate of forty-five years, Agnes. It's understood but not discussed.

That led to a difficult time one day during my sophomore year of high school. I had finally made friends who would talk to me at school. It felt so good to have friends! Well, if not friends, people who let me sit with them at lunch. Okay, to be totally honest, these people were mean to me too, but in a different way. They would pick on me sort of jokingly—but they didn't hit me! I counted it as a win. These people went to church on Sundays (it was Texas in the '80s; we all went to church on Sundays), but they didn't like it. They certainly didn't volunteer to be at church when they weren't forced to go there by their parents. They thought it was weird that I loved going to church. I went every day, so I could never hang out after school. They were annoyed by my busy schedule and the core belief system that saved me from existential dread.

One day at lunch, they asked if I believed in hell. I told them I did, but when they pressed further, I didn't have much to back up my belief. I muttered something about "free will," but they kept asking why God would create evil people just to send them to hell for eternity. I had no answer. When you stop and think about it, the concept of hell really does make God sound like a jerk: *Okay, you guys, I'm gonna give you a test that you cannot pass, and then when you do fail, I'm gonna burn you. Forever!*

Yikes. Somewhere in that lunch period, those mean friends introduced the concept of doubt into my life for the first time. By the end of lunch, I no longer believed anyone went to hell. Except for Hitler. It would take more than one lunch period to convince me that Hitler was in heaven!

Oh, yeah. I guess it's confusing that I stopped believing in hell but not in heaven. Since I loved God so much and the church was a rare place of acceptance for me, I decided that God was love, so why would

God allow hell, a realm dedicated to hate, to exist? I was giving up on hate, not on God. And even though a seed of doubt was planted, it hadn't sprouted yet. I still felt called by God to serve.

I even went to a Christian college—Texas Lutheran University, which everyone knows is the Harvard of Seguin, Texas. Now, TLU was definitely not Berkeley, but it *is* a liberal arts school. They teach science. I once asked a woman who went to a Bible college what her major was, and she just stared at me blankly and then said, "Bible." Honestly, shame on me for asking.

TLU required students to take theology classes, but they weren't like the confirmation classes I took at my church growing up. They were rigorous and intellectual. The professors asked provocative questions and encouraged us to really think about the Bible as ancient texts to be interpreted. They introduced the concept of contextual theology, in which you considered who wrote the Bible and when it was written. Theology majors had to study Greek and Hebrew so they could read the text in its original languages, and students were encouraged to study Jewish and Roman customs in order to understand the parables in the framework of the time. For instance, I remember one professor telling us that the Samaritans were an oppressed group, so the parable of the Good Samaritan, in which a man is robbed and left on the side of the road and a Samaritan helps him when priests would not, was a radical tale about antiracism. *Whoa!*

Many of my fellow students were pretty rough around the edges and did not like what the theology professors were teaching. They would shout loudly in their Texas accents, "Y'all make Jesus sound like a commie!" But the louder they shouted, the more I realized that these radical views they were protesting were the ones that Jesus espoused. Just as I had decided that hell didn't exist, I also decided that the traditional interpretation of Christian doctrine was too staid and conservative. I started to think that Jesus was a badass, and I wanted to be one just like Him. I believed I was called by God to be an ordained minister to help change the systems of oppression in our world.

The only problem was I was a big old homo.

At the same time I was researching which seminary God was calling me to, I was also getting real about who I was. A gay li'l flower. You can read more about my coming-out stories in another chapter, but the gist is this: I wanted to kiss boys real bad.

I should mention that even though I was gay, I didn't feel—what's the opposite of *called*? *Uncalled*? *Hung up on*? *Sent to voicemail*? This metaphor is labored, but the point is I still wanted to be a pastor. In my mind, social justice and Christianity worked hand in hand. But the church as an institution had a different vision.

At that time in the Lutheran Church, gay people could be pastors but they had to be celibate, while heterosexual pastors could get married, which felt like a double standard. I heard several different explanations for this. One pastor told me that being gay was wrong in God's eyes, but people who had those feelings weren't wrong themselves. It was only a sin if one acted on those feelings.

I hadn't acted on them. I was a twenty-year-old virgin, but my gayness was still intrinsically a part of me. I thought about it all the time. Even before I told anyone I was gay, they all assumed. I had been called all manner of gay slurs since roughly 1979. I was confused about what it meant to "act" on these gay urges. Did masturbation count? What if I had a partner but we didn't have sex with each other? There were probably lots of heterosexual pastors with that type of relationship. Also, why had God given me these urges if I was supposed to squash them? Another test? A spiritual SAT exam?

Another explanation I heard was that straight pastors were not permitted to have sex outside the confines of marriage, and since gay marriage was not legal at the time, gay clergy members could not have sex. This was an especially dumb explanation. The marriage that was illegal was a matter of state government and had nothing to do with a covenant with God. It's like saying God doesn't want you to baptize someone because you don't have a city permit to install a hot tub.

I found the policy toward gay pastors rather rude, and it hurt my feelings. I was surprised to hear the church was discriminatory. Yes, this is *very* naive, but I didn't grow up thinking of the church as restrictive. I thought of the church as a social justice organization. A safe space if you had no money, no hope, no friends. In small towns, the church is often the only place to get help when you need it. It provides the food pantry and housing assistance. In my world, churches advocated for dismantling racism and fought against economic inequality. I know that wasn't the case for many people, but in my bubble, it was. When I heard this double standard for gay clergy, it was exactly like when I realized the concept of hell made no sense. The seed of doubt bloomed, though it was less about God than about the institution.

So, in my senior year of college, I announced the decision I had made months ago: I no longer felt called to ordained ministry. I threw away the applications to seminaries, and I dropped my level-two Greek class. (It was a difficult class, and now that I no longer needed it for my major, I wanted to get out before it ruined my overall GPA.)

I kept attending church. I found gay-affirming churches when I moved to Denver and then to New York. They were good places filled with good people doing good things. Still, I had lost the trust in the church that I'd had while growing up. I stopped attending altogether around the time I met the man who became my husband, in 2008. He didn't ask me to stop going, but he's Jewish, so he had no interest in joining me either. I discovered I would rather spend time with him on Sunday mornings.

I haven't given up on God. I just look at God differently than I used to. Instead of seeing God as an old man in the sky or any kind of personified being, I now see God as hope. God is love and peace and sunsets and kindness. I know that sounds like a basic-B thing to say, but that *is* how I feel the presence of God.

And though I don't go to church on Sunday mornings, I haven't given up on it either. There is a scene in the last episode of the first season of *Somebody Somewhere* in which Sam, Joel, Fred, Irma, and Tiffani are driving around in Fred's party bus, the Growler. Sam has just sung

"You Brought Me Home," a song about how Joel rescued Sam from the swirling waters of grief threatening to drown her. After that tender and heavy moment, they're all blowing off steam by laughing, dancing, singing, and being a little dirty. In the chaos of the party, Joel screams, "This is church! *This* is church!"

That line wasn't in the script. I improvised it. I tell you that because I want to brag that I improvised a line that made it to the final edit and also because I believe that deep in my core. I felt it in that moment, and that's why I shouted it out. I felt safe with Bridget, the other actors, the crew, the director. In the same way that I reimagined God, I reimagined church. Community, friendship, showing love and compassion, helping people when they need help, laughing your ass off after three glasses of wine—that *is* church. Some people don't like church, so if you don't want to call celebrations with your close friends church, that is totally cool. But for me, reclaiming the church as a safe space is a wonderful gift in my life.

I Don't Know What You Know Me From

by JUDY GREER*

This is a strange thing to write in a celebrity memoir, but I'm not famous. *Somebody Somewhere* is helping me be known to some people, but before that, I was just an actor who was in a few TV shows you had heard of but only for thirty seconds at a time. I would get so embarrassed when my credits were listed at stand-up shows. Yes, technically I was on *Difficult People*, but only in one scene, where I sang "June Is Bustin' Out All Over" in the middle of a subway fight. My time on television screens was often too brief for folks to remember me in a specific role but long enough to plant a seed. They'd seen my face, so they recognized me, but they weren't sure *where* they'd seen my face that they recognized.

When you are a character actor who has a . . . uh, let's go with a

---

*Judy Greer was twenty-four when she was cast as Fern in *Jawbreaker*.

unique-looking face, and you have briefly appeared in lots of TV shows and commercials, people become very frustrated when they're trying to place you. To relieve this frustration, these people will look to you for help.

Them: You look familiar.

You: Yeah, you too.

[This isn't true, but I always say I recognize people because it seems rude not to.]

Them: How do I know you?

You: Uh, not sure.

Them: You remind me of my cousin.

[Their cousin is gay.]

Them: *Where* did we meet?

You: Well, I'm an actor, so maybe my face played in the background of your living room?

Them: *Yes!* What were you on?

[I'm warning you right now, don't take the bait! You will regret it! Do not take the bait!]

You: Oh, lots of little parts in things.

Them: But what? Or were you just my waiter once? *Ha-ha-ha!*

[Uh-oh. Your ego is gonna make you take the bait.]

You: Well, I was on *30 Rock*. Twice.

Them: No. Not that show. I hate that show. That lady pretends to be Sarah Palin. I hate that show.

[Oh God. They're a Republican! Butch it up!]

You: Well . . . bro . . . I was on *Community*?

Them: *I love that show!* Yes! But wait, what were you?

You: Well, it was just a tiny scene in that musical episode about the glee club?

Them: I don't remember that.

You: Oh. Well, I was in that.

Them: I don't remember it. What else were you in?

You: I've been in several commercials, maybe that?

Them: Nope. I never watch the commercials. But I know I've seen
you in something. *Tell me what it is!*

It's painful, and there is no way to come out of that conversation without feeling like you've begged them to validate your existence. Don't even try—they will never validate your existence.

Unfortunately, the listing-credit game isn't the only possibility for humiliation. Sometimes you bring it on yourself. Like this doozy that I wish was a hypothetical example but is a verbatim conversation I had that has been burned into my brain by the hot fire of mortification.

Improv teammate: Jeff, have you seen Adam?

Me: Oh my God, that's so weird, but I was actually *in* Adam! I
played the waiter who waits on Rose Byrne and Hugh Dancy
in the restaurant.

Improv teammate: No, I mean *Adam*. Our piano player? I don't
think he's shown up yet.

I could've died from embarrassment. I wish I had. Or at least fainted and then gotten amnesia. That incident happened over ten years ago, but with therapy, I think about it only once or twice a day now.

I had a similar encounter at a season-three screening of *Some-body Somewhere*. I was approached by a kind-faced woman in her early forties.

Her: Excuse me, I'm sorry to bother you . . .

Me [Making a beatific face as if to say, *Here we go, I'm getting recog-nized again*]: Yes?

Her: You have tags sticking out of the back of your collar.

Me: Oh. Thanks. Yeah. I needed to wear something nice but I can't
    afford this shirt so I'm gonna return it tomorrow . . .
Her [After a very long beat]: Okay.

There are also times you are recognized and do not want to be. This
is perhaps surprising to hear from someone who found a way to brag
about being in a movie no one has heard of when the improv pianist was
five minutes late, but it's true. Once, after a particularly difficult therapy
session, I was feeling a bit peckish. Oh, all right. I wanted to use food to
suppress the feelings that had come up in my session, are you happy?
I stopped at the newly opened Eataly. Is Eataly a chain that everyone
knows? Sometimes I explain what I think is a quintessentially New
York–y thing to my sister and she's like, "Oh, yeah! We have a few of
those here in Austin!" Just in case Eataly hasn't invaded your town yet,
it is sort of like a bougie grocery store where you can buy fresh ingre-
dients but they also sell prepared foods and have sit-down restaurants.

The New York flagship store for Eataly happens to be in the part of
Chelsea that is Shrink Central. I believe this is intentional.

There are thousands of food options at Eataly, including vegetables, fine pastas, and elegant four-star dining, but I didn't get any of
those things. Instead, I got a foot-long sausage on a stick. It also came
with a piece of bread. No, *piece* is not the right word. It was a *loaf* of
bread. I do not remember where I was going so quickly that I couldn't
sit down and eat this meal for four at a table for one, but apparently
I was in a rush, and so I—oh God, this is so painful to admit—I ate
it while I was walking down Broadway. I alternated bites of the gamy
meat with bites of the gigantic loaf as I loped down the street *not* thinking about therapy. Can you imagine this sight? A gay man gnawing on
a twelve-inch sausage lubed with mustard! Think of the children who
saw me with my lips wrapped around that phallic object or, worse, the
gay men who saw me eating carbs.

As I crossed Twenty-Third Street by the Flatiron Building, I saw
an incredibly attractive man approaching. His face had the glow of

exercise, and he had a yoga mat slung casually over his back, which caused his tight T-shirt to hug his chiseled chest. I stared at his beauty for a moment. I knew him, didn't I?

Oh my God—the realization came to me in a flash! It was Broadway star, badass *Mindhunter*, and avatar of all gay millennials from his time on *Looking* Jonathan Groff. He must've seen me see him because he smiled, took a beat, and said, "Hey! You're really funny!" This was long before *Somebody Somewhere*, so I guess he had seen an improv show or something? It was so sweet of him and exciting for me.

I was so flattered that I said, "Ohmmm, yousotalented!" but my mouth was full of sausage, so to make room for the words, my lips let loose a large piece of meat that dribbled a shameful trail of mustard down my light-pink shirt. Mr. Groff kindly kept walking.

How could something so personally humiliating happen outside of a Ben Stiller movie?

I've met Jonathan Groff at a couple of work functions since that day and he didn't seem to know who I was, so maybe he doesn't remember that incident. But since he also didn't say, "Hey! You're really funny!" at the subsequent meetings, I fear he does remember it and is afraid to engage lest I produce a large gulp of my consumed lunch to dribble down my shirt like from a mother bird to her babies.

I doubt Anya Taylor-Joy has these kinds of stories. People with extreme beauty and poise are called stars for a reason. They shine like burning-hot lights that you can't get too close to. If their light briefly dims, you are grateful for the shade it provides your eyes. When Jennifer Lawrence tripped on the way up the stairs to collect her Academy Award, her ethereal beauty and Dior haute couture gown made the gaffe and therefore *her* relatable and lovable. Unfortunately, I just look like some dude you'd see in the waiting room at your dentist. I have nothing that makes me *not* relatable, so when I trip, you are not relieved. You expected it.

When *Somebody Somewhere* started airing, people began recognizing me more frequently.

Them: Oh! You're on that show! The one with the friends! Is it
    called *Friends*?
Me: It is not called *Friends*, but I think there is a show called that.

Another:

Them: Oh my God! I love your show!
Me: Thank you!
Them: *Life and Beth* is my favorite. What's Amy Schumer like?

A woman came up to me after I did a stand-up set and said, "I love
your show, but you need to change the title."

"Okay, I will," I told her. "Because I totally have that power."

You must admit, this was an out-of-the-box suggestion. This was
after the second season of the show had aired. I can't think of any show
that has changed its name after two seasons. Not even *Cougar Town* did
that, and one can argue it should have.

She was not wrong, though. People have a really difficult time with
the name of the show.

Them: Oh, yeah, you're on that show *Somebody, Somewhere, All at
    Once*, right?

I was a guest on a podcast where the host tried to do that serious
NPR intro voice that Terry Gross does on *Fresh Air*. She said, "My guest
Jeff Hiller is on a new show on HBO called *Somebody Out There*. Jeff,
I loved *Somebody Out There*. I loved *everything* about *Somebody Out
There*."

Everything?

One day, my husband and I were walking along the South Street
Seaport. The first season of the show had just finished airing, and my
husband was really celebrating the win of me being on a show that
he loved watching himself (my previous oeuvre wasn't always up his

alley). I was being a bit of a crab apple and wondering to myself if anyone was watching it and whether we would do well enough to get a second season when suddenly a man approached.

He pointed directly at my face, shouted, "*Nobody Nowhere,*" and kept walking.

To this day, I'm not sure if he had seen the show or if he could just hear my inner monologue.

Around the Way Girl

by TARAJI P. HENSON*

I was born in Texas. I went to college in Texas. A college in Texas where 80 percent of the students were also from Texas. A campus of a thousand students in Seguin, a town of twenty-five thousand people forty-five minutes away from the town where I was born and grew up.

Seguin's claim to fame is having the world's largest pecan, only the pecan is not an actual pecan, it's just concrete painted to look like a pecan. In theory, any other city could make their own, slightly larger concrete pecan and steal the town's primary tourist attraction.

I felt stifled in Seguin. I needed to get out of that small town, out of Texas, and, for the first time, out of the United States. Well, technically I had been out of the country before. When I was growing up, my family went to Mexico, but only to border towns. Our primary cultural interaction was buying brand-name toothpaste at cheaper prices.

---

*Taraji P. Henson was thirty-one when she made *Baby Boy* and thirty-eight when she was nominated for an Oscar for *The Curious Case of Benjamin Button.*

I needed to grow! I needed to learn! I needed to go far away so I could be gay!

That was the foremost reason for wanting to study abroad. I was looking for growth through light kissing and maybe some hand stuff. At my college, there was one out gay man and one out gay woman, and they were dating each other. This sounds like I am making fun of them, but you cannot imagine the cruelty that these two freedom fighters endured to live authentically. That torment was what drove them together. Neither one seemed to be looking for a beard—more like a comrade in arms.

So I felt my only option was to get out. I knew exactly where I would go—Ireland! The predominant reason for this was the 1992 film *Far and Away*. If you held a gun to my head and asked me to describe the plot of *Far and Away*, I would tell you to pull the trigger. I'm not sure if I even saw the movie. I just saw the music video for "Book of Days" by Enya, and in it, there is a scene where Nicole Kidman is spying on Tom Cruise while he changes, and you see the top of his butt crack. This was before internet porn, when a hint of crack could make a man swoon! Or at least a closeted kid at a Christian college. I wanted to drink green beer, learn to dance a jig, and kiss a redheaded boy! This goes to show you how little I knew myself. I hate beer, I can't dance, and I had barely kissed any boys at that point, so why was I going for some gay-kiss bingo card?

As it turns out, the logic was even more flawed because I just looked up the plot of *Far and Away* and apparently the film begins in Ireland but the story is primarily about the adventures of immigrants Tom and Nicole in the United States. I probably should have watched the movie rather than just the Enya video.

I went to Dr. Hoppe, our study-abroad adviser (he was also a sociology professor because hardly anyone at my school studied abroad, so the adviser role couldn't have taken up that much time). I need to confess something to you that is slightly embarrassing—I am a nepo baby. I'm not related to anyone famous and powerful, but I am distantly related to Dr. Hoppe, the TLU study-abroad adviser. I discovered this familial connection when, in 1995, I walked into our study-abroad consultation and he said to me, "Hiller? You and I are distantly related!" Consequently, our meeting started with a twenty-minute interrogation about my paternal grandmother's side of the family. I didn't know anything about them, and I certainly didn't know more than he, an actual genealogist, did. He was obviously disappointed, and I felt nervous that we had gotten off on the wrong foot, but I pressed on and told him I wanted to study abroad.

"Oh, that's a very good idea. I think you should. Where would you like to go?" he asked.

"Ireland!" I shouted, perhaps too loudly.

"Interesting. Why do you want to go to Ireland?"

This sort of threw me. I mean, I knew why I wanted to go to Ireland, but "Tom Cruise's butt crack" did not feel like an appropriate response to give this man of academia who I had just discovered was a family member. I had already disappointed him with my dearth of ancestry knowledge, so I had to think quickly. I needed to cite a reason that sounded academic so he would think I was smart and like me again. If I had chosen London, I could've said I wanted to study theater history because I had just taken a class on that. Why didn't Enya write music for *American Werewolf in London*?

Wait! I had just taken a class about liberation theology! "Well, I am thinking of being a theology major and I would love to study the conflict between Protestants and Catholics in Northern Ireland as well as the church's role in social norms." I threw in that last part because I knew he taught sociology. Can I just take a moment here to pat myself on the back? I mean, I pulled that out of my ass! I barely even knew there *was* a conflict between Catholics and Protestants in Ireland. I had only heard about it because TV dramas in the 1980s and '90s loved plots about the Irish Republican Army. This allowed handsome white actors to play villains and justified their characters having knowledge of bombs. So for me to pull that out was *pretty* damn impressive, if I say so myself.

Dr. Hoppe hummed in approval and said, "Oh, that's a fascinating topic to study. Unfortunately, we don't have a program like that in Ireland. But we have one in Namibia."

I'm glad I took that moment above to celebrate, because this was when that brilliant improvisation backfired. I couldn't backtrack now after I had already disappointed him at the beginning of the meeting, so suddenly I was going to Namibia.

The first order of business was to answer the question "Where is Namibia?" It was the days before the internet, so I went to the library. There was only one book that even mentioned Namibia. It was about sub-Saharan Africa and discussed Namibia in a chapter titled (and I swear to you this is real) "The Land God Made in Anger."

You might have heard of Namibia in pop culture because it's where they filmed *Mad Max: Fury Road*. It is also where Angelina Jolie and Brad Pitt went to have their twins because it was so remote, no paparazzi could get to them. It is roughly the size of Texas and Oklahoma but has a smaller population than Houston. It is a desert nation, home to Dune 7, one of the highest sand dunes in the world. So, basically, *exactly* like Ireland.

Namibia was once a German colony, which is why it is a predominantly Christian country and also why it has towns that look like Ye Olde Christmas Village but with sand instead of snow. Namibia's history is harsh. After World War I, the territory was ruled by South Africa, which instituted the racist and brutal policy of apartheid. The country gained its independence in 1990 after a deadly war. South Africa elected Nelson Mandela in 1994, so apartheid was not ancient history when I arrived in Windhoek, Namibia, in August of 1996.

As I sit here typing, I am sort of flabbergasted that I traveled all that way when I was just twenty years old (December birthday!). I had been on a plane only two times before this, and never by myself, but that summer, I took a flight from San Antonio to Dallas, from Dallas to London (where I had a fourteen-hour layover, during which I left the airport and just hung out in a park all day clutching my carry-on luggage), from London to Johannesburg, and from there to Windhoek on a plane so tiny, they asked passengers how much they weighed. No wonder the paparazzi left Brad and Angie alone.

The study-abroad program was called Societies in Transition, which was appropriate because in 1996, Namibia was in a serious transition phase. In addition to the twelve or so American students in the program (all white), there were two Namibian students of color. The Namibian students were in their early twenties like the American students, but unlike us, they had seen the effects of apartheid firsthand. The rules of Apartheid were both ridiculous (Black people couldn't eat white bread) and unbelievably cruel (Black people could be beaten to death for eating white bread).

The program was led by a white American man named Bryan and a Black Namibian woman named Olivia. Olivia had grown up in Namibia but left to get an education in England (there was no higher education for Black students in Namibia during apartheid). She had returned to her home country and taken this job educating mostly white American college students on Namibian history. Bryan was a former hippie who said he had been "radicalized by the Vietnam War." He asked me, "What caused you to become socially aware and progressive?" and I didn't have the heart to tell him I'd come to Namibia because I got lost on my way to Ireland, so I just said, "Oh, uh, I guess the Gulf War?" I mean, I was against it, but I wouldn't say it had made me socially aware or progressive. In fact, I wouldn't say I knew that much about it at all. What I didn't know then was that the thing that *would* make me socially aware and progressive was studying in Namibia.

I wanted to be a new person in this country. No one knew me here. Even in college, there were several people who'd known me from my church growing up. I should have adopted the out-gay-guy persona, but being in a program with other American students made me scared to be that open. Instead, I adopted the persona of the granola Christian, a Jesuit type who believes in social justice and wears Birkenstocks. No, that is too cynical. I wanted to be this type of person, but I wasn't successful at it. I didn't know much about the world, and the Birks were cheap knockoffs. At the beginning of the term, the staff asked if anyone was a vegetarian. I raised my hand, which was odd because I wasn't a vegetarian. Well, I guess I was, but I had been for only the past thirty minutes. In the same way I made up a reason for wanting to go to Ireland on the spot, I made up an entire personality. I told my fellow students that I wanted to attend seminary and that my thesis would be on the theology of the oppressed. It was the opposite of the boozy-slut version of myself I had pictured in Ireland, but it was still better than the person I actually was.

We had two stays with host families during our semester, one in the city and one in the rural north. My urban-host stay was with a delightful family of five boys, ages five to thirteen, and a single working mother. She was a pastor at an apostolic church, which I guess was why they put me with her. The boys all wore school uniforms and washed and ironed their shirts every night. Their version of casual Friday was not having to wear shoes to school. The oldest brother spoke perfect English, but the younger boys spoke only Khoekhoe, a language that uses clicks and tongue pops. I've been a comedian for more than twenty years, but the best audience I ever had was those boys listening to me try to master the slight nuances between clicks. At my host mother's church on Sunday, the congregation sang in perfect three-part harmony, and when they clicked in unison, the loud sound filled the high-ceilinged building with a satisfying pop.

My rural stay lasted longer as it was much farther away from Windhoek. My fellow students and I took a combi (that's just the Namibian word for *van*, but isn't it fun to have geographic specifics?) for several hours to Ovamboland, which is high desert. I stayed with an Ovambo family, again headed by a single mother; I was told to call her Mime. She was a teacher at the local school, which was a fifty-minute walk from home. She lived with her five kids, a cousin, Martha, who was staying with her to help with the farm, and a young man named Simon whose relationship to the others I never really understood. He was from Angola and spoke only Portuguese. Olivia had asked if I spoke any languages other than English, and I told her I'd taken Spanish in high school. She said, "Perfect! You'll be able to speak with the cousin from Angola, then." Her assumption of my mastery of language was a bit too optimistic and I never really found a way to connect with him. He had crafted a guitar out of an old paint can, though, and he would play songs and I would sing and dance along. My dancing killed as much as my attempt at the tongue clicks.

However, Mime's cousin Martha spoke English very well and loved to laugh. She laughed with me and, often, at me. We developed an instant sibling relationship. She would ask me to carry water, and I would struggle to lift it. She would laugh, hoist the fifty-gallon jug on top of her head, and keep it there with only the strength of her neck muscles to hold it. Then—and this was really the showstopper—she would climb a fence with it on her head! I have a video of it, and it is a real shame that you can't put videos in a book 'cause you would be so impressed.

I bonded with the family quickly. I herded cattle and goats with them and pounded a grain called mahangu into flour for the oshifima— a traditional porridge that is a staple of every meal. The home was inside a large fenced area with a fire pit that was basically the kitchen, a thatched-roof lean-to that was sort of the pantry, a cinder-block main house for Mime, and individual thatched-roof huts that were like additional bedrooms. There was a partition blocking a large red bucket where you bathed, and for the bathroom there was a hole about three hundred feet from the house surrounded by modesty sticks roughly three feet high. At first, I was shy as I crossed the large field toward the literal shithole, but eventually I embraced the fact that, indeed, everybody poops. I would start the day with a truly joyous crap that came with a breathtaking view of the sunrise.

Martha and I worked on the farm while Mime went to teach. We would walk about thirty minutes each way to pick up water and bring it home (this was separate from the fifty-gallon jug of water that Martha carried on her head; that was provided by the exchange program for my delicate American gut). Then we would herd goats to some brush for them to munch on, pound mahangu for dinner that night, and, finally, sit in the shade of the house, moving every so often to avoid the heat of the sun as it moved across the sky.

After a month living with Mime, Martha, the kids, and that guy who spoke Portuguese, I felt like they were my family. I was sad to leave. The one thing that softened the blow was that I was going on a safari with my classmates and stopping in Swakopmund to see the Skeleton Coast.

On my last night, Mime said to me, "When a member of our family leaves on a long trip, we sit in a circle, pass around the traditional beer, and tell stories about our loved one so they can take a part of us with them." I won't lie—I cried a little when she said that. We sat in a circle and people told stories about the dances I couldn't dance, the words I couldn't say, and the water I couldn't carry on my head. I loved everything about it.

Well, almost everything. Part of the ceremony involved passing around a cup containing my host family's homemade beer. It was made from the mahangu and had been fermented in clay jugs for a month or so. It tasted very bad to my American taste buds, but all the students had gotten strict instructions from Bryan and Olivia to respect the culture we were entering. That meant if food looked or tasted unusual, you should experience the food and keep your opinions to yourself. So I gulped the beer down, trying not to smell it, so I could experience this beautiful time with my new family.

Once the ceremony was over, I packed up, hugged everyone goodbye, and headed off with my classmates to Etosha National Park. That night, we sat around sharing stories of our host families and eating fresh fruits and vegetables, which the program provided as a treat after we'd lived in a desert for a month. I ate strawberries, green beans, and carrots. I ate a whole avocado, scraping the skin with my teeth for the last bit of green goodness. Having moisture-filled produce felt like such luxury after a month of eating nothing but sandy porridge. The campsite had clean restrooms and a view of a watering hole where animals came to drink. That night we saw a white rhino, cheetahs, giraffes, warthogs, and elephants. It was magical.

I shared a tent with Lester, one of the Namibian students. We were friendly and laughed a lot together. He liked saying politically provocative things to shock me and send me into a tizzy, which he found hilarious. That night was no exception.

"You know, sometimes I think Namibia was better off under apartheid because you were aware of rules. Nothing was hidden," he said, looking at me like *What are ya gonna say to this?*

"I know that there is still racism in this country, I agree with you, but you must admit that *bleeeeeeeccccchhhhhhhhh!*"

I puked. There was no warning; it just came out of me with shocking force, like Linda Blair in *The Exorcist*. It was even a similar color. I vomited all over Lester. And my sleeping bag. And his sleeping bag. And the door to the tent. I can still see the puke outside the tent on the ground. It landed on the earth in the same mesh-like pattern of the screen on the door.

Poor Lester! He had wanted to get a rise out of me, but not like this. He was incredibly kind, especially considering what I had just done to him. He helped me clean up and get to the bathroom. I stood fully dressed in my soiled clothes in the shower and washed off the vomit as best I could. I felt something in my nose, so I held one nostril and blew out an entire green bean. It landed on the floor of the shower. I remember thinking, *How did I swallow that bean whole?* I also remember thinking that it must have been that avocado I ate that had made me so violently ill because—*bleeeeecccchhhh!* I threw up again, this time just outside the campsite shower. As I tried to push my vomit into the shower drain, Lester gave me a look that said *Okay, you made your point, stop already.*

We went back to the tent and saw the horror left for us. There was nothing to do but completely hose it down. I tried to turn the tent inside out for better access—*bleeeecccchhhhhh!* I vomited inside it again.

There was so much puke! How could I have had all this liquid inside of me? And it wasn't a controlled stream either. It was vicious and strong. When I saw the first Pitch Perfect movie, the one where Anna Camp's character vomits, I remember thinking, *That's how it was for me in Namibia.* My vomit looked as if it were made by CGI.

Lester and I washed out the tent in the showers and retired to the combi, where I lay across the front seat. The back seat would have been more comfortable, but I couldn't open the sliding door as easily as I could the driver's side so I could vomit every half hour. I ended up puking somewhere in the neighborhood of fifteen times that night, eventually just coughing up bile. Lester probably never uttered a politically provocative statement again.

The next morning, I staggered over to the campfire and explained what had happened. Olivia looked at me and said, "I heard that, but assumed someone had drank too much." A fair assumption when traveling with nineteen- and twenty-year-old American students in a country with no minimum legal drinking age. I told her that the avocado was rotten, but in her wisdom, she dug further.

"You didn't drink any of the water at your host family's house, did you?" she asked me.

"No. You said not to." I follow rules.

"Did you eat something that was made with uncooked water?" she asked, but her eyes said, *This is obviously from dirty water and not an avocado, you dum-dum.*

"Oh. I did a ceremony with Mime where I drank her homemade beer. But that couldn't be it 'cause it was fermented, right?" I wondered aloud.

That could be it. It turns out you need to boil the water, not just ferment it, to kill parasites and bacteria that American tummies can't handle. I was so mad at myself because, as I said, I really like to follow rules. I had followed the rule of not mentioning that a food didn't appeal to me, but technically I hadn't followed the rule of not drinking the water.

Even though my body was empty, I continued to gag and retch all morning. Olivia said I needed to go to the hospital for fluids. I wanted to go to Swakopmund and have a fun time with the rest of the group, so I protested, "I am fine. I just need to—*blecchhh!*"

The hospital in the north of Namibia was located about an hour away from Etosha National Park. The students and Olivia dropped me off and waved goodbye, grateful to be rid of the human puke machine (Lester especially, no doubt), and continued on with their trip.

There were some big differences between this hospital and an American one. The most obvious difference was that this hospital didn't have electric lights after a certain time at night. There was very little electricity in the northern part of the country because it was so sparsely populated, so I guess the generator had time limits for the lights. You went to sleep at eight p.m. because it was dark. They didn't have air-conditioning, but they did have ceiling fans that slowly turned to circulate air. I don't know how those fans turned. Maybe they used the generator or a tiny mouse running on a tread-mill? They moved consistently and languidly like in an old noir movie. They were beautiful but so slow, I didn't understand how they could make any air move. I thought about the fans a lot because this was before cell phones and I had already read my book, so for forty-eight hours, my entertainment was a show called *As the Slow Fan Turns*.

There were twelve beds in the room, but I was the only patient. I think I was one of only two patients in the entire hospital. The other patient was a woman, so she was in another room.

When it came time to bathe, I was taken into a very large room with ten claw-foot bathtubs lined up in a row. It was beautiful, like something out of a high-end spa.

The doctor spoke English, as did one of the two nurses. I had learned a little bit of Ovambo and spoke that with the nurses, who seemed to enjoy my mispronunciations and appreciate the effort. I got IV fluids and rested a lot, and I was finally released after two nights. I was told that the program would send someone in a combi to take me back to my fellow students, and indeed a man picked me up at the hospital to drive me down the coast.

I assumed this would be a private ride. I assumed incorrectly. As we traveled along, the driver frequently pulled over and picked up passengers for a small fee. I was in the van with people of all ages, and we began to talk. Most didn't know English, but one woman who did asked me about America, whose film and television cultural exports are all over the world, even somehow in the rural deserts of Namibia.

"Do you know Pamela Anderson?" she asked. "She is a real American woman."

I told her I did not know Pam but that she wasn't the best example of the typical American woman. Of course, this was before I read *Love, Pamela*, her incredible memoir, and realized she really *is* all of us, though she is Canadian.

At first, I was disappointed in my driver. Was he being paid to take me alone and making extra cash on the side? But as the trip continued, I realized this was simply custom in Namibia. When you live in a desert and you see someone who needs a ride, you offer it to them out of courtesy and safety. It is dangerous to be alone in a desert. The driver wasn't being shady; he was being kind. I mean, he was also taking a fee, but why shouldn't he be rewarded for kindness?

I was reconnected with my fellow students and we made our way back to the school in Windhoek. I missed seeing the Skeleton Coast, but I did get an evening in Swakopmund, where I tried calamari for the first time in my life. I remember thinking how exotic that was. Calamari! It wasn't even prepared in a unique way. It was just fried, like you would get at a crappy bar nowhere near an ocean in Middle America. Perhaps the Skeleton Coast would have proved just as banal as eating fried calamari, which makes me even more grateful for a long trip across the Namib desert with a van full of strangers from the country. While on the ride, a woman shared something she called crunchies, which were kind of like granola bars but really not like anything we have in the States. It's much more unique than calamari, I'll say that.

When we Americans finished the program, we went as a group to the airport, even though I wasn't flying out with everyone else. I had decided to tack on a trip to London so that I could see theater in the West End. I mean, if you're halfway around the world anyway, why not swing by?

Unfortunately, there was a problem in customs because I had an American passport but I was traveling to the United Kingdom. The woman from customs was annoyed with me and told me so explicitly. Because of my trip, she had to fill out more forms. She argued with me and I argued back. It was a stressful experience, and when I returned to my group, I yelled, "I hate this country and I can't *wait* to leave!"

Why did I say that? And why did I say it to Linda, of all people? She was one of the Namibian students in the program and the only one I hadn't vomited over repeatedly; I really loved Linda. Her face fell. That was how I was leaving her country?

I felt shame wash over me. I apologized. "I do not hate this country. Namibia will always hold the most special place in my heart."

It does.

I've lost contact with my host families and my Namibian friends. We wrote letters back and forth for a year or two, but, as happens, after that, communication waned. That isn't entirely true, though. I was afraid to write them once I came out. My Namibian host families and friends were all very Christian. I was too when I was studying abroad, so it was the basis for my relationship with many of them. I was scared to come out to them and lose their friendship, so instead, I let the friendships fade. I am mad at myself for doing that. I gave my birth family the chance to know the real me, so why didn't I give my found family that chance?

Still, the trip taught me more about myself than anything else had in my young life. Travel is fun, but it is also a path to personal growth. I learned that I'd grown up in a world that believed in white supremacy and that, especially as a white person, I needed to fight archaic racist ideas every day. I learned kindness was the ultimate virtue and one I wanted to put first in my life. I learned I was much more capable than I had assumed. And perhaps most important of all, I learned I needed to chew green beans more thoroughly. It was a trip of a lifetime, even if I didn't get to see Tom Cruise's butt crack.

So, Anyway

by JOHN CLEESE*

I was on the last season of *Ugly Betty*.

I was on the last episode of *Law & Order: Criminal Intent*.

I was on the last week of *Guiding Light*, which is a show that ran for *seventy-two years*. I don't *want* to kill your show, but I probably will.

In all the theater I have done, I have never had my own dressing room. I was even in a one-person show Off-Broadway—a *one-person show*—but the theater was so small that my dressing room was the stage manager's office. It isn't just Virginia Woolf who longs for *A Room of One's Own*.

My neighbor making chitchat at the elevator asked me about improv. "So, you still working with Citizens United?"

To be clear, I improvised for many years with the Upright Citizens

---

*John Cleese was twenty-four when a sketch show he was in went to the West End and then Broadway. He was thirty when *Monty Python* first aired on British television.

Brigade. I had nothing to do with the controversial Supreme Court case that declared that corporations were people.

I got my Equity card at the Jekyll and Hyde Club. Either this means nothing to you or it fills you with a deep sense of dread and sympathy. Equity—the Actors' Equity Association—is the stage actors' union. You can't just join the union. In order to get into Equity, you must first be hired by a professional, unionized production. Once you are a member of Equity, you have access to more auditions and receive protections that non-union productions do not always offer. There are protections around safety and pay, benefits (including health insurance), plus a cot for naps. Every union theatrical production must provide the cast with an Equity cot so they can take naps between the matinee and evening show. The production is required to provide only one cot, as far as I'm aware, but, wow, does that cot mean a lot to a young actor. It is a sign of extreme professional development to be able to nap if no one else in the cast is napping.

In the same way that queer people share their coming-out stories, theater people share how they got their Equity cards. It becomes a bragging game of who has the most inauspicious beginnings.

"I got mine in grad school as a spear carrier doing Shakespeare in the Park!" an NYU grad might say, shaking his head at the humiliation of not having lines in *King Lear*.

"Mine's way worse!" a musical-theater star might say with a laugh. "I got mine on a TheaterWorks tour of *Curious George* right after college! I was playing the monkey!"

"I got mine at the Jekyll and Hyde Club," I will mirthlessly confess. "I was twenty-seven."

"Oh." They gasp. "That's much worse."

The Jekyll and Hyde Club was a restaurant on Sixth Avenue and Fifty-Seventh Street that has since closed. There was a pub version downtown, but was much less theatrical than the original. I worked at the four-story restaurant that employed waiters, bartenders, and—this is where I came in—actors who roamed around interacting with the patrons. Ninety-seven percent of the patrons were families with young children.

Somehow, the actors there had unionized in the early 2000s, and thus being a roaming actor at a restaurant became a back door to get into the stage actors' union. The restaurant paid us eleven dollars an hour and specifically looked for actors with experience in improvisation, since you had to interact with children in character. The club made sure that no actor worked enough hours a week to be eligible for health and pension benefits, but it was still a good deal for actors because you got to join the union. And if you got a job out of town, you could leave to do it and then get right back on the schedule as soon as the production of *Bye Bye Birdie* in which you played "mayor understudy" closed in St. Louis.

I had mailed my headshot and résumé to the club because I wanted my union card, and I was a great improviser. My résumé had only two scripted shows on it, from the New York Fringe Festival—the rest was improv! I got the job. I would play Cornelius Shroud, a butler at the "mansion." I received a biography of my character and was told to *never* break character.

"You *are* Cornelius," the acting supervisor told me. "You are *not* . . . uh . . ."

"Jeff," I reminded him helpfully.

"*No!* You are Cornelius!"

Oh, brother.

This might surprise you, but the job was awful. Most of the time I was on the floor, which just meant I walked around to different tables and talked to people. Since my character was a butler, I carried a feather duster. I would use the prop as an intro by pretending to dust something up high and then bringing it down on a child's head and tickling their nose with the feathers. I would say something like "Oh, dear, this statue is *especially* dusty." I used an accent that sounded very similar to Dame Joan Plowright's.

Sometimes the parents would join in good-naturedly, sometimes they would let the children do the talking as they watched, and sometimes, the parents would be completely checked out, seeing me as a babysitter so they could get some GD peace and quiet, thank you very much.

Actors at the club also worked the door. You would stand out on Sixth Avenue and beckon people inside. What a nightmare. New Yorkers in Midtown aren't the friendliest bunch, and if I saw people I knew walking down the street, I tried to hide so they wouldn't see me.

Once people came in, you would usher them into a hall and show a two-minute video about the history of the house. In the middle of the video, the ceiling above the guests would lower in an incredibly benign way to insinuate that we would all be crushed! Then I would open the back door of the hall and they could enter the restaurant. The ceiling was a divisive part of the floor show. Children found it terrifying and would often weep, scream, and beg to be let out. I felt like such a jerk putting babies through trauma. We weren't supposed to open the door unless the video had finished, there was a safety concern, or the parents demanded it, but I opened it a lot anyway because I didn't want to be someone's reason for therapy.

Meanwhile, the adults who came to the restaurant (and, strangely, there were some who came without kids) found it not at all terrifying. I was working one shift when Hugh Hefner and seven young, beautiful Playmates came in. He told me they were his girlfriends. I can't explain why Hefner (who was either seventy-nine or eighty at the time; I just looked it up) was dating seven gorgeous women, all of whom were roughly sixty years his junior. I cannot explain why these seven women all went out with him simultaneously, and I definitely cannot explain why they came to a children's theme restaurant. All I can tell you is that when I played the video and the ceiling came down, one of the women looked at me and said, "This isn't even scary."

A couple of other celebrities came while I worked there. Patti LuPone came in with two children. She was one of the nicest people I interacted with in my six months at the club. I think she was familiar with humiliating acting work and took pity on me. She did have chapters in her book, *Patti LuPone: A Memoir*, titled "A Working Actor" (parts 1 and 2), so she knew this craft keeps you humble.

Britney Spears came in too! I would love to tell you about an interaction with her, but when I approached her table to do my job, a security guard stood up and shook his head. I guess he thought I was coming over to be a lookie-loo, but I had been instructed by my manager to go to the table. I loved that he turned me away. I hated going to people's tables just as much as the people at the tables hated having me there.

In addition to working the door and the floor, you could also work the booth. This was the most coveted position for roving actors. You sat in the control booth on the fourth floor and looked at video screens showing patrons in the restaurant who were sitting next to mechanical puppets, like suits of armor or wolf heads mounted on the wall. You could make the puppets talk by using a microphone in the booth and pressing a button to move the mouth. Kids *loved* talking to the puppet! They would *freak out* when you responded. Parents didn't mind talking to a puppet like they minded talking to a clearly American actor faking a British accent. There was a remove that just made everyone more comfortable.

I wanted *that* job, but my manager wouldn't put me on that shift. I finally asked him why.

"Well, when you're on booth duty, you have to do the show," he said as if this made sense.

"The show" was done every hour. An actor climbed into an elevator and descended to the main dining room's atrium. He (it was always a male actor) wore an overcoat, a top hat, and a scarf over a rubber mask that was meant to look like a man wearing a monocle. It was meant to look like that, but it did not succeed. A track played a man's voice saying that he was Dr. Jekyll and he was going to drink a potion for science or whatever. The actor lip-synched to the recorded track, but you couldn't see the actor's lips because he was wearing a rubber mask, so there was a lot of moving arms like silent-film acting. Then the actor pretended to drink the potion and choke, put his head behind the red velvet curtain, and quickly changed into a different mask that was meant to look like a hideous monster. This mask was successful. A villainous voice stated that he was now Mr. Hyde, and the actor moved his arms as if he were going to get you even though he was in an elevator easily twenty feet away from the closest patron, and then the elevator rose up. The show lasted roughly ninety seconds.

That wasn't *Hamlet*. You didn't even have to memorize lines. The only skill involved was taking off and putting on a rubber mask quickly.

"I can do the show. I watch it eight times a day. I think I got it," I said with *Put me in, Coach* energy.

"Well . . . Dr. Jekyll, you know, he's a— I mean, you're a . . . ," my manager stammered.

This was confusing. This manager was a lot of things, but tongue-tied was not one of them. I waited for him to finish his thought, genuinely confused as to what Dr. Jekyll was that I was not.

"He's, you know . . . a *leading man*."

The words on the page do not fully reflect what he was saying. His tone and awkward shuffle told me a fuller story. What he was actually saying was that I was too gay to play a character in a rubber mask.

"Nope," I said before I could stop the word from escaping my lips. "Nope. I will be playing him. I can play him. Let me play him. Today at four p.m. The club is empty at four p.m., post-lunch and pre-dinner. Let me prove to you I can play"—I sighed, stifling a shudder of humiliation and a flood of fury—"Dr. Jekyll."

He let me play him. Guess what—no one noticed any difference between the way I played him and the way anyone else played him. In fact, a month later they even started letting women play the role of Dr. Jekyll, as long as their floor costumes were fully hidden under the overcoat.

I left the Jekyll and Hyde Club a few weeks after that. I had gotten everything I needed—entry to the union, a command performance for Patti LuPone, and, perhaps best of all, the opportunity to play the leading man.

This Will Only Hurt a Little

by BUSY PHILIPPS*

I realized I needed to live my life out of the closet, so clearly becoming a pastor wasn't my calling. I decided to pivot from ordained ministry to social work, which is sort of like non-ordained ministry. They are both helping professions, and I wanted to help people. I was going to miss the costumes that pastors got to rock, though. The paper collar alone!

When I graduated from Texas Lutheran, in May of 1998, I applied to be part of a program called the Urban Servant Corps in Denver, Colorado. The program placed young people in full-time volunteer positions in social-service agencies throughout the city. It was sort of like AmeriCorps, only with a church affiliation.

You might wonder why I didn't just do AmeriCorps. I also wonder this. I guess that even though I wasn't feeling called to be a pastor, I

---

*Busy Philipps was twenty when she was cast in *Freaks and Geeks*.

was still very entrenched in the church. Plus, I loved the promise of community that came with this program. I would live with nine other full-time volunteers in an old mansion in Denver's Capitol Hill neighborhood, all of us sharing meals, support, and accountability. In fact, the program billed itself as an "intentional Christian living community." A Jesus commune!

Okay, it never called itself a commune, much less a Jesus commune, but I like calling it that. Doesn't it sound like something you totally understand while simultaneously not understanding it at all?

I like the word *commune* because it makes us sound like we all ate vegan food and had naked Fridays, but that wasn't the case. In fact, in comparison to the binge-drinking frat parties at my Christian college, it was tame. Rather than smoking pot or swapping partners, commune members spent most of the time fighting over who'd eaten all the peanut butter. After we fought, we prayed about it. Our lives were like MTV's *The Real World* if it had aired on Pax TV.

My social-service placement was at a shelter for people under twenty-one. This shelter was important because young people who had been kicked out of their houses or had run away from scary home situations needed a place to stay, and adult shelters were often too rough. This shelter aimed to provide a safe space for young people who had run into difficult situations at home. Half my time at work was spent as a jobs counselor. I helped the youth staying in the shelter complete applications, practice for job interviews, and pick appropriate interview outfits from donated clothes. I also worked as an outreach counselor, which meant that I would walk the streets of Denver (primarily the 16th Street Mall), find young people, and provide them with resources. This was often a peanut butter and jelly sandwich, but we also provided condoms, bleach kits for cleaning needles, and, of course, referrals for places to sleep at night.

Here is the thing about helping people: I was bad at it.

I wish I could tell you I immediately helped everyone under twenty-one who was experiencing homelessness, but that was not the case.

Almost every young person had multiple issues, and these issues banged up against each other, making it difficult for anyone to provide the help they needed.

Take, for instance, the time I tried to help a young woman named Patricia. She told me she wouldn't mind working at 7-Eleven. She enjoyed working nights and had passed by a store that was looking for a nighttime cashier. I looked into how to apply for the job and discovered that to complete the application, you needed to answer some questions over the phone. I called Patricia into my cubicle, and we called the 7-Eleven employment line and put it on speaker. The first question was "Have you ever been convicted of a felony? If yes, press one; if no, press two." I knew Patricia had been convicted of a felony. She was arrested for selling drugs, which she'd done because it was the only way she could make money after her father kicked her out of the house.

Patricia looked at me and asked, "What should I say?" I told her she needed to tell the truth because eventually they would find out anyway. She pressed one.

"Thank you, goodbye," said the speakerphone.

"Damn," Patricia said, staring at the phone. "They didn't even ask my name."

Patricia wanted to work, but I couldn't find a way to get her a job.

Another time, I was doing outreach and ran into a large group of young people skateboarding around a city park with stairs that must have been very fun to jump. One young woman came to me and asked quietly, "Do you have any of those bleach kits?" I did and was happy to give her one. I had been studying up on harm reduction. When someone is addicted to heroin, they cannot stop immediately, so if they're provided with bleach kits, they can properly clean their needles and avoid contracting HIV, hep B, and hep C. That way, if and when these young people kick heroin, they won't be saddled with chronic illnesses.

I gave the young woman a bleach kit, a sandwich, and a brochure on drug-treatment programs that were low or no cost and I kept going, confident that she would contact me in the coming weeks to get into rehab.

I've wanted to perform my entire life. This was from an early show staged in the screened-in porch of my childhood home—a site-specific piece with "all-singin'-all-dancin'-no-reading-cause-I-hadn't-learned-yet."

"Jock."

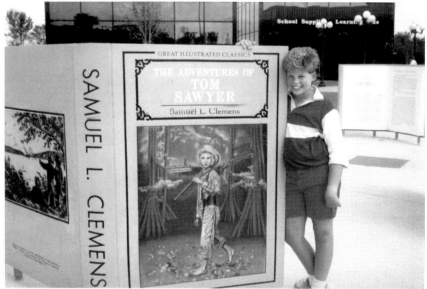

At SeaWorld in San Antonio, Texas. This is one of those pics that reveals a deep truth: "If a child has a beveled leg in a photo, he will be bullied."

My mother standing between my sister, Melissa, and me (with matching perms).

Studying abroad
in Namibia, trying
unsuccessfully to hold
a basket on my head.
My host families were
genuinely shocked
that I couldn't get it
to stay up there.

This was at a time when
I was really leaning in
to being "natural," so
I "grew" a "beard."

Having a mountaintop experience in the Poudre Valley. Being a social worker drained me, so I would recharge with hikes with friends. It's the only sporty thing I've ever liked to do.

My desk at the shelter in Denver. You might be asking where my computer is, but—*you have to remember* cliché alert—this was before people had computers at their desks.

9

Backstage at the Delacorte Theater while performing *Love's Labour's Lost*. This costume makes it look like a traditional production, but it was not. The Shakespeare play was rewritten by Alex Timbers with original music by Michael Friedman. I came in on page 56 and so I started a book club with costar Rachel Dratch.

10

On the set of *Ghost Town* wearing a flesh-colored thong. Can you see the scars on my abdomen? No?! THANK YOU FOR LYING!

My husband, Neil, and me after our wedding, missing a nice piece of cake but feeling surprisingly emotional after making our commitment to each other.

This is "Jeanette," my tiny wiglet from season one of *Somebody Somewhere*. I appreciated that her name was so honored by the hair department.

(*Left*) This was taken during the season two finale episode. I got so sweaty dancing to "Gloria" as sung by Bridget Everett that I had to put my head directly into a large tube on a portable air conditioner afterward.

(*Right*) My daughters Beverly and Yvonne De Carlo. I know I sound like one of those people who treat their pets like human children, but that's only because I am one of those people.

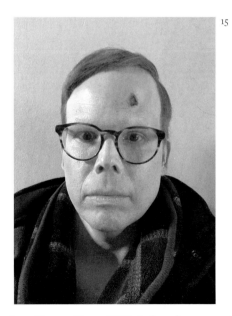

On the set of *American Horror Story: NYC.* I played a gay serial killer who dismembered corpses of his gay victims. It's nice to play a character like yourself.

Bridget's and my mutual friend Larry Krone (*left*), and actor Tim Bagley (*right*, holding Larry's homemade St. Louis Sushi). Tim's character, Brad, made it on *Somebody Somewhere*. For the record, St. Louis Sushi has never given me anything but a good time.

Bridget, Murray, and me on the first day of shooting season three. We couldn't believe we even got one season, even if we were disappointed that we wouldn't get a fourth. Because of our strange shooting schedule, one of the first things we shot in season three was Bridget singing "The Climb," which was the last scene of season three.

As I walked back to my car, I saw the young woman again. She had a shower cap on and was wildly scratching her head with chopsticks given out for free at the King Soopers grocery store.

"Hey!" she said. "How long does the bleach take?"

She was using the bleach kit meant to clean hypodermic needles to make herself into a blonde. A modern-day Jean Harlow. Over the following weeks, whenever I ran into this young woman, she would yell at me, "My hair is orange! I thought it was supposed to make it white!"

I met another who actually was a heroin addict. She told me so herself. She asked if I could get her the money to buy some silver heels, at least four inches high. If she could get the heels, she could get her job dancing back, and then she could go on methadone again and get back into her housing.

I found a way to get her the heels. There was a grant for buying shoes for people who needed them for employment. The funds were usually used to buy steel-toed boots for construction workers and specific black clogs for line cooks, but one time it was used to get a stripper back on the pole. Had I helped this woman?

I feel like I helped only one person in my year working at the shelter. A young woman I will call Bea came to me, and I helped her find a job at a Blockbuster video store. She was a model employee. After she'd worked there for three months, her case manager and I found a transitional living program and she was accepted. I helped her fill out her community college application and she started taking classes at Community College of Denver. She still occasionally sends me messages on Facebook. She's doing well.

Out of roughly one thousand young people who came through the shelter the year I worked there, Bea is the *only* person with a traditional "success story," but I'm pretty sure she would have been fine without me. She was a hard worker and driven, and, like I said, I wasn't good at the job.

Plus, teens are mean. And teens who are experiencing homelessness are even meaner. Staff members at the shelter had to take floor shifts, which required sitting in the office while the young people were in the adjacent common room. That doesn't sound bad, but there were all these rules. The kids couldn't go into the dorms during the day. This was a way to prevent theft, but it also prevented peace. Kids forgot stuff in the dorm, and when they came to you, you had to tell them that they couldn't go in, even though you had a key. Sometimes the thing they forgot was a résumé for the job interview they were going to that afternoon, so you had to let them in, but then another young person who had forgotten their cigarettes screamed at you because you hadn't allowed them to get the thing they needed. A client who came back in the morning after a night shift needed to sleep, so you opened the dorm for them, but then another client wanted to take a nap because the person in the bunk above them snored the night before, and you had to decide whether to let them in to sleep and risk them messing with other clients' stuff or tell them no and get yelled at for the next twenty minutes to four hours until you needed a nap yourself. If kids came in drunk or high, you had to tell them they couldn't sleep there that night, but if they couldn't sleep at the shelter, they might have to sleep on the streets. That is a terrifying type of power.

The clients yelled at me. A lot. I wasn't good at deciding who could go into the dorms and who could not. I wasn't good at deciding who could keep a snack in the shelter fridge and who could not. I wasn't good at gauging who was joking with me and who was straight-up making fun of me. I was only twenty-two years old, and the cutoff to stay at this shelter was twenty-one. I imagine a lot of the clients felt like I was their older sibling babysitting them and wielding power while Mom was out for the night. I was called the F-word every day, many times a day. I was told to fuck off, to fuck myself, and once, rather memorably, to fuck a tree "since you have that long-ass hair!" (I had shoulder-length hair that curved at my shoulders in a perfect *That Girl* wave.)

I sometimes shared these stories with my housemates, looking for sympathy.

"This kid said I should rot in hell today because he didn't come in for a snack and was pissed that it had all been eaten. I told him three times to come in! What a little shit."

"Jeff, these kids are homeless. They need your compassion, not your judgment."

This from the person working for Habitat for Humanity. Of course her clients liked her—she was giving them houses!

There were other problems with my housemates. One of them, Amanda, was not Lutheran. She had grown up as a conservative evangelical, and I could tell she had an issue with the fact that I was gay.

She came into my room, sat on the floor, and asked me this question:

"So, would you say you had an absent father and an overbearing mother?"

I laughed out loud. The way she said it, it sounded like an acting student reciting a precisely memorized line. I also laughed because even back in 1998, it was rare to find someone who believed the myth that your parents made you gay.

I told her my father coached my basketball team (true) and that my mother happily didn't work until I was in the first grade (not true; she'd missed working, but I didn't want to give Amanda the satisfaction). In a dream world, I would have changed her mind and opened her up to accepting LGBTQ people with a loving heart, but she left with the same vaguely disgusted look on her face that she'd had when she came in. Another job I was bad at.

A couple of weeks later, outside my door, I found a brochure from a conservative church that warned that a homosexual lifestyle would lead to an eternity in hell. I asked Amanda if she had left it for me and she said she hadn't. I hope she was telling the truth, because lying can send you to hell too.

When the volunteer year ended, I knew I couldn't work with youth anymore. I hate conflict! Being a case manager for young people requires nonstop tough love. I like people to like me. This is an asset for a comedian but a huge disadvantage for a case manager.

So even though I could have stayed and become a paid employee, I left and took a job at a gay bookstore owned by one of the lunch volunteers at the shelter. It was called Category Six, a reference to the Kinsey scale that describes sexual orientation. It had originally been a bookstore for all LGBTQ people, but when Eve's Garden, aimed at lesbians, opened across town, Category Six became a gay men's bookstore. This happened before I worked there, and I can't defend the decision. I'm just telling you that this bookstore had literature aimed only at gay men, and a whole lot of porno magazines. You really don't realize how much the internet has changed people's lives until you start writing about life in the 1990s. There were men who came in every week and bought hundreds of dollars' worth of old-fashioned gay-porn magazines. Every week.

I was the cashier and spent most of my time scouring want ads for a new social work–y type of job. One day a man who, inexplicably, had both a toupee and dandruff came into the store and asked, "Excuse me, young man, are you available to touch? I'm willing to pay."

I told him, "No, I'm not available to touch, but I am very flattered." And I really *was*! I regret not asking how much he was willing to pay, but it's probably best I didn't. I'm sure I would have been disappointed.

I applied for a job at the Denver Department of Public Health in the infectious disease clinic. I know that to the modern ear, *infectious disease* means respiratory diseases like COVID-19, but think south of that. I got hired at the free clinic. The sexually transmitted infections clinic. The STD clinic if you are Gen X. The VD clinic if you are a boomer.

I was hired to be an outreach worker for a study researching the best ways to prevent HIV infection in men who have sex with men (or MSMs, for short—isn't that a cute li'l acronym?). They used the term *men who have sex with men* instead of *gay* or *bisexual* in case a man didn't identify with those labels. This confused me. I always thought if a man didn't identify as gay, bisexual, or queer, he probably wouldn't identify as a man who had sex with men. The sex-with-men part is sort of the main sticking point that most men deny, you know? It's like saying, "I'm not a cannibal! I'm a person who eats other people!" Not that I mean to compare cannibalism to homosexual sex. Gay men don't eat human flesh . . . but they sure like the bone! (*Nailed it!*)

The study didn't acknowledge gender identity, but this was 1999, and it was a different time. By *different*, I guess I mean "more oppressive"?

The research study was one of the largest of its kind, so lots and lots of MSMs were needed. My job was to go to all the gay spaces in Denver and recruit them to join the study. I went to gay bars, drag shows, the LGBT center, bathhouses, stripper nights, and Cheesman Park on sunny days when gay guys would lie out.

I set up a table with a sign-up sheet for the study and put out literature on how to prevent HIV and other sexually transmitted infections. I handed out condoms, lube, and breath mints. When I was hired, I'd had a fantasy that this was how I would meet a boyfriend, but no one wants to date a guy who has chlamydia literature. It's a real boner killer.

At first, I found the outreach to be a lot of fun, but eventually the novelty wore off, and as with any job, I discovered there were things I didn't love doing.

I went to so many drag shows, and let me tell you, the *Drag Race* queens of today have nothing on the drag queens in Denver in the late '90s—*just kidding!* It was pretty bad drag. The queens wore Shake-N-Go wigs and dresses they stole from their sisters' closets. They lip-synched to ballads standing completely frozen, and even though they did the same number every single week, they often didn't know the words.

The gay bars got old quickly. They were very loud, so while recruiting, I would have to scream, *"Have you had receptive anal sex in the last twelve months?"*

"Done *what*?" they would shout back, scrunching up their faces in confusion.

"Receptive anal sex!" I would shout at the exact moment of silence during a musical transition.

The worst, however, was doing outreach in a bathhouse. The first time I heard what these things were, I was titillated.

"So this is just a big building where men go, take off their clothes, and have sex with anonymous strangers?" I asked my coworkers, a look of naughty delight on my face.

"Yep," they replied officiously.

The first time I went in, I discovered less a bacchanal and more a wet, dirty locker room that hadn't been cleaned in several . . . I want to say years? It smelled of cigarettes, mold, and desperation. I know myself well enough to recognize that my innate prudishness can veer into slut-shaming territory, so I am doing some real self-analyzation here, and . . . nope. It was icky. There were rows and rows of private rooms that each had only a mattress with no sheet. There was a hot tub that screamed *Legionnaires' disease* and there were puddles of liquid all over the floor that I hoped were from the hot tub. There was a dark maze where "anything can happen," and while I could see the appeal of it in theory, I kept thinking, *What if the* anything *is murder?* The worst part, however, was my wardrobe.

As an outreach worker, I was required to dress in the manner of the group I was performing outreach to. This meant that if I was going to the country and western bar, I wore a plaid shirt and jeans, and if I was going to the bathhouse, I needed to wear a towel.

This was not a towel *over* my clothes. The towel *was* my clothes. The study was called Project Explore, and the towel they gave me was emblazoned with that name. I wore a towel with the word *Explore* writ large across my flat ass.

I've never been good at standing up for myself, but this was so ridiculously over-the-top that even mealymouthed Hiller stood up and said, "I cannot work like this!"

Okay, I said something more like "Would it be okay if I wore my street clothes instead of a towel, because it's so awkward and I feel kind of, I don't know, sort of—?" And my boss cut me off and said that was fine and he couldn't believe I had done it even once.

Even when I was fully clothed, recruiting in a bathhouse was difficult. I'm not sure how familiar you are with the culture of gay men's bathhouses, but there isn't a lot of talking. That's kind of its thing. You go there to get your bang on without the complication of human interaction, not to chat with a vanilla twenty-three-year-old about life-threatening sexually transmitted diseases.

I took this job as a professional homosexual in order to become part of the gay community, but ironically, the job put me on the outside looking in. I was in sacred gay spaces but as an observer, not a participant. When I went to bars off duty, I was seen as a guy who handed out condoms instead of a guy you might want to share a candlelight dinner with. Also, I didn't really *want* to go to gay bars on my nights off because it felt like I was going to work.

I did learn a lot about this community, though, even if I didn't feel embraced. I discovered our stereotypes! I didn't know that it was a cliché to like Judy Garland! I didn't realize that it was common to call other gay men Mary. When my coworker called me Mary, I thought he had confused me with my mother, because that was her name.

I was proud that in less than a year, I had grown from a person afraid to tell anyone I was gay to a person who had literally hundreds of condoms in the trunk of my car. I still wasn't dating or using any of the condoms, but it felt like a start.

In addition to outreach, I worked with the "men who have sex with men" on the clinical side. Our primary goal was to test for HIV, but we also did screenings for common sexually transmitted infections. Before the tests, a frank discussion was required with the patient. I asked these men about the most intimate details of their sex lives, and they told me! Public health is gossip in the name of science.

I liked listening to people. I liked being a nonjudgmental ear. Sometimes clients obviously tried to shock me. It was usually a man in his fifties or older talking to this counselor (me) who was half his age and clearly inexperienced in the sex department. There were the scat and piss queens, of course, but others described acts that I had difficulty picturing. Not picturing how someone might enjoy doing this thing but picturing the logistics of *physically* doing this thing. I loved when they tried to shock me. I would nod and say, "Mmm-hmm." When they finished, I would say, "And is this within your acceptable-risk limits?" I liked showing them that I didn't judge them. I could tell I had gained a bit of respect for not freaking out or saying, *"Ew! Why would you do that?"*

As part of the pre-test counseling, I was required to draw blood for the HIV test. Me! Some twenty-three-year-old idiot! It was terrifying. When I moved to New York a couple years later, I investigated becoming a phlebotomist as a day job, but it required schooling, tests, and certifications. In Denver in the late 1990s, you just needed an orange.

My entire training consisted of one of my coworkers handing me a needle and telling me to stick it into an orange. "It kinda feels like that," he told me.

That was it. Hundreds of years of scientific discovery reduced to citrus. And an orange? After everything Anita Bryant had done to our people?

Our study required three vials of blood from each subject, so after the scary part when you inserted the needle, you had to hold the needle in place as you filled all three vials before removing the tourniquet. This was such an overwhelming task that I avoided drawing blood for the first few months. I asked coworkers to do it for me. It was tiresome to find another clinician, but I was terrified of shoving that needle into flesh. One night I was working late and there was no one in the office but me, and I had a client who needed a blood draw. I held my breath and did it. After I was finished, the client said, "Thank you. It's so nice to have someone who knows what they're doing."

Holy shit! I. Was. A *natural*!

I started drawing all my clients' blood after that. I volunteered to help other clinicians with their blood draws. Now, listen, men who have sex with men as a population tend to have thick, visible veins from gym culture, and in the late '90s, they were all wearing T-shirts so tight, the sleeves practically acted as tourniquets, but still, I was good. Sometimes another clinician would come to me and say, "My client says his veins roll."

"Hold my beer," I'd reply.

I was *really* good. But then I got cocky.

I had one client who was a very generous laugher. One of my biggest weaknesses is people who laugh often and liberally at my jokes. This client had a low-grade giggle as soon as he walked in the door, and we were having a kiki! We were talking about the movie *The Talented Mr. Ripley*, which had recently opened. We were joking about how attractive Matt Damon was in the film. "I don't care if he *is* a serial killer," I said, basking in my client's appreciative chuckles, "I'll take my chances!"

We laughed! We laughed so hard! We laughed until I threw my head back . . . and took the needle with me.

Let me interrupt here to give you some scientific facts. When a needle is ripped out of an arm while a tourniquet is still on, there is a sound that is similar to what you hear when you are drinking from a straw and get to the end of your beverage—that sort of sucking noise when all the iced coffee is gone but you can still get a little foam from the bottom. It is an annoying sound at Starbucks, but it is a terrifying sound in an exam room.

Seconds after you hear the sound, blood that was supposed to go into the vial comes *shooting* out of your client's body with great force.

There was blood on my client's arm, blood on my (gloved) hands, and then I noticed . . . there was blood on the *walls of the exam room*! Screw Mr. Ripley; this was Freddy freaking Krueger.

I was able to get the tourniquet off and stop the bleeding. We sat in silence for a moment, and for the first time, my client was not laughing. Then he said the sweetest thing.

"Sorry, I guess I moved."

Then I said the most awful thing. "That's okay."

I let him take the blame. I know, *I know! I am not proud of it!*

My client was okay. He came in for his results and was giggling again, though he did have a rather nasty bruise on his arm. Poor guy.

The vibe in the infectious disease clinic was (and probably still is) intense and stressful. Half of our world told us we should be having a ton of sex, and the other half told us we should never have sex. If any unintended consequences came from having sex, the entire world told you that you were disgusting. We were the epicenter of those feelings of shame and anxiety.

Patients would come in with obvious sexually transmitted infections and tell us that they had never had sex in their entire lives. They would usually blame a hot tub. When this happened, the clinicians wouldn't judge the person, but among ourselves, we did jokingly call it "an immaculate infection."

On the other side of the coin, some people were so terrified of sexually transmitted infections that they would come in for testing when there was a low (or sometimes *no*) chance of their having contracted anything.

That's why when a client of mine requested a full workup even though he had never had anal sex, I asked if he was sure he wanted that.

"A full workup requires a rectal swab. You don't need that if you haven't bottomed," I said.

"Do it anyway," he said. "Just in case."

Okay. No skin off my butthole.

You ready for the second asshole story? You've earned it!

"Undo your pants, bend over, and pull your butt cheeks apart," I said. Isn't it wild that I said that sentence several times a day in the course of my job and it was entirely appropriate?

He did so, and I took out a swab. A swab is just a long Q-tip. I'm sure it's properly sterilized or has some other scientific merit that a normal Q-tip does not have, but it looks like a long Q-tip.

To get a rectal swab, you insert the swab into the anus, twist it, then wipe it on a petri dish that you send to the lab. At this point in my tenure at the clinic, I had done many rectal swabs and was very comfortable performing them.

I inserted the swab into my client's anus, twisted it, and pulled it out, but something was strange. There was nothing to wipe on the dish. It was just a stick. The cotton had come off inside of . . . *him*.

I was confused. How could this have happened? I realized that the cotton might have been twisted to the left by the manufacturer, and

I had twisted to the right, so maybe when I swabbed, I had untwisted the cotton and that was why it got stuck in there. I took a new swab, inserted it, and twisted it to the left this time. I pulled out another empty stick.

On the outside, I remained calm and collected. I told my client to take a deep breath. I was hoping that might loosen him up in a literal sense. On the inside, I was freaking out with a myriad of emotions. I felt bad for him and scared for me, and I was also touched that he hadn't lied about bottoming. That was clear.

I took a third swab. I wanted to be sure to get something, so this time I just sort of plunged it in and out a bit, no twisting. What came out was half a swab, but there was enough cotton to wipe on the petri dish. I counted the exam as complete.

I was still worried about the two and a half cotton balls up my client's ass, though. I went to my boss and asked him for advice.

"Oh, please! Don't worry about it, honey," he said. "You did the guy a favor. He won't have to wipe the next time he takes a shit."

Good Lord in heaven. It's so shocking to see this story in black and white. It was even more shocking to live it.

I hesitate to tell these stories for many reasons, not least of which is patient confidentiality, but it is important for you to see that I was not good at my job. I had not been "called" to public health. I did the job for a little under two years. Sometimes I loved doing it, but I knew there was something bigger calling me. I hated going to work most days. All I wanted to do was play with the improv team I had joined, but we had a show only once a month.

I decided to embrace that long tradition of those who do not know where they want their life to go and applied to graduate school. I was accepted to NYU's master's in social work program. I told my boss, my coworkers, my friends, and my family that I was going to become a licensed clinical social worker so I could do one-on-one therapy.

What I did not tell them was that I was going to defer my enrollment for a bit. I am currently on year twenty-four of my deferment.

Inside Out

by DEMI MOORE*

My hope is that the coming-out story might not be necessary in a generation or two. So many kids today are like, "Coming *out*? I was never *in*." And I love that so many young LGBTQ folks have the security and confidence to be themselves from the beginning. I certainly wish that I had sashayed down the stairs in fourth grade and yelled, "Ma*ma*! She's queer, hinny, get ovah it!" then done that tongue-pop thing followed by a cooter slam. I did not do that. In fact, I had a pretty difficult time admitting I was gay.

There were lots of reasons why. I grew up in a religious household. I feared that my parents would reject me, and I had no one but them. I genuinely believed that God would be angry if I didn't fight this carnal urge. Plus, my peers had assumed I was gay since I was four years old, and I didn't want to give them the satisfaction of being right.

This was also a time before *Will and Grace*. It was *just* before, but

---

*Demi Moore was twenty-two when she got *Blame It on Rio* and twenty-three for *St. Elmo's Fire*. She was on *General Hospital* at nineteen.

still technically before! That said, I just heard a young stand-up say that he had a difficult time coming out because it was before *Glee*. An even younger person told me, "Remember, this was before *Heartstopper*." This was confusing to me, as *Heartstopper* was still on the air. I guess it's difficult to come out no matter when you were born because it is incredibly brave to be authentic and true to yourself. Imagine how difficult it was to come out before that sexy hot-tub scene in *Spartacus*.

I am not brave. I was afraid to put my true self out in the world and face the fear and rejection that might come my way. I wanted to be loved as the perfect little boy and perfect little Christian. I didn't think you could be good and also be gay. I didn't want other people to think I was bad, even though I completely knew I *was* bad.

So I came out in phases.

The first person I came out to was myself when I was about twelve years old. I had gone to a Bible camp in Texas. This was not a progressive camp focused on grace and service to others; this was a fire-and-brimstone Bible camp where you were asked to "accept Jesus into your heart as your personal Lord and Savior." Sometimes people spoke in tongues.

Have you ever seen someone speak in tongues? It's a real shock if you've grown up Protestant, I know that. Basically, people become "possessed" by the Spirit, and they channel a foreign tongue that they do not speak. The tongue is always a language that is conveniently not spoken on Earth and sounds suspiciously like gibberish, but some churches are very proud that their members do it. I'm not completely clear on what the reasoning is behind it, but I think some Christians see it as a way to tap into a new spiritual realm. I found the tongue-speakers both terrifying and interesting. Scary because they looked possessed by a demon, but intriguing because their possession had such dramatic flair!

The camp was not too far from San Antonio and a friend of my mom's had sent her kids there and they loved it, so my mom sent my sister and me there too. My sister was unimpressed, but I snorted this type of Jesus like cocaine. I was all in. They talked about being saved, and somewhere inside of me, I knew I wasn't saved yet and needed their help.

You can always tell conservative evangelical churches by how often they use the word *just*. In prayer, they repeat that word incessantly. Not the adjective *just*, as in "righteous," but the adverb *just*, as in "simply." It's almost a tic, and in my experience, it is present in the prayers at every right-wing church in America and many parts of Canada. It sounds like this: "Lord, we just . . . we come to You, Lord, just . . . Lord, just, we hope, Lord, just be with us today, Lord, as we just . . . praise You and just . . . Lord, we just . . . ." This was a *just* camp.

The camp counselors talked about sex but only to say "don't do it." There wasn't talk of homosexuality. It was as taboo as bestiality to these people. I do remember one male counselor from another cabin who presented as gay. A camper in my cabin called him "fruity" and our counselor overheard and reprimanded him. "Hey!" our counselor said. "He's just a funny guy, he's not bad." Even without saying the word *gay*, my counselor communicated that it was bad. You just know the Florida Department of Education got so excited by that sentence.

This camp also had communal showers. I saw a lot of boys my age—twelve—who had veiny arms and pubes. I didn't know boys my age could even *have* pubes. I felt something in my tummy. Then I saw counselors who had pubes *and* muscles, and I felt something through my whole body. One counselor in particular looked like a blond Marlboro Man, only one who didn't smoke 'cause it was a sin. He would methodically rub lotion from his shoulders down to his toes every night in the bathhouse. He didn't miss one spot. Trust me. He didn't.

One time in the pool house while we were changing into our swimsuits, a counselor bragged about being very tan. He pointed to his dark abdominal muscles covered in tawny gold hair and said, "See how my skin is dark but my hair is light? That's how you know you are a real tanner. Look at the difference between my stomach and my butt!" And he pulled down his swimsuit to show a shockingly graphic tan line.

I almost fainted. The counselors told us that our sexual desires were something we should fight like Christian soldiers in a war of goodness, but let me tell you, his brown abdomen and white ass won the battle that day.

Why was I thinking about the *male* counselors?

Oh no, I thought. *I'm gay.*

I prayed, "Lord, just, just take this away from me, Lord . . . just . . . just . . . Oh, Lord, I just . . ."

The first time I said "I'm gay" out loud was to a waiter at a bar in Cape Town, South Africa. That old cliché!

During my study-abroad program, I spent a month in South Africa and a full week in Cape Town. After three months in rural Namibia, I thought Cape Town was impossibly cosmopolitan. I decided to go to a bar that looked out on the ocean and offered fancy cocktails like . . . the cosmopolitan! It was 1996; the cosmo was having a moment.

The bar also offered karaoke, and a fellow patron got up and sang "I Will Survive." I noticed that my waiter was singing along. In fact, he was singing louder than the person with the microphone. He was dancing and laughing with abandon. I was getting a gay vibe from him, so I started eavesdropping, and some of the things he said to the bartender sounded sort of gay to me. I can't remember what he said exactly, but it was something like "I enjoy having sex and romantic relationships with other men."

I ignored the karaoke and focused my full attention on the waiter. He was utterly fascinating. I wasn't attracted to him; I was attracted to what he meant. He was living his truth, something I wanted to be able to do but just couldn't find a way. I felt an uncomfortable mix of exhilarating freedom, nauseating self-hatred, and recognition in this Cape Town waiter. I wanted him to know that I was like him. We were the same. We were brothers. Sisters? Compatriots.

I got up from the bar and went to the bathroom. I didn't even have to go to the bathroom, but I needed a quiet moment. I looked in the mirror and silently said to myself, *You have to do this.*

I walked right out of the loo and up to the bar, where the waiter knocked back a shot of peppermint schnapps, shouted, "I've got fresh breath now," and kissed a handsome man sitting on a stool. The man kissed him back. He didn't fight it or scream. He seemed to enjoy it. As they kissed, I saw myself! It was my own "Ring of Keys" moment (it's a song from the musical *Fun Home*—google it and weep).

The customer who got kissed left, leaving the waiter alone. This was my chance. I walked up to him, gathered courage from the depths of my soul, and slowly spoke my truth: "I. Am. Also . . . gay."

I let the confession hang in the air. Something so monumental can't be brushed away quickly. How would he react to a fellow member of the queer brood? How would we greet and acknowledge each other? Would he weep from the honor that I had just bestowed on him?

He looked me in the eye and said, "Yeah, gurl, no duh!"

Precious memories.

I left my truth there on the floor and made my way back to the hostel and the closet for the time being.

In the span of two weeks, I saw *In and Out* and *The Object of My Affection*. These were the first films I saw that had gay lead characters in them. They were a road map of sorts. I knew I wanted to be like Paul Rudd's character in *Object*. He was self-assured and knew what he wanted in life. I didn't want to be like Kevin Kline's character in *In and Out*. He was so lacking in self-awareness that he was engaged to a woman! I wanted to be best friends with Joan Cusack, not engaged to her. Tom Selleck was playing a gay man who was comfortable with himself, but the actor seemed so terrified of playing gay that the self-assurance didn't really come across. Wow. I'm just realizing that not even one of those actors is gay, but I guess no famous actors were out at that time, so what were they gonna do, get an actor who wasn't famous but was incredibly talented and emotionally affecting to play the role? Ha-ha-ha-ha-ha-ha-ha! No, silly.

I saw *In and Out* with my friend Sarah and *The Object of My Affection* with my friend Heather. Both were overly effusive about the movies. They said things like "I think it's wonderful that gay people can feel comfortable coming out!" and "It was so sweet and *important* that he found a *man* to love. I wish that for all gay people! *I like gay people! They are safe with me! I would have thrown a brick at Stonewall!*" This was very different from the way they normally discussed movies. Their film criticism up to that point was usually something along the lines of "That was good, I liked the girl's hair."

I got the hint, but I still wasn't ready to tell anyone. I would open my mouth, but no words would come out. I know saying "no words would come out" is a common turn of phrase, but I mean it literally. I really did open my mouth to say it, but I couldn't produce the sound. I didn't even swerve into a different topic. I just stood there, mouth agape, staring into the distance, frozen in fear of who I was.

Both Sarah and Heather were suffering from serious bouts of clinical depression. They were the first people in my life I had encountered with the disorder, and I confess I wasn't the gold standard in being there for them. I said stuff like "Hey, life could be a lot worse!" and "Let's take a walk and get some fresh air" instead of "It sounds like you are really hurting. I am sorry."

Things got bad. Heather left college and moved back in with her parents. Sarah left for a semester to do an intensive inpatient treatment program. She returned to school at the same time I came back from Namibia. By this time, I had seen the world, and Seguin felt small and backward to me. I hated everything, and so did Sarah. We became very close, bonded by our dislike of this tiny world where we felt trapped.

Sarah was cartoonishly depressed. She made Eeyore look like Ellie Kemper. She would call me at night and we would talk. One evening, after we had been talking for quite some time, she said, "Ugh. I think I cut myself too deeply." I didn't know what she meant, but I went to her. Immediately.

I opened the door of her apartment and saw Sarah sitting at her desk. She said, "I think I did something bad." She showed me her forearm, where there was an incredibly deep wound, a half an inch wide and two inches long. She said defensively, "I wasn't trying to kill myself! I just wanted to see what I looked like inside!" I didn't find that explanation comforting. She didn't want to go to the doctor. I told her I thought we should go to one anyway. She refused. I said, "I think we should go." Finally, I firmly stated, "Sarah, we need to go to a hospital."

She looked up at me and asked, "Were you trying to sound really firm just now?"

I shrugged and said, "Yeah."

She laughed. It felt so good to hear her laugh. Some of the terror subsided. She agreed to go to the hospital, but she wanted to drive herself. I know I should have insisted on driving, considering she had a gaping wound on her arm, but I felt like I had used up all my "demanding" energy. She drove with her left hand while I pressed a rag against her right arm, which she held out like a cater-waiter passing appetizers. Thank goodness she drove an automatic.

"This is just great." Sarah sighed. "Once again, I'm the sad fuckup. The weirdo. People are going to think I was looking for attention, but I am just interested in anatomy!" Her voice was raw, full of rage and sadness.

I tried to tell her it didn't matter what other people thought, which coming from me was ridiculously hypocritical.

"You're just so perfect," she sneered. "You study abroad, and you do the school plays and campus ministry. Don't you ever feel bad? Don't you have any problems in your life?"

I wanted to make her feel better. I wanted to be a good friend and let her know that I had lots of problems. I wanted her to know that I didn't like myself at all. I wanted to finally be truthful.

"My problem is that I am gay, and I don't know how to tell anyone. I'm afraid to." I just blurted it out. All it took to get it out of me was severe depression, a mortal wound, and a harrowing, one-handed drive to a tiny hospital in rural Texas.

"*Yayyyyyy!*" Sarah squealed with glee!

It was jarring. She tried to clap her hands like a little child, but I was holding a rag to the wound on her right arm, and we swerved on the road.

"I'm so glad you finally told me! Have you told Heather yet?"

I hadn't.

"Oh, good! Can I tell her you told me? We had a bet about who you would tell first."

"Sure. You can tell Heather," I said. "Let's just get you to the doctor."

"Are you sure a Band-Aid won't work on this?"

I was sure.

I waited in the lobby until Sarah was done. She came out with several stitches and rolled her eyes as she told me about the ER doctor's questions. "He asked me if I had done 'illicit drugs'! I told him coke and LSD, just to make him feel better."

I got Sarah back home, put her in bed, and sat at her desk. I turned out the lights and told her I would stay with her until she fell asleep. (They had given her some licit drugs to help her do so.) She spoke to me from the darkness.

"I'm glad you finally told me. We still love you." Then, after a long pause, she asked, "Do you think I should get a tattoo?"

We were already back to normal.

A little less than a month later, Sarah was given electroshock therapy to treat her severe depression. A side effect can be memory loss. Heather and I drove to see Sarah at her parents' house. I had come out to Heather since the night in the hospital with Sarah. During the visit, Heather and I agreed that Paul Rudd was very handsome. Sarah's eyes got big and she asked, "Jeff, are you telling us that you're gay?"

I nodded in surprise at this question. She knew. I had told her.

She squealed with glee! "*Yayyyyy!* Heather and I had a bet about who you would tell first. I'm so sad it was her!"

So Sarah was the second person I told I was gay and also the fourth. Her therapy had erased my confession. I was strangely insulted by this, but Heather pointed out that Sarah *was* going through some serious shit and maybe I should cut her some slack.

"Jeff, just so you know," Heather said to me on the drive home from Sarah's parents' house. "We weren't betting on your life to make money. We were sort of competing to see which one of us could make you feel safe enough so that you could feel comfortable to come out to us." Neither of them was even slightly surprised, but they had the compassion to see how monumental it was for me to share this truth. Even while they were both suffering from depression.

Heather eventually confessed to Sarah that I had told Sarah first, so she had actually won the bet. I thought that was classy.

I moved into the Christian commune directly after college. I know that is a weird thing to say, but there was a whole chapter about it, so I'm hoping we can just breeze through this for now. This specific Christian commune was historically on the progressive side of things (as opposed to the general idea of a Christian commune . . . is there a general idea of a Christian commune?). We were called to serve our brothers and sisters in Christ without judgment, not for rewards in heaven but because God calls us to serve one another. So, frankly, I was thinking the gay thing wouldn't be a big deal. In fact, I hoped it might make people like me more. This was naive. There had been a regime change just before our year, and the recruitment team had reached out to Christian colleges that weren't Lutheran. They also reached out to older people who hadn't just graduated from college. Diversity is usually wonderful, but in this case, the commune's politics were pushed much further to the right. Four of the ten volunteers that year were from a "Lord, just . . ." church background.

I didn't know this when I called the new director of the program and told her that I was gay and was planning on being out at the house. I heard her gasp in shock. I had a moment of excitement to finally be surprising someone by coming out, but then she said, "I assumed you were gay but not that you would want to be open about it."

Now it was my turn to gasp.

She spoke to me in measured tones. "It will work out eventually, I suppose, but don't tell anyone about this at first. Let them get to know the real you so that when they find this information out, they will have a relationship with you already, and it won't cloud how they think about you."

I know she was genuinely trying to help, but as I write this now, I understand how bonkers this advice was—she wanted me to *lie* to people so that they could get to know the real me? Like . . . whaaaa? I had come out to most of my friends back in Texas by this point, but I was still filled with buckets of shame about being gay, so I went along with her plan to lie. I assumed she was correct that people needed to like me before they found out I was gay. I think I was also partly relieved that I didn't have to come out right away. It's a hard thing to do, and I often procrastinate when I have hard things to do.

The ten of us moved into the house in August, and during our two weeks of orientation we visited all the sites where each of us would be placed. When we got to my agency, the shelter for youth who were experiencing homelessness, one of the statistics the volunteer coordinator bragged about was that the shelter had a case manager specifically for LGBTQ youth. I wanted to shout that I was serving at the perfect agency! I wanted to scream that young queer people needed help and I was thrilled to be someone who would help them! I wanted to shout at my housemates that there was a big rainbow-colored elephant in the room!

Instead, I stared ahead and pretended this information held the same importance to me as the number of beds in the dorms.

During the first couple of months, there were huge revelations by each of the ten members of the house. Every time someone was vulnerable like that, the director of the program did the same thing: She thanked them for sharing with us. She told them it was wonderful that they felt safe enough within the community to do so. She gathered us together and had us pray. She never told any of them to keep these secrets until we got to know them better.

I was closeted at the house, but at the shelter I never hid my sexuality. I remember on the third day of work, one of the youth yelled to me, "Hey, Pantene!" (I had long hair at the time, and I really did look like I had just stepped out of a shampoo commercial.) She asked, "You gay?"

I gulped and said, "Yes. I am."

She nodded and said, "Yeah, I figured. Can you open the dorm for me?"

I opened the door. Everything was fine. No one told me they hated me. Well, at certain points during my year there, many of the kids *did* shout that they hated me, but it wasn't because I was gay, it was because they were nineteen and pissed at the world.

I began forming real relationships with my housemates. I felt guilty that I wasn't being honest with them. I made a promise to myself that while I might not tell the full truth, I wouldn't lie. I wouldn't pretend to drool over a female celebrity or talk about a hypothetical future wife. At the same time, I didn't talk about a hypothetical future husband either. It was before gay marriage, so it would have been a hypothetical male partner, but you get the gist.

In October of that year, Matthew Shepard was killed in Wyoming, just two hours north of us. When I found out, I cried. I couldn't help myself. My housemates looked at me. They certainly were sad about a young, innocent man's life being taken, but it was obvious that I was having a much more personal reaction. Later that night, my housemate Jess pulled me aside, looked me straight in the eye, and said, "Are you ever going to tell us?"

She knew. They probably all knew. I was so ashamed, not of my gayness but of my disingenuousness. In that moment, I realized that the pastor's plan was obviously flawed. I know she was trying her best to protect me, but wow. It was a *bad* idea. How could I build trust with a group of people when I wasn't willing to be vulnerable with them?

The first community night after Matthew Shepard's death, we gathered in the living room for a Bible study led by the pastor. Earlier that day I'd asked her if I could speak. I was going to tell everyone that I was gay. She wasn't sure it had been enough time (it had been two months), but I told her I couldn't pretend any longer.

It was October 12, 1998. I know because I wrote a speech to deliver to the group and it had the date at the top. I keep it with me to this day, tucked in the journal I sporadically kept that year. Here is what I said:

(1) I am not HIV-positive.

(2) I am not in any way sexually attracted to the other male members of the community.

(3) I do not see this as my brokenness; I see the negative way I am treated because I am gay as my brokenness.

(4) I cannot change my sexuality any more than you can. Trust me, I've tried.

(5) I do not believe that I am an abomination or that I am going to hell. I believe I am loved by God.

(6) This isn't something new or unusual for me; I have been gay all my life. I used to pray for it to just go away. I was very angry at God for making me gay, so I lived far too long in the closet. Now I realize that I am another of God's diverse creations.

(7) I don't think this is something I should have to deal with any more than others should have to deal with their heterosexuality. However, we live in a society that does not grant that luxury to homosexuals, so, please, if you have questions or feel the call to express your feelings (approval or disapproval), come to me in a respectful way as I would to you.

(8) I did not tell you at first because I didn't want to be known only as the gay guy, but I always intended to tell you. I believe this community can work if we are open and honest, and it is my prayer that we can do that.

Rereading that piece of paper makes me sad. It makes me remember being that terrified twenty-two-year-old. I want to tell him it will be okay, that there is a much bigger world out there. Seeing how scared I was shows me how much the world and I have changed in the past two and a half decades. I was working so hard to prove I had value despite being gay—that is so terrible. Also, I originally misspelled a lot of words.

Afterward, my housemates were kind. They were not surprised, and they'd suspected that I wasn't telling them about myself fully. One of my housemates was from Holland and said to me, "I love gays. They had the gay games in Amsterdam and when they left, the city was cleaner than it had been when they arrived."

"Thank you?" I said.

Jess, who had earlier asked me point-blank if I was gay, gave me a big hug. She thanked me for coming out. That meant a lot. I was glad my deception hadn't turned her against me.

I did notice that my housemate Amanda said nothing to me. She was the most conservative among us and had been one of the four people I was most concerned about telling. The other three said something encouraging, but as I wrote in my journal at the time, *They seem to tolerate more than accept, but I guess that's all I can ask for.*

After that night, I was completely out in my day-to-day life in Denver. There was only one more coming-out to do. I had to tell my parents.

That November, I flew down to Texas for a wedding. I promised myself that I would not return to Denver without coming out to my parents. I broke that promise.

The following spring, I went to Texas for another wedding. Same promise; same outcome.

In September of 1999, I knew I *had* to tell them. I was twenty-three years old (December birthday). I hated that there was this wall between me and my parents. We were close. I loved them. They loved me. That was actually the problem. I was afraid I would lose that love if I was completely honest about who I was.

I returned to Texas for *another* wedding. You know that time in your early thirties when you're invited to a wedding every other weekend?

Well, when you go to a small Christian college in Texas, that time of your life happens in your early twenties. If you're saving yourself for marriage, there is less incentive to play the field.

On the plane, I rehearsed a speech in my head, but every time I got to the part where I was about to say the words *I'm gay*, I stalled. I couldn't even come out in my imagination. I was working at a gay men's bookstore at the time, so I'd bought a book called *Now That You Know*, which was a manual for parents navigating their children's coming out. I also brought my worn copy of *Stranger at the Gate*, written by a former evangelical pastor who came out of the closet after being a speechwriter for the televangelist Jerry Falwell. That book had helped me reconcile my faith and my sexuality, and I thought my mom might be helped by it too.

That night, I went to my friend's rehearsal dinner and returned to my parents' place but I never worked up the courage to tell them. The next day my parents and I attended the wedding. We had a nice time, but when we got back home, once again I couldn't tell them. On Sunday morning, we went to church, but at breakfast after the service, I found myself tongue-tied again, incapable of saying the words. I was literally shaking with fear.

At the wedding, I had given my parents' home number to my college friend Suzie, and she called me that afternoon to catch up since we hadn't had a chance to talk to each other all weekend. I came out to her, and I told her I felt like I was going to vomit because I needed to tell my parents but I couldn't.

"I've met your mom," Suzie said. "She's nice to everyone. Why would you think she wouldn't be nice to you?"

Suzie made a very good point. I went into the living room, where my mom was watching a rerun of *Cheers*. Isn't it wild that I can remember that? I asked my mom if I could talk to her. I could tell she recognized this was an important moment. She turned off the TV and un-reclined her chair. My dad was ten feet away at the kitchen table. I sat down on the couch, looked my mom directly in the eyes, breathed deeply, and said, "Uh . . . how can I say this? I'm scared to say this."

My mom said, "It's okay, just say it."

"I'm gay," I said.

"I know," she said.

"You *know*?"

"I suspected. Just for a few years."

"Why didn't you say anything?" I asked.

"The pastor said not to," she replied.

"You talked to the pastor? *Our* pastor?"

"Oh, no." She shook her head. "I talked to a gay pastor at a church downtown. It's a gay church, I guess? He said you needed to tell me first and I shouldn't ask."

This was a classic move for my mom. Of course she had researched this issue that was weighing on her heart. Of course she made it easy for me to say what I had to say. Of course she was accepting and loving and told me it was okay.

I gave her the books; she thanked me for them. She told me I never had to worry about telling her anything. "My love is unconditional," she said.

My dad was present for the entire conversation but didn't say anything. At all. No words, sounds, or breath escaped his lips. My mom and I went out on the porch and drank some wine, and he went to bed, still saying nothing.

My mom and I talked for a couple hours. It was a warm conversation. For the first time, we felt like two adults talking rather than a mom and her son. She told me about friends from high school she suspected were gay and floated the idea of setting me up with the son of a woman at work because "he's gay too." We talked about faith and her belief that God is love first, before anything else. She told me she'd read a pamphlet called "What the Bible *Really* Says About Homosexuality."

"Sodom and Gomorrah was actually about punishment for inhospitality!" she declared.

It was a wonderful conversation, but I couldn't stop thinking about my dad and his silence. "Do you think he's mad?" I asked.

"He loves you," she said. "He just needs to get used to it. I've been thinking about it for most of your life."

"I thought you said you've only known for a little bit! When did you first suspect?"

She smiled and said, "Remember you were in that soccer league when you were four and the coach kept yelling at you because you were picking flowers instead of keeping your eye on the ball? Around then." Who could argue with that logic?

The next morning, I woke up early for my flight home. My dad was waiting for me in the living room, ready to take me to the airport.

"You got everything?" he asked.

I nodded.

During the drive we talked about nothing but the weather and traffic. At the airport, he parked the car and got out with me. He helped me get my bag out of the trunk. We stood there in silence.

"You got everything?" he asked again.

"I think so," I said.

"We can mail it to you if you forgot something."

"I think I got everything," I said.

"Okay. Well . . ." His voice broke, and he pulled me into a hug and squeezed my whole body tight. My dad was always loving, but a hug, and such a tight one, was unusual. "We love you. We just want to make sure you have everything."

In that moment, I did.

S'Tori Telling

by TORI SPELLING[*]

When I first moved to New York, in the summer of 2001, I forced myself to go to open-call auditions. These are auditions where you don't need to be invited; anyone can show up, so they are always very crowded. They almost never lead to a job. Maybe it's different if you are a fierce dancer or super-gorgeous or if you have a special skill needed for a job, but I don't play the fiddle at all, much less on a roof, so it never worked for me. I guess it's good to get out there and experience rejection because learning how to handle that is a skill you need as an actor. Learn how to handle rejection I did.

One particularly educational audition was for an Off-Off-Broadway musical about young single people. The casting director gathered the hundred or so actors who'd shown up and explained that there were simply *too many people* there.

"Y'all! There are too many people here!" she said. Several times.

She told us she would be typing us out, which meant she'd tell

---

*Tori Spelling was seventeen when she was cast in *Beverly Hills 90210*.

people who were not physically right for any of the roles to, well, get the fuck out. This casting director said over and over again that being typed out would be a *good* thing for the actors.

"Y'all, this means you will get a free day! 'Cause this audition will go on *all* day! We hear songs in the morning, then call back people to read, and then a dance call after that! Y'all, I am doing you a favor if I type you out! You will get a free day!"

An assistant walked up and down the line of actors, looking each person in the face. When she came to me, she scrunched up her nose like she was smelling something awful.

Of the more than one hundred actors at that open call, about five were typed out. It took roughly forty-five minutes.

Y'all! I got a free day!

My first Off-Broadway show was called *The Awesome 80s Prom* and it was an immersive prom experience set in the 1980s. Sometimes a title tells you a lot.

I played the class president, who was modeled after Alex Keaton, Michael J. Fox's character in *Family Ties*. The show was mostly improvised, and the actors walked through the crowd mingling with the audience as if we were all at a prom in the 1980s. The high school was called Wanaget High, so that gives you a clue as to the tone.

I have always wanted to be a great actress of the stage. Just because I was doing an immersive show didn't mean I would take any shortcuts. I had been hired to play a Republican in the late 1980s. I studied up on issues of the time so I could seem authentic. I praised Ronald Reagan, trying to be subtle and subversive. I said things like "I like trickle-down economics 'cause tax laws benefiting the rich are gutters that bring the money to society at large. Plus, they allow me to stay rich." I was really good at it.

Here is the truth, though: Subtlety doesn't work on a crowd of drunk bachelorette partyers. And any New Yorkers who came without a bacchanal agenda were Democrats, and this was in the middle of the

2004 election, so they became very angry when you mentioned having Republican allegiance. I would say, "I like George Bush . . . 'cause he's our vice president!" and the well-meaning attendees would forget we were supposed to be in the eighties and shout about how George W. Bush stole the 2000 election. I did that show every Friday and Saturday night for a year. We got fifty dollars a show, so I was still working at my day job and performing improv shows for free during the week. One hundred bucks a week isn't enough money to take abuse from drunk people, so I found a way to get the audience to like me.

Over the course of a couple months, I morphed my character from smug Republican into hapless virgin. I danced off the beat, stared slack-jawed at the actors playing the cheerleaders, and held a book over my crotch when the Swedish exchange student character gave me a hug. People liked me more! The bachelorette partyers felt sorry for me, and the politically active people didn't pay attention to me anymore.

All I really wanted the audience to do was not yell at me and maybe vote for me for prom king. (It was an interactive piece of the show billed as being different every week, but the nerdy girl always won queen, and the gay kid modeled on Duckie from *Pretty in Pink* always won king.) Instead, large groups of women, usually the bachelorette parties, began taking me into intimate dance circles, where they would try to—and I know this sounds dramatic but I can't think of another word—*deflower* me. Anonymous women grabbed and squeezed my butt, many of them tried to touch my genitals, and one of them kissed me. With tongue. I realize the kissing thing doesn't seem as bad as the grabbing-the-penis thing, but I play by *Pretty Woman* rules. When the woman kissed me, I said, "Please stop!" She looked at me, confused, and slurred, "But you're a virgin?" Obviously, this was before the #MeToo movement more concretely defined what *consent* means. It is the only time I have ever been sexually harassed. I believe all women. Even the ones who sexually harassed me.

Straight men were also bad. They tried to take me under their wing and offer advice on how to get women. I suppose that was sweet enough, but when they started talking about the other characters in the show, things became very strange. They offered blunt critiques of my female castmates' bodies. Often positive but occasionally not. Even the positive critiques were disgusting. I didn't know how to balance playing a character and defending my castmates and women everywhere because these guys were reprehensible. Lots of very specific comments about very specific body parts, most unseen by these creeps. Seriously, is this how straight guys talk to each other? Don't do that!

I really didn't like being grabbed and pinched by groups of bachelorettes or hearing the secrets of straight-male bonding, but there were two good things about changing my character from politically savvy capitalist to boner-wielding sad sack. The first was that I was able to avoid getting screamed at by angry Democrats. The second was that I learned that in extremely low light, when loud eighties music is playing and groups of women are dangerously intoxicated with alcohol and the spirit of having a fun night out, I can kind of pass as a sexually deprived, cartoonish version of a straight guy, and somehow, embarrassingly, that makes me feel good.

In 2017, I auditioned to play a maître d' in a movie called *The Widow*. The character was the boss of a young waitress who was being stalked by the titular widow. It was depressing to see I had aged out of waiter and into maître d', but that didn't stop me from auditioning. I booked the gig! The widow was played by Isabelle Huppert and the waitress by Chloë Grace Moretz! Nothing like famous faces to ease the pain of aging.

The film took place in New York City, but it was shot in Dublin, Ireland, because the director, Neil Jordan, was Irish. I didn't think it made financial sense for them to fly me over and put me up in a hotel for three weeks when I was only on set for four or five days, but I was not about to argue! As you know, I had been trying to get to Ireland since my first study-abroad meeting in 1996. Twenty years later, I was humming Enya and finally living my dream.

Well, sort of. I didn't kiss any redheaded boys or watch Tom Cruise changing through a crack in the wall, but I used my time off to the fullest. I went to the Trinity library, took the Guinness beer tour, and spent a weekend in County Cork! I did everything but take an Irish step-dancing class. I was living my tourist fantasy so hard that I would get annoyed when I had to work on the movie.

One day I was called in when I hadn't been scheduled to shoot anything. The assistant director told me I had to meet with the stunt coordinator.

What? Surely I had misunderstood the words she spoke in her gorgeous Irish lilt, because asking me to perform a stunt felt a bit like asking the Rock to do a Broadway musical—it's technically possible but doesn't seem like a great fit.

I met with the stunt director in a dance studio. He called it a gym, but there were mirrors and a ballet barre. The next day we would be shooting a scene in which the widow charges at the young waitress. The director thought it made sense for my character to restrain the widow when she does this.

"Okay . . . ," I said tentatively.

The stunt director gave me my instructions. "Ya graberbah de shoulders, ra? Pushnback, but really ya catchin' ha ahrms? Follah?"

I nodded, hoping that was an appropriate response to whatever he'd just said.

We practiced for about an hour. A stuntwoman stood in for the widow and I got the idea of how to restrain her. I grew to love the challenge of it. They cautioned me that the actor might not fight as hard as the stuntwoman, so I might have to adjust on the day. I was just starting to feel confident when the stunt director spoke again.

"Ya know de widow is Isabelle Huppert, ra? She's a feckin' livin' legend. Don't hurt her." The last part he said completely clearly, and the words echoed in my ears.

The next day on set I could think of nothing other than the fact that I would have to restrain France's greatest living actress. I looked at her tiny frame compared to my own. I thought about my klutzy gait, of all the times I'd bumped my head because I didn't have great control of my body, and how when I was in a regional production of *Li'l Abner*, the woman playing Daisy Mae got stepped on by the actor playing Abner and never danced again!

Ms. Huppert was a delicate flower—a foot shorter than me and a size 0. She was costumed in a matronly Dior suit, delicate and soft. I felt like I was Lennie in *Of Mice and Men* and my bunny rabbit had the most César Award acting nominations of all time.

It came time to shoot the scene. I stood at my maître d' lectern, palms sweating. They called "Action" and the widow started her scripted freak-out. She ran toward me. I tried to make myself as soft as I could, and—she ran over me like a freight train.

I literally fell over. The director had to cut and we had to do it again. The idea I'd had that I'd need to pull punches with Isabelle Huppert was comical. In fact, I wish she had gone a little easier *on me*!

The film was renamed *Greta*, and the way the scene came out in the movie is hilariously awkward. You can see my fear as I barely touch her and the two stunt performers playing restaurant-goers tackle her to the ground. Isabelle Huppert continues kicking, spitting, and fighting, but if you look closely, you can see my flaccid arms trying to get out of the way, not out of fear of hurting her but out of fear of being hurt *by* her.

I'd been worried about what it meant that I had aged out of waiter and into maître d'. Meanwhile, here was a woman playing a widow who could knock me over and not lose one of her Gucci heels. Lesson learned. Thank you, Mme. Huppert.

Baggage: Tales from a Fully Packed Life

by ALAN CUMMING*

I remember arriving in New York City on the Greyhound bus! I had to hold my wide-brimmed hat close to my head with my white-gloved hand just to look up and see all the tall buildings.

JK—my arrival in the big city was slightly less cinematic. When I deferred my acceptance to the NYU master's program, I told my friends and family that I wanted to spend a year getting to know the city and earn a bit of money before I started school. The truth was that I wanted to perform.

I didn't tell people about my desire to become an actor because it was difficult to find a way to spin my life transition from helping people to making fart jokes. Even I thought I sounded like a jerk. Can you imagine me trying to tell someone else about it? *I used to help young people who had nowhere to turn find housing and jobs, but* now I *do* improv!

---

*Alan Cumming was thirty-three when *Cabaret* made him an international star.

I did tell one person, my friend Catey, who was still working with vulnerable populations back in Denver. I told her I felt guilty and self-ish about focusing on performing instead of helping people.

"You're still helping people," she said. "You're making them laugh!"

"Does that mean I'm *not* helping people if I have a bad show?"

Bless her heart—Catey took a deep breath and said, "Yes."

Although I was afraid to tell people about my desire, I couldn't suppress it. It felt very similar to coming out. My need to perform was something I'd wanted to keep in the closet, but I could no longer do it no matter how hard I tried. I was living authentically as a queer person, so now I needed to live authentically as a performer.

I knew I couldn't become a professional actor in Denver, San Antonio, or, especially, Seguin. Or maybe I could, but not on the scale that I wanted. So I had to move to one of the big cities—New York, LA, or Chicago. It was now or never; after all, I was getting so old—I was twenty-five!

In my mind, getting to the city was the biggest obstacle to becoming an actor. Moving across the country for a dream certainly makes you feel like you are committing. I thought the grad-school ruse might help ease this difficult transition, but since I had deferred my acceptance to NYU, I didn't have access to student housing. In retrospect, I am so glad I deferred. If I hadn't, I would have had student-loan debt weighing me down for decades.

So in 2001, without a place to live, I went to New York City and began the adventure of setting up a life there. It is difficult to move anywhere, but it is *really* hard to move to New York City. Perhaps you've heard that "the rent is too damn high"? It is.

You also have to learn about subways and bodegas and that Houston is pronounced How-Sten. (That point will land better in the audiobook.)

Just to give you an idea of how different it is to live in New York City versus other towns, let's look at buying groceries, which I think we can agree is a mundane occurrence in our lives. It isn't that New

York doesn't have grocery stores—it does, but they are different from grocery stores in the rest of the country. They are much, *much* smaller, but somehow have many more people in them at all times of day. You will never find an aisle that doesn't have a person standing completely still in it, and due to the store's microscopic size, there is no way to pass someone standing still in an aisle. You must completely leave the aisle, let the other person out while they give you the stink eye, then reenter the aisle. A shopping trip without constant pleas of "Excuse me" is a true suburban privilege.

But before that, you must consider how to *get* to the grocery store. If you are lucky, there is one on your block, but more often than not, you will need to walk several blocks, which means that you will need to carry your groceries several blocks back to your home. Remember, you do not have a car because there is nowhere to park.

And if you live in a neighborhood that isn't all that developed (that is, gentrified)—and you *will* live in a neighborhood that isn't all that gentrified, because that is the only neighborhood you'll be able to afford—then you will most likely be in a food desert and have to take a subway to a grocery store. That means you'll need to carry bags of groceries onto a train or get one of those grandma carts and learn to maneuver it up and down steps with it *ba-bump-bump-bump*ing behind you as you climb and descend the endless staircases that you encounter in New York City public transportation.

Once you get to the store, you will discover that it does not have something you think of as a completely common food item, like, say, pecans, but it *will* sell MSG in the spice section. Oh, and everything is wildly expensive. The plums that look like they were delivered via golf club are $7.99 a pound. People in Texas jokingly called Whole Foods "Whole Paycheck," but those prices were comparable to and sometimes cheaper than the prices at the Fine Fare down the street from me in the East Village.

If you move from Texas to New York City, you will encounter a radically different approach to customer service. In Texas it's all "Yes, sir" and "Let me get that for you," and in New York it's steely glares and monosyllabic responses. Of course, the person in Texas is gossiping about you immediately after you leave the store, and the New Yorker never thinks about you once you leave. Or while you are in the store, for that matter. I'm not saying New York is worse. It is just very, very different.

The thing about New Yorkers and customer service—in fact, about New Yorkers in general—is that language and tone are completely different than in Middle America. It's like learning a new dialect. New Yorkers *are* polite, contrary to popular opinion, but they have different cultural ways of showing it. For instance, one day in my first few weeks of living in the city, I sat down on the subway and crossed my legs, which caused the loose change in my pocket to fall onto the floor. I didn't notice, but the young woman behind me on the train did. She poked me forcefully and said, *"Hey! Ya dropped ya change!"* I was taken aback by her tone—she was screaming at me. I looked down, saw my quarters and nickels, and picked them up, apologizing. "Sorry, I didn't realize they fell." She nodded and said, "I *know*! I didn't want you to lose your money 'cause change adds up."

I was so confused. She was being nice? Then why had she screamed at me? Because New Yorkers just have a different affect, and once you learn and accept that, you will see that they aren't rude as a whole; their tone is just harsh. It's probably because crowds are everywhere and a cup of coffee costs nine bucks.

"Wow, Jeff. You make New York City sound horrible. Why do you live there?" you may be asking. To quote Lin-Manuel Miranda, "It's the greatest city in the world," so "I am not throwing away my shot," and "Excuse me." (Lin-Manuel Miranda said, "Excuse me" to me once at a restaurant.)

The things this city does well make up for the difficult grocery runs, the expensive rents, and seeing other humans' fecal matter on a surprisingly regular basis. New York is where dreams happen, where you can see glitzy musicals on Broadway and also a gritty modern ballet that is "site-specific" (that usually means it takes place in one of the dancers' apartments). New York is where you can find your people because all the weirdos in small towns come here and join forces so that the "normal people" back home who were mean to you growing up become the new weirdos.

So that's why I made the effort to move here. And why I make the effort to stay.

Before I moved here for good, I came for a week and stayed with a married couple I *sort of* knew but not well enough that it was a good idea for me to stay on their couch for an entire week. I had done improv in Denver with the husband. He'd told me he was moving to New York City to try to become a full-time screenwriter. His wife supported his goal and arranged something with her company in Denver that allowed her to work remotely from New York. This was a beautiful thing for her to do for her husband—and a huge sacrifice.

"It's hard to work from home," she told me. (This was before working from home was normal.) "It's a sacrifice in pay and quality of life, but I do it because I love him."

Unfortunately, she hadn't signed up to make a sacrifice for a guy on her husband's old improv team. I was sleeping in their living room. Which was her office. It was also their kitchen, dining room, and entire home. The only other space was the bathroom and the very tiny bedroom. She was on the phone all day and needed quiet. So I would leave their house at nine a.m. when she started working and stay out until ten or eleven p.m. so that when I arrived home, I could immediately lie down. I thought I would be able to hang out with the husband during the day, but he was extremely focused on writing in the tiny bedroom, so that week I was on my own. They never said anything mean to me, but you can tell when you're a burden, and I was a burden. One night, a rainstorm suddenly dumped sheets of water from the sky, so I stood under the elevated subway in Astoria trying unsuccessfully to stay dry. It was too early to go back to the apartment and too expensive to sit down in a restaurant. So I just got wet and pretended I was Gene Kelly.

I learned how to get from their place in Astoria, Queens, to Manhattan by subway only. I didn't take a cab in New York City until I had lived here for two years. That week I would take the subway to Manhattan and then walk around all day looking for housing and work. I found a job at Barnes and Noble pretty quickly, but the apartment was elusive. This was just before you could rent apartments on the internet, so I walked around neighborhoods looking for For Rent signs to avoid paying a broker fee. Even without the fee, you had to fork out first and last month's rent and put down a security deposit, and most of the apartments I looked at were in the nine-hundred-a-month range—an astronomical sum for rent at the time. Now, however, that is so cheap, it has become a joke about my advanced age.

Most of the apartments required you to put down two months' rent up front—in cash. It was very difficult to get upwards of three thousand dollars in cash. ATMs allowed withdrawals of only five hundred a day, so I'd had to take the money out little by little over the course of a week before I came to New York. Once I had the cash, I was scared to have it in my wallet. What if I was mugged? So I put it in my shoes. I had fifteen hundred dollars in each shoe, the most expensive inserts in history.

I remember going to one open house on Charles Street in the West Village that I found through an ad in the *Village Voice*: "Studio apartment, W. Vill, 250 square feet, $1100/month. Open house June 3, 11 a.m.–2 p.m." It was out of my price range, but it was my dream neighborhood. I put the three thousand dollars in my shoes and went to the open house on June 3 at ten a.m., a full hour early. There were easily fifty people in line already, and the line continued to grow behind me. At eleven a.m., we all filed into the incredibly tiny apartment (that had exposed brick!) and milled around in bumper-car fashion as we saw the bathroom (no storage), the kitchen (no oven), and the living room/bedroom (no closet). It started out orderly, but about six minutes in, everyone went bonkers.

"I will give you cash for this place right now"; "I have three months' rent *plus* deposit!"; "I have *four* months' rent and I'll suck your dick real nasty!" Okay, maybe I exaggerate, but it was competitive. I told the landlord I had a wad of sweaty cash in my shoe and he said, "Fill out an application. Stop offering me cash!" A decent guy. It probably would have been a great place to live if I'd had a job that paid more than nine dollars an hour. I filled out an application. I am still waiting for a response.

I finally found a place in Harlem. My good friend Meredith had moved to New York six months earlier. She'd worked at the teen shelter at the same time as me! We were best friends! Well, in truth, she'd worked the night shift and I'd worked the day shift, and I had never spoken to her except at the all-staff meetings, and I wasn't exactly sure of her last name. When I reached out to her and she told me there was a sign in her building about an apartment for rent upstairs, this woman I kind of knew was suddenly my best friend! Bonds are formed quickly from the bondage of moving to New York City. The apartment was $750 a month, which was almost double my rent in Denver, but it was the cheapest thing by far I had seen in New York City. We were located on 142nd Street and St. Nicholas in the heart of Harlem.

My apartment had one window, which faced an air shaft. There was also a door in the kitchen that overlooked an abandoned lot. It was just a door and a platform; I don't think it was a fire escape because there were no stairs down to the ground. There was definitely a fire escape in the front of the building facing the street, but my apartment faced the back. There were stairs to go *up* from my little platform but not down. Oh. I'm just realizing that maybe I was supposed to climb *up* the burning building, over the roof, and down the front? That doesn't seem especially safe. Thankfully, there were no fires during the time I lived there.

I signed the lease and flew home to my parents' house in Texas. We loaded my clothes and personal effects into a rented minivan for the drive to New York City. I had taken nothing from Denver because all my furniture was hand-me-downs from local churches that were given to the full-time volunteers when they left the Jesus commune. My bed was stained by a previous owner, and my chair had a spring in the seat that you had to carefully negotiate to avoid being sodomized when you sat, so it seemed right to leave them behind. I had saved money and bought IKEA furniture, which at the time felt like a very grown-up thing to get. For twelve hundred dollars, I got a futon, a bed, a table that doubled as a desk, and a TV stand. I took dishes from some church lady in Denver and towels my sister no longer needed after she'd gotten fancy ones at her wedding. I was set!

For the first three or four months in New York, I felt so alone. I slowly became friends with Meredith downstairs, but she had been living in the city for six months and had already created a life. My friends in Astoria were also too busy for social time (no doubt they had had enough of me during the week I'd lived in their home). I would walk around the city moodily during my free time. Occasionally I bought a ticket to a Broadway show from the TKTS booth, but that was too expensive to do on a regular basis, so usually I just walked from Harlem down to Times Square. Then to Herald Square. Then to Union Square. Then to Tompkins Square. Then back up the way I'd come— Tompkins Square, Union Square, Herald Square, Times Square. A circle of squares.

At night when I got home, I'd realize I hadn't spoken all day, so I would speak aloud to myself in my apartment. "Hello. Hello. I. Am. Speaking. This is my voice! I have a voice!" It was a pitiful soliloquy, both emotionally and dramaturgically.

I told Meredith I was feeling lonely, and she suggested we take advantage of the amazing world just outside our front door. We needed to do something quintessentially New York. We decided to see Shakespeare in the Park. It was free, culturally fulfilling, and, best of all, this show had famous people! These were not just any celebrities—these were A-listers! Shakespeare in the Park was doing a production of *The Seagull*, which is actually not Shakespeare but Chekhov. I found this confusing but got over it because of this cast: Meryl Streep, Kevin Kline, Natalie Portman, Marcia Gay Harden, Christopher Walken, Philip Seymour Hoffman, John Goodman, Larry Pine, Debra Monk, and Stephen Spinella. It was directed by Mike Nichols and had been adapted by Tom Stoppard. It was the hottest ticket in town! I couldn't believe it was *free*!

Then I learned that it wasn't free. You didn't pay money for these tickets, but you paid with your time. The way Shakespeare in the Park's free-ticket system works is that people line up outside the Delacorte Theater in Central Park and tickets are handed out at noon on each day of the show. There are a limited number of tickets, and the number varies from day to day, so you are never sure if you will get in, but you have a much better shot if you get in line early and wait for the handout. For a show with this starry cast, people were waiting in line for hours. The park doesn't open until six a.m., but Meredith had read in *Time Out New York* that people were lining up on Central Park West and Eighty-First Street at five a.m. to get a great spot in line.

We decided to get there at three a.m.! We would leave our apartment at two thirty a.m. after a disco nap when neither of us had to work the following morning. Meredith packed food and water. I packed joie de vivre! We would each get two tickets. She would give her extra ticket to her friend who was a nanny and needed a night out, and I would give my extra ticket to the wife of my friend who had let me sleep on her couch for a full week. A wonderful way to say thank-you!

We left our apartment at two forty-five a.m. (Oops! Late starts happen, but how much difference could it possibly make?) and walked into the surprisingly warm summer night. The streets were relatively empty, but it was New York City, and, as they say, she never sleeps. I quibble with this statement because when you are hungry at one a.m., there aren't all that many options for food, but it is true that you will never be completely alone on a street in New York City no matter what time it is.

This was why we weren't surprised to see someone approaching us as we crossed 142nd Street. The person was short but wide. It was unusual, but I'm not one to body-shame, so I just kept walking. As we got closer, it became apparent that the thing coming toward us was not human. It was a group of dogs. I know this is hard to believe, and if I hadn't seen it with my own eyes, I would call bullshit, but I swear to you that this was a pack of *wild* dogs. They were dirty and wolf-like. They traveled in a triangular formation with the largest dog at the front, two larger dogs flanking the back, and puppies with swollen tummies in the middle. They swerved around us and disappeared into an overgrown section of St. Nicholas Park.

We had moved from the mountains of Colorado to the most populated city in the country, and *now* we were seeing wild animals roaming the streets? It was shocking, and Meredith and I couldn't stop talking about it as we approached our subway stop at 145th Street. I was commenting on how dirty the dogs were and wondering if we should call a rescue organization. I was so lost in thought I didn't notice Meredith stop or feel her tapping me on the shoulder.

She later told me she was trying to get my attention, but I kept walking and found myself in the center of three men standing in a triangular position. Two of them were on my left and they were holding up their hands, palms out.

That's funny, I thought. *It almost looks like they are being held up by a man with a gun.* I had that thought at the exact moment I caught a glimpse of the man on my right. He was holding a gun.

I. Walked. Between. The people. And. The gun.

It made sense that we were going to see Chekhov now, because I had seen his gun. It didn't look like a robbery, more like a fight with very high stakes, but I didn't feel like I should stick around to ask about specifics.

I quickly ran down the subway stairs, but as I descended, I turned and saw all three men looking down at me in confusion. I wonder if they all laughed about it as soon as I left, defusing the tension that had called for the gun in the first place.

Can you believe that queen just walked in front of my gun? one would say.

Yeah, and what was he saying about wild dogs? the other would reply.

Then they would forget whatever it was they had been fighting about and go have a beer to laugh about the dumbass from out of town on the streets of Harlem at three a.m.

Meredith had come down a different set of subway stairs across the street and yelled at me, *"Did you see the gun?"*

Yes, I'd seen it. Eventually. We saw a police officer sitting on a stool just outside the ticket booth. We ran to him and screamed, "There's a guy upstairs with a gun and he's holding up two other men!"

This is another part of the story that doesn't seem believable, but I swear to you it happened. The cop looked at us, tilted his head, then let out a long, slow sigh. It wasn't a sigh that said *What has the city come to?* or *How can people be so cruel to each other?* It wasn't even a sigh that said *These idiot kids walked into a gunfight!* It was the type of sigh that you would give if you were in the break room at Target and your boss came in to tell you to get back to work 'cause a kid had puked in the Greeting Card aisle. The police officer placed his hands on his legs, stood up, gave a little stretch, and slowly walked up the stairs. Meredith and I looked at each other, unsure what to do next. We settled on shrugging. It was a shrug that said *I guess we should just get on the train and go see Meryl?*

We did just that. The train took a while to come, but we finally got to Eighty-First Street at 3:40 a.m. It was later than we had hoped to arrive but earlier than *Time Out New York* told us the line started. We walked up the stairs and glanced across the street to the park to see a line of 178 people. Yes, 178 people. I know this because when we got to the end of the line, we were each handed a piece of yellow legal paper with the names of everyone who was currently in line. Meredith was 179 and I was 180. The man in front of us said that this wasn't an official list sanctioned by the Public Theater, but the group had agreed to honor it when we transitioned to a line inside the park when it opened at six a.m. Tensions were high. Each person could get two tickets, which meant there had to be at least 360 tickets for us to get ours. The man in front of us said that the Delacorte had eighteen hundred seats, so we should be fine, but the woman in front of him pointed out that members of the Public Theater got free seats, actors were assigned comps, and employees of the Public also had access to tickets, and with such a starry cast, many people were using back-channel connections to get in, greatly limiting the number of free tickets handed out to the public. The woman's speech was very detailed and felt to me like it should have been delivered in front of a bulletin board with red string connecting pictures of all the important players. These people were serious about Shakespeare tickets—er, Chekhov tickets.

As the night continued, more people joined the line behind us. We gave them the same speech we had just received. This was serious, but we started joking with our line mates about things, although only certain things. You know how at airports they used to have people who checked you in rather than those little machines? And sometimes you would have great rapport with the airline attendant at the check-in counter, and you would be silly about how early in the morning your flight was or about your fear that your bag would be too heavy or about how you wished you were flying first class? But as much as you joked about those things, you also knew that the one taboo subject that you must *never* joke about were bombs and terrorism? Well, there was also a subject you did not bring up in that line. You could laugh and joke about wild dogs and walking in front of a loaded gun and how your butt hurt from sitting on cobblestones all you wanted, but if you even hinted that you would let someone cut in front of you, you would be taken away by security and put on a metaphorical no-fly list.

A community formed. We became a new group: line people. Laws were made. Cutting in line was forbidden, but you could hold the space for someone who was there already so that they could run to get coffee or use the bathroom. It was unspoken that you shouldn't be gone for more than five minutes or so, but some leeway could be given here and there. The man in front of us was chatty and polite. He told us he was visiting from some state that I can't remember. Missouri, maybe? He and his wife had come to New York specifically to see this show, and his gift to his wife for her fortieth birthday was that he would wake up early and secure the tickets. He was a sweet guy. He was the one who told us about the Starbucks bathroom over on Columbus and gave us the code to use it. He talked about his two kids back home in . . . Montana? He told us how his wife took care of the kids while he worked and how she was such a great mom and needed an adventure like the one he was providing for her. We loved him, were charmed by his nerdy affect and dopey devotion to his wife, who was sleeping in a hotel room forty blocks south in Midtown.

At six a.m., the park opened and a woman at the front of the line shouted that there had been a line forming on the east side of the park too, so *run!* Everyone did. I knew the legal-pad list was unofficial, but I thought we had all agreed to honor it among ourselves and not cut in front of anyone from our west-side line. I was wrong. The community that we had formed fell apart as people knocked down old ladies to get a better space in the new line.

Meredith and I didn't run, per se, but we did power-walk. So did the guy in front of us. We made a show of rolling our eyes at the other people in line, but it's telling that we weren't strolling. Indeed, some of the people from the east side of the park got to the line before us, but we beat some of them too!

We were still in line behind our guy as we started the second leg of our journey. Is it a journey when you are just standing and waiting?

At ten a.m., I got a call from a company I had interviewed with earlier that week. They were offering me a job! I was making only nine dollars an hour at Barnes and Noble, and this was an administrative assistant job where I would be making more, although I wasn't sure how much more. I'd told myself I needed to earn *at least* what I had earned at my last job in Denver, which was thirty thousand a year. I had managed to save a lot of money on that salary, and if I could make that again, I thought I could really survive in the big city. Meredith agreed and so did the man from (maybe) Maryland. "Stand firm," they coached me when I told them who was on the phone. "It's the only way to negotiate!"

After the HR director told me I'd gotten the job, she asked about my salary requirements. I took a deep breath and stated my case. "The job posting said that salary was commensurate with experience, and while I haven't been an admin assistant, I do have a lot of experience with organizing schedules, creating spreadsheets, and in customer service, and for this reason, I do not feel I can accept the job unless I am making the same amount I did at my last job, which was"—*gulp*—"thirty thousand a year."

There was a brief silence. Had I shocked her? When she spoke again, it was in a tone you would use with a child or a naughty kitten.

"Oh, well, the salary can't go lower than thirty-five thousand a year. So . . . you okay with that?"

So much for my negotiation techniques, but who cares? I now had a job with health insurance that paid thirty-five K a year, and tonight I would be seeing Philip Seymour Hoffman and Natalie Portman under the stars!

The line finally started moving around noon. We all stood up and took one step at a time to fill the gap in front of us, like the orphans in *Oliver Twist* collecting tickets instead of porridge, only we were smart enough not to ask for more than what we got.

We were about halfway to the front of the line when we noticed a woman ahead of us who we hadn't seen in the previous nine hours. She was wearing an ironed linen suit with black stockings and her hair had very clearly been brushed recently. She was too clean to be one of us.

The sweet man from Minnesota or wherever asked, "Excuse me, but are you in line?"

"Yes," the too-clean woman replied without looking him in the eyes. "I'm with her."

She pointed to the woman in front of us who had been there all along, the one who had explained that eighteen hundred tickets were simply not enough. That woman looked back at us and said, "She's my sister."

The man from Mississippi changed from a sweet guy with a hard-working wife into a rabid beast. He shouted at the top of his lungs, *"Are you trying to get four tickets?"*

Suddenly, two men joined the two women. Holy shit. They were trying to get *eight tickets*!

"Calm down, sir," said the woman who had recently slept in a bed.

In my experience, telling someone to calm down has the opposite effect, and, hot damn, was that true for the guy from Maine. He yelled that they were being horrible, that he was ashamed of them, that they were going against the spirit of Shakespeare in the Park (which was currently Chekhov in the Park, but let's not talk about that at this moment).

The dismissive woman in the linen suit said, "We couldn't wait in line; we were at a funeral."

Meredith and I stopped short. She'd played the death card! How can you come back from that? The guy from Massachusetts knew exactly how. He said, "Well, that means that today isn't a day you get to see *The Seagull*—go mourn somewhere else! *Security! Security!*"

In seconds, the security team approached and asked everyone there who had cut. We pointed at the offending group, and they were all removed except for the woman who had given the speech about the scarcity of tickets. We couldn't argue with her since she *had* been there the whole time, but I was still shocked by her chutzpah.

We finally got to the front of the line and received our tickets. The two people behind me got the last four tickets. We had just made it and it was thanks solely to the man in front of us. He had told us he was from someplace that started with an *M*, but on that day, he was from Manhattan. A real New Yorker. I wondered if I would ever feel that way myself.

I have now lived in New York City for twenty-three years. I have lived in Harlem, the East Village, Woodside, Prospect Heights, Carroll

Gardens, Astoria, the East Village again, Hell's Kitchen, and the Lower East Side, with four years of being a bicoastal traveler between New York and Los Feliz in Los Angeles. I have seen actual Shakespeare at Shakespeare in the Park, and I have even been in four productions at the Delacorte Theater. When I first made it onto that stage, doing *Love's Labor's Lost* in 2013, I thought about that crazy night in 2001. I thought about wild dogs, the guy with the gun, and the exhausted cop. I thought about Meredith, who had aged out of her career as a dancer, moved on to being a CPA, and gone back to Denver. I thought about Meryl Streep and Kevin Kline treading these boards. I felt proud to be an actor working at this prestigious place, but mostly, I was proud because I knew that, just like that guy from wherever, I was now definitely a real New Yorker.

Yes Please

by AMY POEHLER[*]

When I was still working at the clinic in Denver, I joined an improv team called Mile-Hi-Larity. The name was a play on Denver's nickname, the "Mile-High City." That is my favorite kind of pun—a stupid one. My friend Catey had asked me to accompany her when she auditioned for the team in case they were actually a multi-level marketing scheme or a secret cult. I agreed to go with her and audition, but I assured her that I would not get on the team. She had done improv in college and told me it was fun and easy, but I felt sure it would be too difficult for me to master.

I was wrong. I was great at it right away. At the audition, I realized that even though I had just tagged along with my friend for safety reasons, I was going to get on this team. Do you see where this is going? Well, Catey got on too, so I surprised you! We loved performing with the team, doing shows on Tuesday nights at a Mexican restaurant,

---

[*]Amy Poehler was twenty-seven when *Upright Citizens Brigade* debuted on Comedy Central. She was thirty when she first appeared on *Saturday Night Live*.

playing to a house of coworkers and former members of the Jesus commune. This success planted a seed in my mind that I could possibly move to New York City, do improv, get on *SNL*, transition to a sitcom, and eventually surprise the entertainment industry with my incredible Oscar-winning dramatic film roles. (My dreams are very specific.)

When I told another person on my improv team that I was moving to New York, he told me, "Take classes at the Upright Citizens Brigade Theatre. They are the place where everything is happening."

A woman on the team said, "No! UCB is a scam! They make you take all their classes before you can perform!"

Two things can be true at once.

I had a simple agenda when I moved to New York City: Get an apartment, get a job, and sign up for classes at the Upright Citizens Brigade Theatre. The first task I checked off my list was signing up for a class. What seemed like a scam to the woman on my improv team in Denver seemed to me like a logical way to break into a community that I wanted to belong to. I loved the classes.

I would call the UCB Theatre my artistic home if I weren't so embarrassed to refer to a place as my "artistic home." The UCB Theatre wouldn't really like it either. It prides itself on a punk-rock aesthetic and an F-you attitude.

One of the best things about reading memoirs is hearing that famous people knew each other before they were famous. Also, this is a subtle brag on my part to show you that I know famous people. Just kidding! It's not subtle.

The theater started in the late nineties when four improvisers from Chicago moved to New York City to star in their own sketch show, which they called, rather unsurprisingly, *Upright Citizens Brigade*. The UCB4, as they are known, are Matt Besser (who hosts the *Improv4-Humans* podcast), Ian Roberts (who was the head writer of *Key and Peele*), Matt Walsh (who was Mike in *Veep*), and Amy Poehler (who is Amy Poehler). They started an improv school and theater, and a *lot* of today's comedy stars came out of the theater. A lot. I tried to list the names here and my editor told me, "We don't have enough paper." So here's just a tiny sprinkle of names: Aubrey Plaza, Donald Glover, Natasha Rothwell, Nicole Byer, Bobby Moynihan, and Ellie Kemper. Oh, I have to write one more: Pam Murphy. My friend Pam is the voice of Stupendous on *Krapopolis* and if I don't mention her, she will hound me forever. In fact, I know the first time she opens this book, it will be exclusively to search for her name, so let me say, loudly and clearly, that one of the *very* talented people who started at UCB is Pam Murphy! (Sorry to make you read all that, but you saved me from a lot of future turmoil.)

In addition to UCB's acting talent, mentioned above, every writing room on every sitcom you have watched in the past twenty years has had a UCB alum in it. That is an exaggeration, but a slight one. For some reason, the spirits aligned in the early 2000s and created this hot spot for comedic voices in New York City.

The first day I was in New York, I signed up for my first class. It was June 1, 2001.

My level-one class was inauspicious, although there *was* a person in that class who went on to become famous, though I don't think he even took level two, so I wouldn't say he got his start at the UCB. Obviously, I still want to drop his name, though. It was Michael Zegen from *The Marvelous Mrs. Maisel* (he was Mr. Maisel). I do not blame him for not continuing, because our class was pretty rough. My teacher, Sean Conroy, told me years later that it was the worst class he had ever taught. I'm proud of that fact. I do not know why. The students were argumentative, and they performed scenes that were boring and offensive, but despite how bad they were, I discovered that I was *really* good at improv.

This was unusual for me. I rarely think I am good at something. I usually spend my time apologizing for taking up space. I knew I was good at playing short-form improv games for Denver audiences, but I wasn't sure I would be good at improv with fancy NYC people. But I was! I was really good at it!

A lot of people hate watching improv. Fair. When you see bad improv, it is *so* bad. If you see a bad musical on Broadway, there is usually one number that has great choreography or at least a character actress wearing a ridiculous wig. Not so in improv. If it's bad, there are no bells and whistles to save it. You feel terrible for the performers, but you feel worse for yourself because you have to sit through it.

But when improv is great? It is *transcendent*! When eight people come on a stage and transport you to magical worlds with wit, verve, and character, it feels spiritual—as if you are all plugged into the same life source of group mind!

Unfortunately, great improv is less than 1 percent of all improv.

Still, that isn't the main reason people hate improv. People hate improv because every television show from *The Office* to *The Comeback* has done episodes set in the world of improv, and the improv world comes off poorly. They show Michael Scott (played by Second City alum Steve Carell) refusing to perform a scene without a gun and Valerie Cherish (played by Groundlings alum Lisa Kudrow) hearing she is in a candy factory and saying, "I don't know what kind of candy you're making, but I'm a coal miner!" Off the top of my head, I can remember scenes making fun of improv on *30 Rock*, *SNL*, *Broad City*, *The Other Two*, and *Community*. They rip improv to shreds, but remember what I said before? Every TV sitcom you can think of has a UCB alum in its writing room, so these TV shows that rip on improv are being written by people who got their start in improv! They are making fun of themselves, but the audience doesn't realize that.

Do I sound defensive? I guess I am. I poured twenty-five years of my life into doing improv several nights a week for free.

At UCB, I was placed on a house team (an improv team that gets to perform on the UCB stage) within a year. I was also on several indie teams, so named because they are not affiliated with a specific theater. Indie teams did shows at any space that would let us. I did two-person improv, musical improv, dramatic improv, improvised plays, improvised reality shows, character improv, improvised movies, and sketch shows. If improv could be snorted, I would have cooked it and injected it. To put it mildly, I was all in.

My first house team had the same eight members for the two years we existed: me, Katie Dippold, Angeliki Ebbesen, Chris Kula, David Martin, Will McLaughlin, Bobby Moynihan, and Charlie Sanders. We called our team Police Chief Rumble. It is a stupid name. All improv teams have stupid names. When you are placed on a team, you spend a week agonizing over the perfect name. Then, after you and your teammates have fought and each of you has pleaded your case about the name you love the most, you all choose a name that no one is all that passionate about. Then you never think about the name again. Our name was Police Chief Rumble because Bobby was on the subway when a fight broke out and someone yelled, "It's a rumble!" Then an older police officer approached and the same person yelled, "Oh, shit! It's a police chief rumble!"

The members of Police Chief Rumble (or PCR) became my family. We practiced every week. (It seems counterintuitive to rehearse improv, but you aren't rehearsing lines, you are learning the group mind. You are getting to know each other. That's why we call it practice, not rehearsal.) We also had a show at the theater and sometimes performed at outside venues in Brooklyn or uptown Manhattan. We decided to write a sketch show together and got a weekly slot at midnight on Fridays. With sketch, you have to have a technical rehearsal to test out lights, sound, and costumes. Our sketch show changed every week, so we had a tech rehearsal every week on Thursday after the eleven p.m. show. That means we started at midnight or twelve thirty a.m. and finished at one thirty or two a.m. So, to recap, every week we had improv practice, sketch rehearsal, a sketch show, a tech rehearsal, and one to three improv shows. And we all had full-time jobs (most of which ran on a nine-to-five schedule).

I do not mean to romanticize this time. It was *so* hard. I was exhausted. Always. I cannot fathom doing even one of those days now, much less many years of them, but this was twenty years ago, and youth was on my side. Or maybe I was just stupid? Thank goodness we were in New York and I didn't have to drive. I sometimes fell asleep on the train, missed my stop, and woke up in the Bronx at four a.m.

But also, it was *so* fun. It felt like we were creating something—not just a show, a lifestyle! We loved putting up sketches that were only half thought out. We would hone each one and try to make it better the next week. We would take improv scenes that went well and turn them into sketches. We wrote down ideas while we were at work, on the train, on the toilet. We were great friends and we were making— I almost said *art*, but no one else would call it that 'cause we were punk-rock comedians. Oops. I think I just romanticized that time. Sorry.

Katie used to love playing pranks on us. One of her favorites was to place her hand just to the side of your ear and call your name so that when you turned around, your face got poked by her finger. As I describe it, it doesn't make a lot of sense, but it was funny. "You got poked!" I guess as humiliations go, it wasn't bad. She did it to everyone, so it became part of our team's language. One day I tried it. I put out my finger and called Bobby's name. He turned, but I had misjudged my finger placement and my hand went inside his mouth. I could feel the ridges of his teeth as I slid across them with my index finger. That is intimacy.

The group met for dinner at cheap places—diners when New York still had diners and sometimes Dallas BBQ, where we'd split rib plates and baked potatoes. We got off work around sixish but didn't have a show until nine thirty p.m., so we'd kill time and bond with each other. I was particularly close with Angeliki and Katie. I've always had closer bonds with women than men in my life. We would talk about their love lives, 'cause female improvisers are always dating someone. The ratio of heterosexual men to heterosexual women is tilted in heterosexual women's favor. I never dated anyone at the theater because there were so few gay people. I didn't date anyone at all at that time because my entire life was office work by day and improv by night.

On house teams, you were required to practice with your team weekly, which meant you had to reserve rehearsal space and pay a coach (or director) to watch you and give notes on your performance. You got these notes in your rehearsals and also immediately after the show (which I mention for a reason). Coaches charged around sixty dollars for three hours and rehearsal rooms cost about the same.

At that time, performers were not paid. Most of the audiences at the shows were current students who got in for free, and the tickets people paid for were only five dollars, but still, it is twisted that we were required to pay for rehearsal every week but we were not paid for the show we put on at their venue. I could tell you something along the lines of "They held the power and I needed to play the game to get stage time," but the truth is worse.

The truth is that I never considered it a bad deal. It never crossed my mind. It took a long time for doubt to reveal itself in my faith journey and also in my UCB journey. Things have changed, thankfully, and improvisers are now paid for their shows. This came about after the pandemic and the racial reckoning of 2020. One of the reasons the improv world is homogenous and white is that economic racism keeps it that way (if you don't have a financial safety net—if you can't go home to Mom and Dad when you run out of money or take off from work if you have a big show—you can't do something you're not paid for). Having disposable income allows you the freedom and privilege to pay for your coach and rehearsal space. So now, house teams are paid.

In fact, in the show I sometimes play in now, we make around sixty dollars a performance. We are very experienced improvisers, which attracts a nice audience, but still, we make sixty dollars a show! If I had earned sixty dollars for every improv show I did in my life, I could have a country house. Two! Even if I got only thirty dollars for every show. This chapter should be a rousing story about organized labor, but again, it *never crossed my mind* that we deserved to be paid for the shows we were doing. I felt like I was getting paid in laughter, which is just about the grossest thing I can say, but it is true.

All the house teams would get notes immediately after every show, and inevitably, I would come off the stage feeling *great!* The audience loved me! They laughed at my scenes! They clapped when I made fun callbacks to previous scenes! I would feel great about the show, but then the coach would inform me that I was wrong to feel that way.

"Well, yeah, the audience liked it, but was it good improv? It was a pretty niche idea," the (always male and always white) coach would say to me.

I once referenced the musical *Wicked* in a scene. It is one of the longest-running musicals on Broadway and has made millions and millions of dollars. This was when it was only a few years old, but it was very po-pu-lar (that's an inside joke for fans of the show!). The thing is, though, that the people who know and love *Wicked* are women and gay men. The straight men in the audience did not know that Idina Menzel flies at the end of act 1 or that Kristin Chenoweth floats in on a bubble, but a large portion of the audience did, and when I was picked up by my teammates (this happens way more than you would expect) and began flying, I referenced the musical *Wicked* and got a huge laugh from the many fans in the audience.

The coach didn't like the move. He said, "You got a laugh, but no one understood that reference; you can't make these niche references." Then he went on to commend another teammate for doing a long scene about *The Legend of Zelda*. I do not know anything about Zelda or her legend, but I was expected to learn about it because most of the straight male improvisers apparently spent hours a day playing it.

I wish I had called this coach out and told him that it was homophobic and misogynistic to value entertainment targeted at men over entertainment aimed at women and gay men. I didn't do that, though. In fact, I took his stupid note to heart and didn't make another reference to a musical for the next ten years, which, I cannot stress enough, was *very difficult for me.* That's, like, 60 percent of my references!

He wasn't trying to be homophobic. It didn't occur to us that we should be paid, and it didn't occur to us that different people might find different things funny.

I was the only gay person on a house team for many years. There was at least one person before me, Mark Sam Rosenthal, but the moment I was put on my house team, he was removed from his. It was a zero-sum situation in 2002.

Eventually more queer improvisers showed up on the scene, and about seven years into my UCB tenure, I was on a team with my friend Eric Bernat. Things had changed so much that there were two openly queer improvisers on the same team at the same time! Actually, we were the only gay people on any team at that time, so maybe it was less progress and more containment.

On house teams, I tried to play to the straight male audience, which was ridiculous because there were plenty of women in that audience who would have loved my comedic point of view (though there weren't that many queer folks). Many of that straight male audience weren't going to like me no matter what I said. I buried my comedic voice to try to fit in, but there were other people who kept up their weird point of view and found success without changing their identity to suit the typical audience. Kristen Schaal, Rachel Bloom, Ilana Glazer, and Abbi Jacobson—they all thrived because they refused to suppress their beautiful and original voices.

Around 2014 or so, something changed. I went to a sketch show starring Josh Sharp and Aaron Jackson called *Fucking Identical Twins*. It was a two-person parody of *The Parent Trap* that was filthy. I mean *filthy*. It was also unapologetically *gay*. I mean *gayyyyy*. I thought it was hilarious, but here is the wild thing—so did the rest of the crowd. I looked around and saw a typical UCB audience. They hadn't brought in gay ringers. These two queens were up there having the time of their lives and didn't care one bit if you didn't like them, which, ironically, was the thing that made you love them. I continued to see smart queer performers refusing to suppress their voices to find mainstream success. These young people were my teachers. People like Cole Escola, Matt Rogers, Bowen Yang, Mano Agapion, Oscar Montoya, Drew Droege, and Justin Sayre used their authentic voices. Even some straight lady named Bridget Everett showed me you do not need to change yourself to accommodate an audience—don't hide your unique point of view, show it off. I hadn't been in the closet about my sexuality, but I *had* been about my comedy, and it was time to come out! I'm here, I'm hilarious, get used to it!

Do I sound like I am shitting on the UCB Theatre? I am not. There has been a huge cultural revolution in comedy in just the past ten years. I don't believe that everything is okay now for queer, female, or nonwhite performers, but at least we are questioning the way things have always been and allowing different voices to shine (sometimes). The UCB gave me so much. My greatest skill as an actor is that I am always present, and I owe that to years of doing improv. I made so many of my dearest friends at the theater. My IMDb page is filled with roles I got from knowing people at the UCB. Some of my closest friendships came from the UCB. I love the UCB.

I also love improv. It is revolutionary.

As an actor, you play roles that are limited by what you look like. I have to play someone white, male-presenting, middle-aged, and, most of the time, nerdy because my vibe screams *I am not a cool person!* I am obviously gay, so I can't play anyone in a romantic relationship with a woman. I am six five, Nordic-looking, and I have a huge mouth. I can't hide those things, so I have to play characters who look like me because I am not as famous as Bradley Cooper or Nicole Kidman, and nobody is gonna make me a prosthetic nose.

Those are the facts of acting, but in improv, the entire world is open to me. I can play a woman. I can play ages zero to one hundred fifty. Actually, I've played both sperm and ancient witches, so there is no limit on age. I can play the president in one scene and thirty seconds later play a cockney chambermaid. I can play a cockroach or a lamp or be the voice of my teammate's left pinkie. You can improvise anywhere without costumes, props, wigs, or sets. You don't even need an audience! Trust me. All you need are two people willing to listen and collaborate to create something together that they could never create alone. I'm so happy that I have improv in my life. It is play, it is creation, and I apologize to my fellow UCB improvisers for saying this, but improv is art.

Out on a Limb

by SHIRLEY MacLAINE[*]

In every celebrity memoir I read, the celeb skips over a really important step: How did they find an agent? It was so frustrating because before I had an agent, that was 75 percent of the reason I was reading those books. So let me tell you exactly how I found mine.

I performed in several musicals at the New York Fringe Festival and the New York Musical Festival. I got the first one because it was written by someone in my improv class. One day after class, he said that he was having open auditions for non-union actors, so I went to his apartment and sang "Blister in the Sun" a cappella. I got the gig because the talent pool was only the sixteen members of my improv class. The show was moderately successful, and the other musicals I was in stemmed from that. Once directors know you are willing to do theater for free, they ask you to do it frequently.

*Shirley MacLaine was twenty years old when she went on for the injured lead in *The Pajama Game* and was seen by an executive from Paramount who signed her to a film contract.

In 2006, when I was in the fifth or seventh musical in a festival, I played a character who was a woman, but not a glamorous one. She was a sad middle-aged lady who waitressed in a greasy spoon and had an unrequited crush on the main character. It was a small role, but it had a great song. I also played lots of other small parts in the show, because playing lots of small parts in a show was my niche before I played waiters. The character probably should have been played by a middle-aged woman, but so few of them were willing to put in 120 hours of rehearsal for a show that would be performed five times, so I got the part. The festival gave awards for individual performances, and I got one! I think they singled me out because I was funny but also because I was brave for wearing the dowdy wig and costume; it was sort of like a very low-stakes version of Charlize Theron winning an Oscar for *Monster*.

Around the time I won that award, my friend Harry, an actor I met in a musical version of *The Silence of the Lambs* (Fringe Festival show number 3), invited me to his birthday party at his apartment in Manhattan Plaza. The location doesn't matter all that much, but Manhattan Plaza is a rent-stabilized apartment house for artists, and I feel cool knowing people who live there 'cause if you put your name on the list to get in, the wait time is over a decade.

Anyway, one of Harry's friends at the party happened to be an agent and the *owner* of a talent agency, but (and this is important) I did not know that. If I had known, I would have been all tongue-tied, trying to work into the conversation my recent award and that I could sing a high G, even though it's inconsistent at best. Instead, I was just being Party Jeff in a group of gay guys. I talked about this porno movie my friend Eric Bernat and I had both seen. We laughed a lot about how the bottom said, "I love getting fucked so much," but when he started bottoming, his face told a completely different story. He was practically crying and kept pushing the top away, looking like he might be afraid he was going to poop on the bed. I called it pornographic realism and did an impression. Would I have told this story to a potential agent? Not in *one million years*, but again, I didn't know he was an agent.

The party ended and I texted Harry on my T-Mobile Sidekick (Back in the Day cliché!) and said I'd had a great time at the party. When I looked at his return text, angels began singing, because Harry said that the guy I was talking to at the party was an agent. He suggested I write him a letter. Not an email. An actual physical letter. This was a time when you had to buy stamps. RIP, US Postal Service.

I had been working with a career coach named Betsy Capes, who was helping me set career goals. I had taken her class called The Path that lots of UCB folks took, and Betsy was so good at explaining the networking side of the biz. She and I sat for an hour crafting the perfect letter and I sent it off to the agent along with my headshot, résumé, and a mention of the award I had just received.

A couple of weeks later, I got a call to set up a meeting with the agents in two weeks! Waiting for weeks and weeks is very common when you are starting out in your career. You will never get a call setting a meeting. If for some reason you do, know that it will be re-scheduled. Twice. I assume that changes when you are really famous, but let me assure you, the waiting for weeks and weeks still happens even when you are on a television show on HBO. Or anyway, a television show on HBO that isn't *Game of Thrones* or a spin-off of *Game of Thrones*.

When the meeting finally came, I sat in a tiny Midtown office with the agent and two of his younger colleagues working for this company. They asked me about myself. I could have said that I'd grown up in Texas and used to be a social worker, but I knew these people were agents. I was no longer Loose-and-Fun Jeff, I was *Glengarry Glen Ross* Jeff trying to make the sale. So when they asked me to tell them about myself, I remembered what I had said in my letter and spewed out this:

"I was a regular on MTV's *Boiling Points* and a voice on *Teenage Mutant Ninja Turtles*, and I have been in over fifteen web series that you can watch on YouTube. I have been in many Off-Off-Broadway musicals, including the hit *Silence! The Musical*, a parody of *The Silence of the Lambs*, which will hopefully have a commercial run in the fall. I am a member of a house team at the prestigious Upright Citizens Brigade Theatre, and I know with the assistance of an agent, I could work a lot and make you money."

They looked as if I had vomited on them, which in effect I had. But then—a light! One of the younger agents said, "Oh! You played the old lady!" I had thought of the character as middle-aged, but I wasn't in a position to quibble. I was just thrilled that this person had actually seen me perform, rather than tell dirty stories at a birthday party at Manhattan Plaza!

"Yes, that kind of role is my specialty," I told him.

"Women?" he asked.

"Oh, I meant ensemble tracks where I play lots of different characters in one show." I laughed out loud. Once he joked with me, I was able to get back to Party Jeff (albeit slightly less irreverent) and talk like a normal human being. They liked me. They told me I had an impressive résumé for someone so young (I did not tell them I was thirty-one because even though you and I know that thirty-one is young, that is very old in youth-obsessed show business). They said they'd like to represent me, and they did for the next five years until I moved to LA and needed an agent there.

So, let's recap. If you are an actor and you want to get an agent, put in five to ten years of free work while you hold down multiple survival jobs, then meet an agent at a party but (and this is important) do not know that they are an agent, then tell a dirty story accompanied by a filthy impression. Hire a career coach who you have already taken a class from so that you can craft a perfect letter stating your goals and why you would make a good candidate for representation. Once you get a meeting, make sure that said agency has a younger agent who saw your award-winning performance as a middle-aged woman unlucky in love. Make a few missteps in trying to sound professional, but then allow some confusion about what types of roles you typically play to lead to a more comfortable conversation, and presto—overnight success!

The truth is that this business isn't fair and there is no rhyme or reason to it whatsoever. Anytime someone asks for career advice in showbiz, I say: "It is not fair." I know people who have an MFA from *Yale* (the place where Meryl Freaking Streep went!) who gave up on acting because they couldn't get their foot in the door, and then you have Kristin Chenoweth, who went to her first audition on a whim with a friend and booked the role. Some people sign with big talent agencies like CAA and are completely forgotten by their agents; other people book roles in major films because a friend is a producer on it and then get an agent from that.

So if you want advice on how to get an agent, mine would be this: Don't worry about the agent. The agent will come. Worry about performing. Find places to act. Make a web series with your friends. Take acting classes and perfect your craft. Try stand-up or improv. And, most of all, do not compare yourself with anyone else. Even people who've written memoirs. Especially those people. There isn't one way to get an agent or become a full-time performer. There are one million ways. A career is built on longevity, not on making the Top 30 Comics Under 30 list. We aren't models, dancers, or professional athletes. There isn't an expiration date on performance.

And if you talk to someone who tells you they got an agent when they were a freshman in college doing a sketch show with their sorority, congratulate them on their good fortune and remember this: There is a middle-aged, profoundly homosexual, doughy white guy who is the second lead on an HBO show that isn't *Game of Thrones* or a *Game of Thrones* spin-off who is also waiting for several weeks to get an appointment for a general meeting with a casting director. We're all doing our own thing, and our thing is valuable too.

The Greatest Love Story Ever Told

by NICK OFFERMAN and MEGAN MULLALLY[*]

My assumption is that one of the main reasons you bought this book is my incredible sexual magnetism. If there is one word that every person would use to describe me, it is *fuckable*, so let me satisfy your cravings for my wild and tawdry adventures. A warning: If you're squeamish about frank depictions of sex, you should be totally fine reading this chapter.

My family didn't talk a lot about sex. I can remember three times in my childhood when it became an unavoidable topic: (1) When an episode of *The Golden Girls* talked about it "too much," according to my mother; (2) when a friend of the family *had* to get married by September; and (3) when we visited the AIDS quilt on its tour through San Antonio. By the time I reached puberty, I had learned that sex was not

---

*Nick Offerman and Megan Mullally were each thirty-nine when they were cast in *Will and Grace* and *Parks and Recreation*, respectively.

something to talk about and that it would bring shame to your family or kill you if you had it. In short, we were Protestant.

My high school had a sexual education unit. In retrospect, that was quite progressive for the Texas Department of Education. My guess is that sex education has been discontinued in that very red state, but in the early 1990s, a three-day-long unit was taught in tenth-grade health class. I guess it wasn't all that progressive, because the school nurse came into the classroom to teach it in a way that could be described as "exclusively clinical." Our health teacher was the women's volleyball coach and an old-school butch lesbian. Okay, I don't know for a fact that she was a lesbian. It is an educated guess. If you had met her and she told you she was a volleyball coach, you'd be like, yeah, that makes sense. I say this as someone who is often clocked as queer, so ga(y)me recognizes ga(y)me, okay? (For audiobook readers, I spelled *game* with the word *gay* in it—isn't that fun?) The coach wasn't a complicated woman. You could tell she was *pumped* to have a few days off from teaching class. She went to the back of the room, sat at a table by the door, and settled in with a newspaper. She had the attitude of the grocery store cashier who gleefully puts down the Lane Closed sign as you approach with a cart full of groceries.

At the front of the room, the nurse set up a large Plexiglas board with images of every type of birth control you can imagine. A museum diorama, but instead of dead butterflies, it was a diaphragm, the pill, and condoms. The nurse relished describing these items in the least sexy way possible. "A condom is a latex sheath stretched over the male phallus in order to collect the sperm at discharge." I began to question whether I knew anything about sex at all, which I think was the nurse's point.

Her description of the IUD was especially graphic. "The IUD, or intrauterine device, is a wire or a coil that is inserted into a woman's uterus." She held up her right hand, extended the index finger, and bent it at a ninety-degree angle. Then she moved it up and down and said, "The wire scrapes at the walls of the uterine lining, causing . . ."

I saw lights that were like fireworks shimmering against a completely black background. Then I had this exact thought: *Wait. I'm in health class. Why am I looking at lights that look like fireworks?* The reason was that in the middle of the description of the IUD, in front of thirty of my peers, the school nurse, and a definitely bored and possibly lesbian gym teacher, I had fainted.

When I opened my eyes, I discovered that I was no longer sitting at my desk. I was lying on the floor of the classroom. The nurse was shouting at me, demanding that I tell her who the president was—clearly living her ER fantasy. The desks had been pushed back, and all of my classmates were standing in a circle staring down at me. Their faces had a mixture of pity, concern, and disdain. I should reiterate that I was not a popular kid, so I didn't have the option to be the fifteen-year-old who laughed this off as one of my cool quirks. There could be no living this down. I was the virgin who flipped out when he heard the word *uterus*. Or, worse, the kid who was so profoundly homosexual that even the mention of a vagina brought him literally to the ground.

My first attempt at self-preservation was denial. Maybe I could just get up and sit down in my chair, and the class could go on as if nothing had happened? The nurse was not having it. Someone fainting is always difficult to ignore, but I had fainted in a particularly showy fashion.

In addition to the fact that I was in the front row (assigned seating, I assure you), I had fainted while sitting down, causing my body to droop forward and close my airway. Apparently, I'd let out a long, wheezing, guttural moan to get oxygen. When that hadn't worked, my body did what bodies do if the airway is closed—it seized. So in the middle of a discussion of birth control, my slumped body made a long, loud snoring noise, shook violently, and fell to the floor. Even unconscious, I play it to the back of the house.

The nurse, still high on the drama of crisis, yelled that I needed to go to her office, lie down, and wait for her to finish the class, at which point she would come back and . . . I'm not sure. Cure me? She asked the coach in the back of the room to put down the newspaper and walk with me to the nurse's office. I could tell that Coach was pissed. I had ruined her free period because I couldn't handle hearing about periods. She sighed and said, "Okay, come on, then."

I walked over to the coach, unsuccessfully willing the earth to swallow me up and save me from this mortification. When I got to the back of the room, just as I was about to escape from their prying eyes, the nurse yelled across the heads of all my fellow students, "Oh, and check and see if he soiled his pants. That usually happens."

I promise you, that did not happen.

Obviously, sex is a complicated subject for me. I thought it would get easier once I came out. Surely, once I declared myself a part of the gay world, other gay men would accept me and allow me into the secret society of blow jobs and butt stuff. Sadly, sex and relationships were somehow just as complicated over the rainbow.

I know I have already said this too much, but this was before the internet. The internet really changes how one lives! When I came out, I couldn't even watch porn, much less look up Reddit threads for tips on anal douching. I didn't even know you *could* douche. This was the time of gay bars. You had to go there and speak to people in person. There is a lot of talk about the lack of civility on hookup apps like Grindr—"He blocked me as soon as I sent my face pic!" People forget or don't realize that this rudeness happened in the bars too, only you had to see the person who harshly rejected you dance with a guy who was a lot hotter than you for hours post-rejection.

Gay male culture is not a monolith. Gay men love to specify the type of homosexual that they are and the type of homosexual that they want. Maybe young queer folks today are more open to different types of people, but in the late nineties when I was first coming out, there were strict groups of gay guys, and you needed to declare your tribe. The problem was that I did not fit into any of the common types of gay men. I was too big (both physically and emotionally) to be a young, slim twink. And while I am big like a bear, I am not hairy. I have body hair like a dolphin, which is to say, just enough to qualify me as a mammal. I don't have the gravitas to be a daddy, the money to be a sugar daddy, or the conceptual understanding to be whatever a zaddy is. I am too fat to be a gym bunny, too thin to be a chub, too prissy to be a leather queen, and too repressed to be a sex pig.

The only gay group I belong to is the show queen. A show queen is a femme-leaning, musical-theater-loving, prissy type of gay man who has been lampooned in film and then television from the 1920s up until last night. It is nice to be a part of a group, but unfortunately, the show queen is a category of gay men that is universally declared to be un-fuckable. Almost every other group has a fetishization, and while this can be a disturbing and problematic sexualization, at least you get freaky once in a while.

Show queens are the most classic of stereotypes. Think *The Boys in the Band* or Paul Lynde (if you do not know who that is, google *Paul Lynde* and *Hollywood Squares*. You are welcome). Show queens like a pristine apartment, always have their hair *just so*, and relish being judgmental and comically harsh. That isn't really like me at all, but here's the thing: I can tell you the differences between the styles of Stephen Schwartz, William Finn, and Adam Guettel. This knowledge makes me a de facto show queen. Consequently, I didn't get much play in the 1990s. Or the 2000s, for that matter.

When I lived in Denver and worked as a professional homosexual, I dated exactly zero people. I did hook up with someone once. Kind of. Sort of a half hookup. It still counts, right? A man was definitely interested in me. The only problem was that he was so intoxicated that he passed out mid-hookup. Okay, early hookup. It was mid-kiss. It is very humiliating to have someone pass out *during* a kiss with you. It is the exact opposite of a fairy tale.

I still count that hookup, though, because the difficult part is connecting with someone enough to decide to go home together, not the actual grinding-of-bodies part. So I did the hard part. I just didn't get the reward. Instead, I left this man sleeping in his apartment and walked home alone. Thank goodness he lived in my neighborhood. Well, I thanked goodness until later when I saw him during a walk and he didn't remember who I was.

Once when I lived in New York City, my improv friend Katie asked me to take her to a gay bar. I think she was looking to have an experience with go-go boys in cages and shirtless men dancing in a sea of glitter, but I never went to gay bars then because I spent my life doing improv comedy. I thought Katie might be an in for me to meet other gay men. Maybe she could be the Karen to my Jack and be delightfully flamboyant and attract all sorts of suitors. I grabbed an *HX* magazine, a gay rag that listed all the gay bars in the city. I found the one that was closest to Under St. Marks, the theater where we were doing a show earlier in the night. It was called Dick's. That seemed like a pretty good name for a gay bar!

We walked inside, through the cigarette smoke and neon lighting, and made out a pool table and two men sitting at the bar. They were easily seventy years old. They sat stone-faced, staring straight ahead as they drank light beers.

We approached the bar and the bartender gave us the side-eye. It was ten p.m.; maybe he was afraid we would make him have to stay longer? Or maybe he thought we wouldn't tip well since we were so young? Or maybe Dick's meant less *penis* and more *jerk*? Whatever the reason, he came over to us and snarled, "What do you want?" We ordered two Bud Lights.

"This isn't what I thought it would be," Katie whispered, slight terror in her voice.

"Yeah," I agreed. Then we sat just like our elderly compatriots, thoughts of a *Queer as Folk* bacchanal fading from our minds.

I once had a showmance while doing an Off-Off-Broadway production of a show aptly titled *Slut*. It was my first time dating anyone. I had taken a slight break from my improv addiction to do this musical about a straight guy who accidentally gets a straight girl pregnant. I played a pirate. I could explain it much better than this, but when the show went Off-Broadway and paid its actors, they didn't bring me with it, so they get only this cryptic description.

The actor who played the straight impregnator got really drunk one night after the show and told me he was about to have a threesome with one of our other castmates and his boyfriend. He asked if I wanted to join a foursome. This would be a bold move for me, going from 0 to 100 without stopping at 10, you know? But what was I gonna do? Turn down the opportunity because it was too advanced? I would fake it to make it. I went along to the couple's place in Astoria, which was a very long trek from my East Village apartment, but I was so lonely and longing for sex, I would have walked to Canada for the possibility of holding hands.

The four of us got into a cab in front of the theater and headed out. Have you ever been in a cab with three other people? One person is always separated from the rest of the group because there is not enough room. I am six five, so I am often told that I should take the front seat for my long legs. People say this as if they are doing you a favor, but the truth is, no one wants to sit in the front seat of a cab. The driver rolls his eyes passive-aggressively as he moves his bag and water bottles full of his urine from the passenger seat. Once you're up front, there is a big Plexiglas wall between you and the rest of the group. It's always hard enough not to be able to hear your group, but it's especially difficult to be separated from a group you are supposed to be having sex with later. I would occasionally hear smacking from the back seat and crane my head around to see three-way kissing and groping. Then I would turn to the driver and he would grumble, annoyed that I was in his private space and that a gay orgy was taking place behind him. When we finally got to their address, the driver asked me where to drop us off. "Oh. I don't know. Hey, guys? Where should he drop us off? Hey, guys? Guys?"

Inside the apartment, candles were barely lit before the couple got into a huge fight. It seems that one of the partners had given the okay for the foursome but had not gotten permission from the other one. I wanted to give the couple some privacy to work out their issues, but this was New York City. There was literally nowhere to go besides the bathroom. I guess the lead guy and I could have gone in there, but we all knew that two of the four of us sitting in the bathroom would kill the mood. So we did the next best thing and hid under a blanket on the futon while they continued their argument less than five feet from us. The fight was incredibly tense. After an hour or more, we knew we needed to exit this situation. There would be no sex tonight. Somehow without planning it, the guy and I crawled to the door of the apartment with the blanket over our heads, ditching it only when we got out. We ran into the hot Astoria night, bonding over this bizarre, shared trauma. Then we took separate cabs home to our respective apartments, giggly and sexually unsatisfied.

The next day at rehearsal, the half of the couple who was in the show pretended nothing had happened the previous evening. The lead and I were surprised and impressed that he could just ignore this completely awkward situation. During lunch, the lead actor and I laughed about how outlandish this all was, and that laughing bonded us. He asked me to dinner after rehearsal. I can't tell you his name because . . . he's not even slightly famous and you would have no idea who he is. Let's call him Freddy.

Freddy and I started to date. I think? I'm not sure how he would classify our relationship, but I thought of what we were doing as dating. He wasn't a great communicator, which, ironically, made me love him more. When guys don't say much, you get to invent what is going on in their heads and it is always way better than what's actually happening in there. When I tell you that I loved him, I mean I *loved* him. I thought about him all the time. I talked about him all the time. I started drawing hearts in my journal. I put my first name with his last name, and this was before gay marriage was legal!

The relationship was not perfect. We saw each other every night during the run of the show, but once it ended, I seemed to lose his attention. He would cancel plans about 80 percent of the time, often without informing me he was canceling (unless just not showing up was a way of informing me, which I suppose it is). When he did show up, he often got so drunk that he would black out or vomit (rarely in the toilet). So, sure, the relationship had its flaws, but that didn't matter because we were in love.

I think?

One night he told me he had slept with his ex-boyfriend earlier that day. We had made no decisions on monogamy, so I couldn't be angry or demand an apology, but he insisted that he was sorry and that it would never happen again! I assured him it was okay if he didn't want to be monogamous. We had been seeing each other for only a month. He said he loved me. I started crying and said I loved him too. Then he got drunk and passed out. A Nicholas Sparks novel come to life!

After our declaration of love, he didn't call me for two weeks. I called him, but he did not return the calls. I found this distressing, but my optimistic heart felt we had more of a story to tell, and sure enough, he showed up at my door on a Friday night.

When I opened the door, he said, "I'm sorry!"

I loved hearing that. Then he told me that the reason he was sorry was that two weeks ago, he had started dating an ex-boyfriend, which I didn't love hearing so much. I was crushed, but I didn't want to be a drama queen about it.

"Thanks for telling me. I hope you two are happy together." I started to shut the door, but he stopped me.

Freddy told me that he and his ex weren't right for each other and he still loved me. (Thank You, God!) I mean, he was a little high, but full of love! He told me that he wanted to be monogamous and that he wanted us to take our relationship to the next level! He had slept with his ex for the last time. Earlier that day. Oh, and this was a different ex from the other ex that he had slept with two weeks ago. He told me this as if this were a meaningful distinction, so to me, it was.

Despite the fact that it had been only hours since he had seen the (other) ex, I was all in on this monogamy thing. I loved him! We were a couple! This was my first boyfriend. At twenty-seven years old. I told him I loved him too and said we should go out to dinner to celebrate with a real date.

But Freddy wanted to go *out*-out. "With other people."

It didn't seem thematic to celebrate being a monogamous couple by going out with other people, but—*Sure, let's do it! I want you to like me!*

The only gay bar I knew of was Dick's. We couldn't go there. A guy from my day job was celebrating his birthday that night in a loft in the Flatiron area. I didn't really like or trust the birthday boy. He was always talking about doing crystal and bragging about how he would take hookups to our office instead of his place so they wouldn't steal his stuff. I hadn't planned on going to the party, but if Freddy wanted to go out, we could go there, I guess.

If only we had gone to Dick's.

When we arrived at the party, Freddy immediately disappeared. I saw him go into the bathroom with someone else. Who was it, though? The women I was talking to said it was the birthday boy. Huh. Weird. Why would they go into the bathroom together?

How pitiful is it that I hoped they were doing drugs?

A half hour later, another woman asked how I knew Freddy. "Oh, well, this is hot off the presses, but he's my boyfriend!" The words felt foreign but sweet as they swirled around for the first time in my mouth.

"Well, your boyfriend is in bed with the birthday boy."

I turned around and saw Freddy's shoes sticking out from the loft bed over another pair of feet. The feet were positioned in a way that said their bodies needed to be especially close together. I climbed the ladder and saw Freddy giving the birthday boy a present: oral.

He had gone from swearing monogamy to cheating on me *while I was in the room* in a span of forty-five minutes. I would love to tell you I pulled an Angela Bassett in *Waiting to Exhale*. I wish I had burned down the building where the party was and walked away in slow motion. Instead, I told Freddy I was going home and asked if he'd like to join me. He didn't really answer me, what with his mouth being full, but I could tell he wasn't ready to leave.

I walked home. For two reasons: (1) because it felt like the melancholy thing to do; and (2) because when Freddy would *for sure* call, I didn't want to be underground in the subway. When I finally got home, I left my phone on, right by my ear. The phone did not ring.

After three days, I called him because we had plans to see a cabaret show put on by one of our former castmates. The more dignified thing to do would have been to ignore this plan and take the hint, but I had already bought the tickets. When he answered, he did this strange thing where he acted like not only the blow job with my coworker but also our relationship hadn't happened. He just pretended like we had been mildly friendly before, but nothing more. His demeanor was *How did you get my number?* It felt especially cruel because we had first bonded making fun of the half of the couple who had done the same thing.

I asked if we could go out one more time to talk and he said, "I'm kind of seeing someone." I don't know if it was the ex-boyfriend or the other ex-boyfriend or the guy from my day job or some new guy he met while walking down Sixth Avenue, but at some point in the past three days, he had found a new relationship and could no longer be alone with me in public. I should have pulled an Angela Bassett in *How Stella Got Her Groove Back* and taken a trip to the Bahamas with Taye Diggs, but instead I did something much worse. I said to him, "I just want you to know that you were the first person I was ever in love with and I will always remember you fondly in my heart." He responded to this tenderness by saying, "Okay, drama queen," which hurt even though it was quite obviously true.

For three months I walked around New York City sadly listening to Rufus Wainwright's *Poses* on repeat in my Discman. Then I realized that I needed to pull an Angela Bassett in *What's Love Got to Do with It*. Freddy would be Ike with a stalled career, and I would be Tina becoming the most beloved female rock star of all time. The only differences being that instead of a becoming a rock star, I got a T-Mobile commercial, and instead of having a stalled career, Freddy moved upstate and adopted kids with his new husband. Thanks, Angela!

I didn't date for many years after my "relationship" with Freddy. It wasn't my choice. No one was interested. This sounds like self-deprecation, and I suppose it is in part (writing this book has laid out in black and white that I rely on self-deprecation heavily), but it's also an indication of how incredibly segregated from the queer community I was in the early 2000s. I marvel at how I could have lived in New York City—a hub of the LGBTQ+ community since its founding—and still have no gay friends. I mean, I was part of a *theater company* located in *Chelsea*—the gayest neighborhood of Manhattan! I did musical theater on the side! I spelled it *theatre*—with an *r-e*! You would think that gay people would be the norm in my life, not the exception. Unfortunately, the theater company was improv, Chelsea was chosen because it was close to train lines, and somehow, even when I was in a musical—*on Broadway*—I was the only openly queer actor in the cast. What are the odds?

It was time to take my fate into my own hands. On my thirty-first birthday, I realized that the longest relationship I'd had was forty-five minutes at a coworker's birthday party in 2002. I vowed I would have a real relationship by the time I turned thirty-two.

I tried every avenue I could to meet a man. My goal was to do one thing a week that could lead me to finding love. This could be as major as going on a date or as minor as writing a list of qualities I wanted in a partner. I told my friends I was looking and asked them to set me up if they knew anyone who might be interested. I went to speed-dating events at the LGBT center. I joined Match.com, Nerve.com, and Men.com (Grindr, Scruff, and Tinder did not yet exist). I googled gay churches and attended their Sunday services. I went to gay bars and awkwardly drank a vodka soda alone waiting for someone to talk to me. I drank coffee at a place solely because it had a pride flag out front. I treated dating like a part-time job.

I did go on a lot of dates. A *lot* of dates. I also was stood up a lot or canceled on with ten minutes' notice. Once a man talked to me for three minutes and when the waiter came over for our order, he said, "We aren't ordering. This isn't a match." I appreciated that he didn't waste my time, but I would have preferred he'd told *me* that news before the waiter.

I learned some rules about online dating, which I am going to share with you now because lots of celebrities offer advice about subjects in which they have no expertise in their memoirs. I'll try too.

Here are the eight simple rules for dating my teenage daughter (I think of myself as my own teenaged daughter).

(1) Get to the in-person date sooner rather than later. People you turn out to have zero chemistry with can give great email.

(2) You can be picky. If someone mentions something in their profile that makes you think they *might* be in a cult, just swipe left. Don't try to make someone fit just so you aren't alone.

(3) With that said, err on the side of being picky about a potential partner's character, not about their looks. A good personality can make an average-looking person very hot, and a hot person who has really bad breath will never be a match.

(4) Choose a public place for your first meeting. Some people say it should be coffee, but I think a bar is fine too. Sometimes a cocktail takes away some of the scariness, but don't get drunk. You look messy and it can be dangerous.

(5) Tell them you have something to do after. I always told people I had an improv show later. I often did have one, but even if I didn't, I told them I did. This gives you an excuse to leave if the date is a fizzle, and if you want to stay longer, you can say, "I'm having such a great time, I'm gonna skip my improv show!" which makes you seem charming.

(6) Never let them come to your improv show. They need to love you in a deep way before they see you sizzling like bacon on the floor.

(7) If you want to have sex on the first date, I say go for it. Better to know sooner rather than later if the sex is shitty, and I do not subscribe to slut-shaming or sex negativity.

(8) I don't really have an eighth thing, but I wanted to make that joke about the eight simple rules for dating my teenaged daughter because I love John Ritter and the young Kaley Cuoco, so let's just say the eighth rule is to make sure they make you laugh. Unless you hate laughing, in which case, eww, I don't wanna date you!

I was already dating quite a bit when I saw an ad on TV for a website called Chemistry.com. It was like eHarmony in that it asked you hundreds of questions about your personality to pair you with the right person. The difference was that Chemistry.com wasn't owned by right-wing Christians, so they let gay people join too. I still remember the ad: A soft-butch lesbian in leather pants looked directly into the camera and said, "Hey, eHarmony. Why would you reject me? Hmm?" I've tried to find the commercial again, but its nowhere online, which makes me sad because that commercial is how I met my husband.

I've never done Tinder, but friends who have tell me that it is fun and mindless as you swipe right and left with abandon. It's like a video game but if you win, you get laid. Chemistry.com was not mindless. It was complicated. You had to answer roughly a thousand questions, and then the site would match you with five people a day. That was it. Five. You read their profiles and if you were interested, you sent them two essay questions to answer. If they were also interested, they would answer your questions and send you two essay questions to answer. I am not making this up. *Essay questions.* It was the SATs of S-E-X.

You could choose from five questions or make up your own. I remember that I chose one and made up one. The made-up one was something along the lines of "What was a life path you thought you would take when you were younger but didn't?" I remember my husband made up one too. It was "Describe your perfect New York City day."

After the essay questions, you were allowed to call each other. Is this insane or what? This is probably the reason that Chemistry.com is no longer around. It was practically a Victorian dating ritual minus the dowager aunt chaperoning your first date.

Neil (my now husband) had a great profile. He answered one question with wit and the next with sincerity and depth. He had a great picture too, which he captioned: *This is from a couple years ago, but there hasn't been significant wear and tear since then.* We decided to meet at Marion's, a restaurant in the East Village that he chose because of its proximity to his apartment and that I was excited to visit because I knew Amy Sedaris had waitressed there and I was a huge *Strangers with Candy* fan. Marion's closed soon after, but we have a postcard of its exterior framed on our wall as an homage to our love and to the fact that good restaurants never last in this city.

Our first date was March 5, 2008. The eagle-eyed math geeks among you will note that I didn't find a boyfriend by my thirty-second birthday; it was a few months after. Remember, December birthday, so I wasn't thirty-three yet. I put this detail in here for a reason. So many people told me that I needed to stop looking for love in order to find it. Okay. I had also told myself I had a year to find love. Okay. I also told myself if I turned forty before I got a TV show, then I would never get a TV show. Okay. Do you see my point? Life is surprises, not deadlines or fooling yourself into thinking you need to stop wanting something to get the thing you want.

When I finally met Neil, I knew he was special. He hadn't lied— there was no significant wear and tear. He was handsome, especially his blue eyes. We bonded over progressive politics and the fact that we both volunteered at an overnight shelter, he at a women's shelter in the basement of a synagogue on the Upper West Side, me at a men's shelter in the basement of a Lutheran church in Astoria (I had moved from the East Village by that time). He was a visual artist and spoke about creativity in ways I had never considered before.

He was twelve years older than me and I liked that. He was established as an artist, with works in museums and gallery representation.

He seemed stable, compassionate, and intelligent but was also hot. This is an *extremely* rare combination to find in an online date.

We were both creative but in radically different ways, which is emblematic of our marriage as a whole. We both believe in volunteering, but he comes at it from a macro worldview and I do it for the one-on-one interaction with people. We both love animals, but he is interested in their evolutionary history, while I think they're so *cuuuuuttttteeee*!

Perhaps the detail that best illustrates how different we are is how we each came to use Chemistry.com. I had followed the advice of a featured extra from *The L Word* in a TV commercial, but Neil had read an in-depth article in the *New York Times* about the complicated algorithm required to match potential partners. Neil is the intellectual, and I am the softy who wants justice for the rejected lez.

Our courtship was dreamy. We went to museums and the theater and had picnics in the park. We drank cocktails on his East Village rooftop and took walks along the East River in Astoria. We met up with his friends and talked about politics, and we met up with my friends and talked about sketches from *Mr. Show*. A fine romance.

I dated other men from Chemistry too. I liked one of them very much. He worked for an opera company, which felt very classy even though I don't have any interest in opera. He was tall and handsome. He wore tailored suits and made me laugh by making fun of the snooty women who came to the opera box office. I couldn't point to anything wrong with him. I also couldn't point to anything wrong with Neil. I dated them both for over a month and was having a difficult time fitting dates with two men into my schedule. I needed to choose one and let the other continue dating, but I didn't know which one to pick.

Then one night while I was out with opera dude, he kissed me, and all I could think was, *Huh. I really wish I were kissing Neil right now instead.*

That was it. I had made my choice, and I have stuck with that choice for the past seventeen years. I introduced him to my family, and they loved him too. My mother went all out to make him feel welcome and no doubt to show me that the gay thing didn't change her love for me. She got him a blue-and-white Christmas stocking—"For Hanukkah!" I worried that my mom's blending of his Jewish tradition and our Christian one might be offensive, but Neil told me that he found his WASPy in-laws rather exotic. That made me love him more.

On June 28, 2013, gay marriage became legal in California (where I was living); it was already legal in New York State (where Neil was living). I remember watching the news on TV in the NYC apartment Neil and I had shared for several years but that was now primarily his. I knew this was a monumental moment in gay rights, but I wasn't sure it was a monumental moment in my *personal* life.

I had fought hard for gay marriage. I knocked on doors and went to rallies and voted for candidates who supported it, but I'd been fighting for equal rights, not because I wanted to get married. When the opportunity came up, I wasn't even sure I wanted to do it. Wearing a white tux and walking down an aisle held zero appeal. I would look like either 1976 Steve Martin or 2016 Hillary Clinton—neither is a fashion inspo. And if I'm being honest, I didn't want anyone looking at Neil and me and saying, "I think Neil is the groom and Jeff is the bride."

Still, I felt a certain obligation to get married. One doesn't leave rights on the table, you know? And I wanted a connection to Neil, especially since we were in a long-distance relationship at the time. So as we watched the news declaring California's decision, I looked at Neil and said those magic words: "I guess we should do it so I get the apartment if you die?" Then he said the thing I had been dreaming about since I was a little girl! "Before January, for tax purposes."

Swoon!

Our wedding was a quiet affair. We got married at the courthouse. The only guests were my friends Liz and Jeff. I had been a groomsman at their wedding, so it felt like symmetry to have them at ours.

I don't know the exact date we got married. Or I didn't until I just looked it up—December 20, 2013. Straight people are always asking how long we've been married, and I never know the answer. We celebrate the day of our first date as our anniversary. The wedding date is just when we filed paperwork with the state. The marriage was about legal protections, not our relationship, so the anniversary doesn't mean all that much to us.

That's why it's surprising that I got choked up while reciting the standard vows in the bare-bones New York State marriage ceremony. Declaring Neil as the person I wanted to be with for the rest of my life felt special and important.

We had brunch downtown to celebrate. The restaurant didn't have cake on their dessert menu, which was disappointing because that is the one wedding tradition I firmly believe in. This was a fancy place that loved experimenting, so consequently, we had cotton candy for our wedding cake. Liz and Jeff picked up the tab for brunch. How many people can say that their friends paid for their wedding reception? I was touched by how they held a reverence for our relationship and for the commitment we made to each other that day.

We went to Texas for the holidays and my mother had a little party for us, with cake and cards and champagne. When I announced on Facebook that Neil and I had gotten married, I received so many messages of congratulations and genuine joy. My improv teammate Tara Copeland took up a collection for airline miles to go toward a honeymoon trip. We felt so honored and so loved!

These outpourings showed me that marriage isn't just for the couple—it is for the community. It is for family, friends, coworkers, and loved ones to hear you declare your commitment to this person and to recognize you and your love. They love your love. I was worried we were being heteronormative, and we were, but that also meant that we were saying our relationship was just as important as a straight one. Plus, what is less heteronormative than wearing a wedding ring and also having gay sex? I mean, occasionally. It has been seventeen years.

Our proposal and wedding story aren't all that romantic, I recognize that. But storybook weddings don't guarantee solid marriages. If you have to choose one or the other, I'm happy with the one I got.

It took me a long time to understand myself in relation to sex, dating, and love. I had to try foursomes, go to the AIDS quilt, and watch a lot of Angela Bassett movies, but I think I have learned this about relationships: They won't always be good, but the good should outweigh the bad. Neil more than outweighs the bad. It was worth kissing all those frogs who passed out drunk mid-kiss to get such an important education.

Don't Stand Too Close to a Naked Man

by TIM ALLEN*

When I finally got an agent, I told him I was pulling back on improv to focus on getting scripted work. In truth, I had just been kicked off a house team at the Upright Citizens Brigade Theatre, but sometimes you have to spin things your way. My new agent said what agents always say when you call them to ask for more auditions: "It's a weird time right now, what with [X], but things are picking up and we will be getting you out soon."

X is a stand-in for any number of reasons that things are slow: a recent actors strike, the Christmas holidays, a merger of two entertainment conglomerates, the internet taking away commercials, the internet taking away scripted content, the internet creating social media, or an agent's impending wedding, baby, or oral surgery. There is always something that is slowing the business down, but the truth is that a

---

*Tim Allen was thirty-eight when *Home Improvement* first aired.

large part of what an actor does is wait for auditions. Unless you are a gorgeous twenty-five-year-old. There is a role in every script for a gorgeous twenty-five-year-old, but that is the only group that consistently gets auditions.

Somehow, though, this time my agents actually did send me out on an audition! The audition was a surprise, and so was what it was for— a fancy Hollywood movie!

There were no lines and they didn't send me a script; they just told me to go to the casting director's office. For the audition, I had to pretend to tiptoe into someone's bedroom and wake them up gently. I tiptoed in and said, "Psst" a few times. The casting director laughed pretty hard when I kept looking around in mock desperation as if to say, *What do I do? What do I do?*

A week later, I got a call on my cell phone at my day job. I did what I always did when I got an acting call while at work: I feigned diarrhea and took the call in the single-stall bathroom. My agent told me I had just booked the movie! It was a *real* movie! They had a budget and were paying me and everything. My agent said it was for DreamWorks and the project had a star attached. I would get to work with Ricky Gervais! Thank goodness I was in the bathroom 'cause I was about to shit my pants from excitement.

"What is the name of the character I play?" I breathlessly asked.

"Uh, Naked Guy," my agent said.

"Is that an ironic name? Like when they call a fat person 'Slim'?" I asked hopefully.

"No. Your character is naked, but it's PG-13, so they can't show your kibbles and bits."

As you will read many times in this book, I have pretty intense body shame. In fact, the only thing as intense as my body shame is my desire to succeed in my acting career. This was my *Sophie's Choice*.

I decided to prioritize my acting career even though the idea of standing shirtless in front of the entire world was an *actual* nightmare I had several times a month. I had three weeks before shooting started, and I spent that time not eating bread and drinking only vodka sodas because an improv student told me I could lose ten pounds by not eating bread and drinking only vodka sodas. I was mentally unhealthy enough to listen to her advice on physical health.

When I showed up to the set, I marveled at the trailers, crew members, and snacks provided. This was the big time! I felt like I was part of a Hollywood that I had never had access to before. Ironically, in the makeup trailer, I overheard Téa Leoni saying that "low-budget" movies like this were rarely made anymore. I just looked it up and the budget was twenty million dollars, which I guess compared to *Jurassic Park* is small, but the web short I had done the week before had a budget of six dollars, and that was because the script said that all six cast members had to be chewing gum, so to me, this was very high-budget.

I was given a trailer—a real one, because there weren't a lot of actors on set that day! It had a couch and a little heater in it, and also my costume. I can still see that tan G-string draped perfectly on the hanger; it looked like a Barbie bikini on a human-size coat hanger. There was also a modesty robe and slippers so I didn't have to put my bare feet on the urine-covered streets of New York City, but I couldn't help feeling a bit exposed.

I went to hair and makeup. They did my hair and my face, and then the makeup artist said, "Oh! You're going to be naked. Do you have any tattoos or, like, ah, *scars* I need to cover up?" She laughed at her joke about the scars.

"Actually, I do. Have scars. Sorry." I blurted that out and then I opened my robe like Irene Cara in *Fame*.

Look, no one in the audition asked me if I had scars on my body, and I am a good actor who does not provide information that could prevent him from getting a job. I hadn't told anyone but I did in fact have two large brown patches on my chest from an autoimmune disorder I had in high school. They're not like Frankenstein scars; they're more just skin discoloration. I am self-conscious about them, though, so I don't love being shirtless (LOL, this job!), but whenever I'm at the beach and I confess my insecurity, my friends all say the exact same thing: "Oh my God, you can't even see them! No one notices! That's all in your head!"

You know who doesn't have good game at pretending they can't see your scars? Makeup artists. When I showed her my chest, she flinched. She took out her readers and got very close to my gut. She tutted. She moaned. She looked me in the eye as if to say, *How could you do this to me?* She yelled across the trailer to no one in particular, "Tell them we have to rearrange the schedule. And somebody get me my airbrush gun!"

So every day I was on set, I had to stand in the makeup trailer in a thong and be sprayed like a used car getting a new paint job. Worse, I had to do it next to Billy Campbell, who came in every day, removed his shirt, revealing his perfectly chiseled physique, and shaved in the mirror next to mine. Have you seen the series *Once and Again*? The side-by-side comparison of me to him was like seeing a Ken Doll next to a stuffed animal.

The movie, called *Ghost Town*, is about a man named Bertram Pincus (Ricky Gervais) who wakes up from a colonoscopy with the ability to see ghosts. All of the ghosts want to use Pincus to send messages to their living loved ones. Greg Kinnear plays a ghost who tries to get Pincus to break up his wife's new relationship. It's a surprisingly sweet and funny movie that has been forgotten, but if you're a rom-com lover like me, you should check it out, and not just 'cause I still get residuals from it. Not *just*.

One of the central jokes of the movie is that ghosts wear whatever they were wearing when they died, and my character died naked. At one point, a production assistant approached me and said, "The director wants you to wear your glasses." Then he walked away with no further explanation. I thought that sounded so dirty, you know? Like the director had some sort of kink: *This character is completely naked except . . . he's wearing glasses . . . yeah . . . keep the glasses on.*

No explanation of my character's death was given in the script, but he *was* still wearing his glasses, so I took that as a clue. He must not have died in his sleep or in the shower, because you don't shower or sleep with glasses on.

Since no one told me the backstory of my character, I decided to make one up. It felt like something a film actor would do, and now I was one! My backstory was that my character had died in a hot-tub accident. Also, I gave him a name: Theodore. Theo was a buttoned-up, type A kind of guy who, at thirty years old, had gone to Fire Island for the first time to explore his sexuality. That night at the Belvedere, he decided to take a dip in the clothing-optional hot tub; he kept his glasses on, which naturally fogged up and impaired his vision. When he got out of the hot tub, he missed a step, slipped, and knocked his head on the hot tub so hard it killed him.

The script also never explained why Naked Guy, who was actually Theodore, was reaching out to Pincus, so my thought was that Theo wanted Pincus to go to his mother and explain that this had been a first-time exploration and that he hadn't been living a double life. Am I the consummate actress or what? That's a pretty good backstory! Especially for a character that was created solely for Téa Leoni to unknowingly touch ghost dick.

You see, Téa Leoni's character couldn't see the ghosts. Unfortunately, Ms. Leoni *could* see me. I was wearing nothing but a dance belt while shooting this thing. The scene I had with her was on Fifth Avenue—right by Central Park, and also *Fifth Avenue*! At one point, a double-decker tourist bus filled with preteen girls who were excitedly looking at the real live movie set in the middle of the bustling city drove by. I watched as their eyes searched for movie stars and landed on my lumpy, airbrushed frame. They looked me up and down. Their eyes changed. Their faces contorted in confusion. I could see something happen inside them. It was not a good thing. I felt as if I had rocketed them into some sort of disturbing puberty in which the male form was less Patrick Swayze in *Ghost* and more that lump of clay that he and Demi Moore left on the wheel after the director called cut.

My dresser would come over with my robe as soon as each scene was over so I could cover up, but one time, she must have gotten distracted and I was left standing in the buff while the cameras weren't rolling. Ms. Leoni yelled, "Hey, can we get this guy his robe?" which I thought was nice. She was watching out for me because she too had been subjected to the cruelty of objectification by the male gaze. She saw another actor and wanted to make sure he felt safe. She used her power to protect those farther down the call sheet.

But see, I didn't want to get my dresser in trouble, because I fear conflict and am bonkers, and so, feeling self-conscious, I went to my go-to, which is self-deprecating jokes. "No, it's okay! This is my gift to New York City! Feast your eyes, New Yorkers!" I yelled.

Ms. Leoni deadpanned back, "No. The robe is for me. I have to look at you."

Damn.

I know she was making a joke. In fact, she was *Yes, and*–ing *my* joke. I know she was the female lead in a major motion picture, which meant she was under a lot of stress. I know that that day there were wildfires threatening her house back in California. And yes, I know one of her ex-husbands was (is?) a sex addict. Still, though . . . *wow*, that hurt! Somehow, *me* making a joke about being disgusting is fine, but a gorgeous movie star doing it adds a level of cruelty. You know what also sucks? She delivered that line with a cutting tone and perfect timing, which made me understand why she was a star.

Guts

by KRISTEN JOHNSTON[*]

I have filmed commercials for American Airlines, American Express, Bud Light, Chevrolet, Microsoft, Snickers, T-Mobile, Wrigley's, and about twenty other products and services that don't have the name-brand recognition of the above companies.

My first commercial was for a product called the FoodLoop. It was a cooking product made of silicone that one could use as a trussing device instead of single-use cooking twine. It kept stuffed foods like chicken cordon bleu together. Look, between you and me, it was a rubber string. I am sure there are people who cook stuffed meats all the time, and for them, this is a useful tool to have in one's kitchen, but it didn't really seem like a million-dollar idea to my eyes.

I guess it didn't seem like a million-dollar idea to the marketing department either, because instead of commercials, they wrote tiny vignettes that they hoped would become viral videos. In my opinion, it is difficult to intentionally make a video that will go viral. It is

---

*Kristen Johnston was twenty-nine when *3rd Rock from the Sun* premiered.

something that is usually a surprise and organic, but these copywriters certainly tried. The point of the commercials was basically to laugh at the limitation of the product—that there weren't that many uses for it. In order for it to go viral, they needed to show ways to misuse the product that would get people talking. They decided the funniest misuse was murder.

Yes, an advertising genius decided that the best way to market a cooking tool was to create short films in which actors used the product to strangle people. There were three commercials: one where a wife strangled her gross husband with the FoodLoop, one where a father strangled his bratty teens with it, and mine, where I hung myself with the FoodLoop because my lover had left me for someone named Felip. Here is a racist/homophobic thing about comedy writers—if they want to show that someone is really kinky, they make him have a gay affair with a man who has a Latino-sounding name. If you haven't noticed it, start watching sitcoms from the eighties and you will see that off-screen gay men mentioned for a laugh always have a name like Felip, Alejandro, or Rodrigo.

Can you imagine the uproar today if a commercial played suicidal ideation for laughs and giggles? I mean, talk about trigger warning. I wish that I'd found this disgusting and reprehensible at the time, but I just wanted to work. I had been trying to break into commercials for years. My commercial agent had been freelancing with me for two years and I knew he would drop me soon if I didn't get something, so this commercial that included stereotypes about gay men and "exotic" gay people of Hispanic descent and was flippant about taking one's own life was sort of a win for me.

Yikes, this was a win? Yes, because commercials are a great way for actors who get three or four acting jobs a year to make a living. Well, they were. With the advent of streaming, commercials have all moved to the internet and are no longer as lucrative as they were when they aired on ABC between eight and eleven p.m. (seven to ten p.m. central time!). Back then, if you got a commercial that aired during prime time or during football games, you could make tens of thousands of dollars from one spot that often took just a day of work. The FoodLoop commercial did not pay that well because it was non-union and was presented as a video that the executives hoped children would share in whatever way they did in 2006. My hope, however, was that after I did this ad, I would break some sort of seal and get more and more commercials that *would* eventually pay me tens of thousands of dollars.

There was another reason getting into commercials was so important to me: revenge.

A woman I met in one of my first improv classes was very glamorous. She knew what ceviche was and she wore sunglasses that were dramatically large. I even saw her wearing a white coat! Do you know how difficult it is to keep a white winter coat white? It is nearly impossible! On *Scandal*, the president kills a Supreme Court justice as revenge for setting up his assassination attempt, but Olivia Pope's pristine white coat was the least believable thing about that show.

This white-coated woman represented a type of New Yorker that I aspired to be but failed miserably at becoming. She was chic and put together and knew about a restaurant that looked like a hot-dog place from the outside but if you walked in and went through the phone booth inside, you were in a speakeasy. She also worked in advertising as a copywriter! This was pre–*Mad Men* but post-*Bewitched,* so I knew that people who worked in advertising were creative, not poor, and drank martinis.

I wanted her to like me, and she sort of did! It was a patronizing kind of like, but some of my best friends in high school called me Big Bear—"You know, 'cause you're so fat!"—so I could handle her saying things to me like "Oh God. You're drinking Starbucks? I have to teach you about coffee."

Everyone in our improv class became friends and we started an improv team. We performed horribly unfunny shows for an audience exclusively filled with other people who were on the bill to perform horribly unfunny shows. The only saving grace was that I was—ugh.

How to say this? I hope you know by now that I am nothing if not self-deprecating, so the fact that I am saying this without any joke associated with it must mean it is the God's honest truth: I was the funniest. By far. Way funnier than the glamourpuss who hated Starbucks, and I could tell she knew it.

She praised my performing, and my being good at improv seemed to raise her level of respect for me. So much so that I felt safe enough to tell her I wanted to try to get work in commercials. I asked if she had any advice with the hope that she would say, "I'm having a casting next week, I'll call you in!"

Instead, this was her advice: "No. You can't do commercials. You come across as gay, and no product wants to be associated with that."

If that line were in a movie, you would throw popcorn at the screen for its lack of subtlety. It was a *macro*aggression! I knew immediately that I had to do everything in my power to do thousands of commercials so I could shove it down her throat so hard, she'd puke good coffee all over her white coat.

I wish I had never spoken to her, but actually I ran into her in Central Park not that long ago and we talked for a long time about the best farmers' markets in Manhattan for locally foraged mushrooms. She told me she was proud of my success, which I found insulting because it insinuated she had something to do with my success. Oh, wait. Now that I think about it, I might not have pursued commercials as hard as I did if she hadn't told me that I would never be cast in them. So, thanks, I guess, white-coat lady.

Commercial auditions are innately humiliating. They are not about acting, they are about the product, so you must suppress any needs you have as an artist when you audition for them. Just shut up about yourself and tell me how great that bundle of phone, internet, and cable is. When you audition for commercials, the directors all say the same thing: "Just make it really small. Throw it away." They say this because they don't want their commercials to sound too much like commercials. They want their ads to be cool, but the ad companies want to make sure the audience understands what they are selling, so you have to walk a fine line, which can be difficult. Do you know how hard it is to "throw away" a line like "These new Bounce dryer sheets offer so much more freshness without any of the static" and *not* sound like a commercial?

The other thing commercial directors love to say is "Make it your own! Feel free to improvise." This means *The commercial isn't funny, so please make it be.* I got really good at finding what was funny about a situation and not making fun of the product itself. The FoodLoop might be okay with dark and bizarre tangents, but AT&T would like you to keep it clean. Sometimes you were paired with other actors for auditions, and I watched people who I knew were brilliant comedians say things like "Oh, *fucking shit!* This Taco Bell is gonna give me the worst god*damn* diarrhea I've ever had in my *tit-sucking* life!" Okay, I never heard anyone say *tit-sucking*, but I definitely heard people curse and claim the product they were auditioning to sell would do horrible things to them. Surprisingly, none of them booked it.

My first big network commercial (that just means that it airs on actual television) was for American Express. I auditioned to be a German shepherd—as in a guy wearing lederhosen and holding a staff with a crook. The audition had no dialogue. Groups of six or so Aryan-looking gentlemen were called into a room and told to stand in a line, then each of us took a turn to step forward, smile, and step back into the line. I got the job. Suck on that, White Coat! Don't have to be straight to do that!

The commercial was a vehicle for my comedy idol Tina Fey. Before I shot this first commercial, I dreamed I would befriend her on set, we would become fast friends, and we'd meet up for a glass of chardonnay on Friday nights. In reality, I didn't even speak to her that day because she had a TV show to run and a family that included a young daughter, so when we German shepherds filmed our section, we stood in front of

Tina's stand-in (who was really nice). They told us not to talk, but I saw a boom operator holding a mic directly over my head, so on one take I improvised a line. The director said, "Okay, and Tina is saying, 'No, the *other* kind of German shepherd' and you are reacting with your face—just throw it away." I said, "Oh, that makes sense." The line made it into the commercial! Well, it made it into the sixty-second commercial, not the thirty-second one, but the sixty-second version played during the Emmys and a ton of friends saw it and recognized me!

My first Super Bowl commercial was for Chevrolet. (Yeah, I've done more than one Super Bowl commercial! I've done two! What? That is more than one.) The Chevy ad was a play on the *Cool Hand Luke* scene where the sexy lady washes the car. The idea was that this car was so hot, even regular guys would want to rub themselves all over it. It was a loose idea.

When my agent contacted me about the audition, he told me to make sure to wear boxer shorts because we would be stripping in the room and dancing around. "Make sure your boys stay in, you know?" I knew.

So, I went into a room with six men I knew from the UCB, undressed down to our underwear, and danced around to no music. My friend Devlyn recently reminded me he was in that audition as well.

"I can't believe we did that for an audition! How embarrassing!" I said.

"Imagine how embarrassing it was for me," Devlyn protested. "I danced around in my underwear and didn't even get the part!"

Touché, Devlyn. Touché.

In the commercial, I played a water-delivery man. I see the gorgeous new Chevrolet, rip off my shirt, pour the water I am delivering all over my body, then wipe the car with my bare chest. We shot the spot in downtown Manhattan on my birthday. Which, as you may recall, is in December. I poured ice-cold water over my bare body in freezing temperatures roughly twenty times that day. Another guy in that commercial told the rest of us we would be making a hundred and fifty thousand dollars each from that one spot. That is the kind of lie that actors tell themselves to justify pouring cold water over their heads in twenty-degree weather. In truth, I made more like fifteen thousand from that spot. In my mind, fifteen Gs is worth the bronchitis.

The most I ever made doing commercials was for a series of spots I did for Snickers' Feast campaign. The idea for these "high-concept" spots was that Snickers was so delicious, it was a "feast." The premise was that people who were famous for feasting went on a road trip in a twenty-year-old Ford Taurus. There was a Roman man in a toga, a Polynesian man in a grass skirt, a Viking with a horn helmet, a Pilgrim in buckled shoes and a hat, and Henry the VIII. I'm not sure why there were four general people and one specific one, nor am I sure why they were traveling around in a 1980s Ford Taurus in 2008. I was not there to ask questions; I was there to play the Pilgrim.

We shot the commercials over a week, primarily in Staten Island. Did you know that Staten Island is home to one of the largest dumps in the country? Well, after breathing through my mouth for a week, I do.

When you shoot a scene, you have to do several takes. If you are eating something in that scene, you have to eat it over and over again. The common wisdom is that you should take very tiny bites. Andrew McCarthy talks about this in his book *Brat*, laughing about Jacqueline Bisset cutting a microscopic leaf of arugula in half but chewing it like a hearty meatball. It probably comes as no surprise that I am no Jacqueline Bisset. I ate big hunks of Snickers bars.

There were several reasons for this. The first is that in a commercial, you have to look like you really love the product and can't get enough of it. The second is that I really love Snickers and I can't get enough of them. They're creamy and delicious, and the peanuts add a complexity that Milky Way could nevah! The fact that I was two weeks into the South Beach Diet while shooting those commercials probably also played a part. It's not cheating if it's for work.

When you eat food in a scene, the prop department gives you a bucket so you can spit out the food after the director yells cut. I kept on chewing because I was too shy to spit out partially chewed-up chocolate (with peanuts inside). It just felt too . . . fecal. Consequently, I ate a *lot* of candy on that shoot. So much so that I didn't poop for a week. Snickers bars really *do* fill you up.

The Feast campaign was a great job to land. Not only did we get six (!) national commercials, but there was thirty minutes of interactive web content and a national tour to NFL and college football games, where the five of us walked around dressed in character. Take that, White Coat! We were paid very well. I mean, not Elon Musk money, but good money for most people. The previous year I'd made $24,000 from acting work, cater-waiter-ing, temping, and teaching improv. The year of the commercials, I made $175,000! One day I got over thirty checks in the mail and made my roommate John take pictures of me in the pile of envelopes as if I were Margot Robbie in *The Wolf of Wall Street*!

When the football tour began, I was excited. Not for the football games but for hotel life. I know that when you travel for work all the time, hotels become monotonous and cold, but I hardly ever traveled, so being in a hotel felt like the most glamorous thing in the world. Even now, I like to pretend I'm someone else when I am in a hotel. Someone complicated and chic who always uses hand lotion and isn't afraid of the charges from the minibar. I like to press the button on the elevator and sigh—the ennui of the glamorous life. But inside I am thinking, *Do I look like I'm feeling the ennui of the glamorous life?*

The hotels were fine, but the tour was difficult. The man playing the Roman was actually a Roman (as in from the city of Rome), and he hated the tour. In fact, he seemed to hate everything. "This restaurant-e is *mis-era-bull*." "The bed in my room-a is *mis-era-bull*." "The way I say-a mis-era-bull is *mis-era-bull!*" There was no way to engage him without getting a shower of shit from the pity potty. That is a powerful image that I have never used before, which I think should indicate how profoundly negative this Roman was.

The man playing Henry the VIII was a talker and what I think would be referred to today as a "mansplainer." It didn't matter that almost everyone on the tour was a man. He explained theater to a group of actors. He explained jogging to a marathon runner. He explained how commercials work to a group of advertising executives. He explained how football works to . . . well, he did that to me, and I actually didn't understand.

Taki, the actor who played the Polynesian, had never done a commercial before, and he was so excited by this entirely new world. He would yell delightedly, "They gave me money for food! It's called *per diem!*" His sweetness was a lovely antidote to the *mis*-era-*bull* stuff.

My salvation on the tour, however, was Chris Sullivan, who played the Viking. You actually know Sully! He played Toby on *This Is Us!* At the time, he was just an improviser from Chicago, and I was just an improviser from New York. I'm normally afraid of straight men (which made this tour difficult, as you can imagine), but Sully is one of those people who make you feel seen and known. We're both six five, so we joked about starting an improv show called *Thirteen Feet of Fun.* He was a joy to hang out with, but that wasn't why he was my salvation (more on that in a moment).

Before we started going to the football games, I thought they might be fun in a novel sort of way. I never liked basketball, but I'd gone to a Spurs game once a year with my dad growing up and we had fun. Sure, I spaced out a lot and spent most of the night making up stories about the people sitting around us, but that was enough to entertain me. I thought the little shows at intermission were cute and I loved how the music pumped through the entire . . . amphitheater? What's the sports term for *stage*? *Stadium* doesn't seem right for basketball. *Arena*? *Arena* feels sort of correct. I'm gonna go with *arena.* Final answer.

The problem with football, however, is that most of the games are outside and during the winter. Did you know this? That's apparently true every year. It was nice when we went to Phoenix, but I froze my Pilgrim ass off at the University of Michigan. You know what else?

Cleveland's football team is called the Browns. Simultaneously boring and disgusting. I looked it up and it turns out it's a reference to a man whose last name was Brown, but I still think it's a dumb team name. No one else on the tour agreed with me, though. During that game, I entertained myself by coming up with wordplay. "Woof, the Browns are playing so bad, they're giving me the Blues!" I said to the guy next to me. "That joke was *mis-era-bull*," he responded.

At each game, we started by walking around tailgate parties in the parking lot outside the stadium. These parties were surprisingly sophisticated. We're talking full buffets, cases and cases of beer, costumes, tables, tents, fully stuffed furniture. One guy had a four-foot-tall ice sculpture made and hauled to a parking lot in Detroit. An ice sculpture! Like something you would order for your high-end wedding! This guy had one just so he could take shots of vodka from it. "It gets it really cold," he told me, but I knew it was about more than cold vodka. It was about the drama.

Unfortunately, not all the fans were fun. Many of them were drunk, which removed their filters. The commercials were playing in constant rotation at the time, and it isn't often that you see a Viking, a Polynesian, a Pilgrim, a Roman, and Henry the VIII walking around together, so we were recognized frequently. Most of the fans would ask for Snickers or take a picture, but about 3 percent of them smelled gay on me and wanted to let me know they were *not* into it. One guy said, "You seem a little light in your Pilgrim shoes." I thought that was a rather erudite way to be homophobic.

Drunk men sometimes tried to tackle us. Some would yell, "I hate y'all's commercials!" We were not allowed to hand out Snickers inside the stadium because fans might pelt the opposing team with them. Consequently, people got mad that the Snickers people didn't have any Snickers bars. We had tiny towels for them to wave in the air, you know . . . like they just don't care? But they did not want the towels. One man yelled, "What is this? A Snickers cum rag?" I was scared of that man, but I've got respect for that joke.

The most dangerous encounter was in Dallas at a Cowboys game. Sully went to the bathroom inside the stadium and when he returned, he was rattled. He told us we needed to stick together because he was dressed as a Viking, so away from the rest of us, he just looked like a rabid Minnesota fan. "You never know what's going on with drunk people, guys, but there is safety in numbers," he cautioned us. I thought this was sweet. Like a protective parent, he had spun an outrageous scenario as he tried to protect his pack of merry feasters.

I was wrong. He was right.

I know I've leaned into my lack of football knowledge for comedic effect in this chapter. I could have looked up whatever a basketball place is called. So you might be thinking I'm joking now, but I must tell you in all honesty that I did not know there was a team with a Pilgrim as a mascot. The New England Patriots? I assumed their mascot was . . . well, to be honest, I spent zero time considering any NFL mascot besides the Browns' during that one game I just mentioned. Also, I just looked up the mascot and he's wearing a football uniform, not a Pilgrim one. He does have a slightly similar-looking hat, though. I guess a bunch of drunk dudes didn't really want to take the time to parse out our sartorial differences.

So I didn't listen to Sully, and I went to the bathroom by myself to kill some time. (When the clock says there are only four minutes left in the game, it is lying.) There was no line outside the bathroom, but inside, there was a crowd waiting for space at the urinals and stalls. I waited patiently in my black wool Pilgrim outfit, white tights, a large hat, and shoes with a chunky three-inch heel. Just blending in, you know?

The first drunk man yelled, "Who the *fuck* do you think you are? Fucking Patriots?" His words were slurred to comedic effect, as if Foster Brooks were roasting me on *The Dean Martin Show*. "Tell meeee, youooooouuu, uh"—burp—"you *faggot*!" This wasn't the first time I had been called the F-word on the tour, but it *was* the most passionate. The slur seemed to awaken the rest of the crowd. I was some sort of gay New Englander come to force them all to make tender love to Tom Brady.

"Fuck the Patriots!" a second drunk yelled.

"Yeah, don't bring that Pilgrim shit to Texas!" a third said, sounding frighteningly sober.

Suddenly, there was a mill of anger and taunts from the men in the room. They started yelling all manner of gay slurs, though I'm not sure if that was specifically for me or just the meanest things they could imagine calling someone. The first drunk man got in my face and threw beer on me.

I was genuinely frightened. And then, just like in a movie, my hero appeared. Superman to my Lois. Tarzan to my Jane. Bruce Willis to my Bonnie Bedelia. It was Sully, still in full Viking regalia. He grabbed the drunk man and pinned him against the wall in a way that didn't seem to hurt the drunk man but did restrict his movement.

"Did you piss yet?" Sully yelled at me.

"There aren't any stalls open," I meekly replied.

"Go to this one," he said and kicked open an empty stall without letting go of Drunkard Number 1. The stall was empty because there were several rolls of paper shoved in the toilet. How could I do this?

"There's toilet pap—"

"Pee on it, Jeff, we gotta get out of here!" Sully stated firmly.

I peed on the toilet paper.

When I came back out, the men were all cowering. One even said, "Naw, man, we like the Vikings, just not this Patriot shit."

Sully didn't blink. He just let go of the guy and walked me out of the restroom like a Secret Service officer.

Toby from *This Is Us* saved my life. Casting directors take note: He can play the action hero!

It's interesting that the Snickers campaign was my greatest achievement in commercials because it was specifically meant to appeal to straight men who loved sports, hence the tour of football games. I wanted to succeed in commercials so desperately because I wanted to prove that I wasn't too gay to be mainstream. Yet being there in the most mainstream world of male heterosexual bonding proved to me how correct White Coat had been. At one game at the University of Arizona, a man looked me directly in the eye and said with a sneer, "We all know you're gay."

He wanted me to know that even if I had fooled the Snickers marketing team and the fancy New York ad agency, I hadn't fooled him. He wanted to remind me that I was just a guest here, and not a welcome one. The empowering thing to do would be to tell you that this rolled off my back and I laughed all the way to the bank. I can't tell you that. It hurt a lot and it didn't make White Coat respect me. I was a gay Pilgrim who needed saving by a straight Viking.

But also . . . I did make $175,000 that year. And that ain't so *misera-bull*.

Speedbumps

by TERI GARR[*]

In the spring of 2008, I was in love. Neil and I were newly dating and we were disgusting. Full-on heart eyes while we fed each other at dimly lit restaurants that were not dim enough for these displays. Our Saturdays were especially dreamy. We would lounge around Neil's apartment with the windows open, talking about who we were and how in love we were with each other while we "shared breath." I'm sure the neighbors were vomiting, hearing it through those open windows. One Saturday as we were holding each other and reading Rumi or some shit, I got a phone call from Pat, the tech director at the Upright Citizens Brigade Theatre.

"Hey, man, you close by? I told your class to do Zip Zap Zop, but they've been doing it for fifteen minutes."

Oh, shit!

I wasn't supposed to be getting high on young love at that moment!

---

[*]Teri Garr worked as a dancer and comedic actor quite a bit before she found fame at age thirty-eight with her Oscar-nominated performance in *Tootsie*.

I was supposed to be supervising an end-of-class improv show across town!

I told Pat I was close by (a lie) and that I would be there soon—"So, please, don't start without me!" (If they did, I wouldn't get paid.) Then I went from lounging in PJs to fully dressed, hair combed, and riding the subway to the theater in less than four minutes. Neil later told me that my speed shocked him. "All I heard was 'Oh, shit!' and then you were . . . gone."

Of course I was gone. 'Twas not my first "Oh, shit" rodeo. I forget a lot of stuff. Scheduling is not my forte, and those lapses in memory turn me into that Looney Tunes Tasmanian Devil tornado, stopping only when I've arrived where I was supposed to be in the first place.

Neil has come to call these trials my "Oh, shit" moments. The truth is, I am a mess. A semifunctional one, but a legit mess. I cannot remember dates, times, addresses, or birthdays. My mind becomes foggy with details, and my palms sweat if someone expects me to oversee a committee or plan a travel itinerary or remember which queen was on which season of *Drag Race*.

I am good at listening! I remember names and faces. I have comforted more than one friend through the grief of losing their parents. I am an incredible conversationalist at a dinner party! But if I planned a dinner party, I would forget something major, like food. When it comes down to details and plans, I am a nightmare wrapped in pitiful wrapping paper (and the paper isn't taped down because I never remember to buy things like tape).

Neil has marveled that I can go in front of an audience without a script and improvise for an hour without feeling any stress. It's true, I do not get stage fright. I feel comfortable in front of a large group of people. You know when I *do* feel stressed? When I have to plan things.

I'm not proud of it. I come from a family of detail-oriented taskmasters. My mom graduated with a 4.0 GPA while raising two kids and holding down a part-time job. My dad designed hospital beds for special-care patients. He figured out things like how to perform CPR on a patient who is sleeping on an air mattress to prevent bedsores. My sister has two kids, a full-time job as an HR director overseeing one hundred employees, a part-time job running billing for a lawyer, another part-time job as a property manager, and a thriving social life with multiple friends; she decorates for every holiday and crafts on the weekends.

Meanwhile, I once made an appointment to get my teeth cleaned with a dermatologist. I showed up, realized this was not a dentist, and made up a story about getting my moles checked. I come from organizer stock, but like a redhead with two brunette parents, I got the recessive gene. And just like the redhead, I do a lot of skin-cancer checks.

To celebrate their fortieth wedding anniversary, my parents took our entire family on a Caribbean cruise. My sister packed up her husband's suitcase, her toddler son's suitcase, and her own while she was six months pregnant. My dad planned the route from San Antonio to Galveston, where we would be setting sail, by printing several pages of Yahoo! Maps that he placed in a manila folder organized by route with alternatives in case of traffic. (This was pre-Waze, but my dad didn't *need* Waze!) My mom, meanwhile, planned the whole damn trip. She researched cruise lines by price/destination/amenities, figured out the most cost-effective way to bring six (and a half) people on a cruise, and found coupons for each of our preplanned excursions as well as itineraries for excursions when she felt the preplanned itineraries weren't preplanned enough.

The *only* thing I had to do was get on a plane from New York to Texas (a flight that was researched by my mother to arrive not too early and not too late and also be the cheapest possible 'cause she was paying for the cruise too and what was she, a Rockefeller?). Oh, one more thing: I had to bring clothes and my passport. Actually, I could buy clothes on the ship. Just remember the passport.

I forgot my passport. When I arrived in San Antonio the night before we left, my mother asked if I had my passport as soon as I got in the car at the airport. I remembered placing it on my dresser in New

York so I wouldn't forget it. It was still sitting there. My poor mom. She just kept repeating, "Jeff, you are almost thirty years old. You are almost thirty years old! *You are almost thirty years old!*" It was a mantra of disbelief and disappointment.

I called my friend Mark Sam who lived in the neighborhood and had keys to my apartment because he was watering my roommate's plants. I had no plants because I do not have the executive function to remember to care for them. Thankfully, my roommate, Amy, not only cared for her plants but also had an extra set of keys made and gave them to our mutual friend in case of emergencies. He got into our apartment, found my passport, and FedExed it overnight to the cruise ship itself. We were able to get on board and celebrate my parents' blessed union. Even if it had yielded a disorganized spawn.

Other "Oh, shit" stories have less happy endings. On my way to the Denver airport to catch a plane to Houston for a friend's wedding, I somehow dropped my wallet without noticing. I say *somehow*, but I need to come clean. I dropped the wallet because it wasn't a wallet. I was in an especially granola phase at the time and I carried what I called a satchel but what anyone with eyes could see was a purse. It hung around my shoulders and had everything I needed for my trip, like my ticket, my ID, cash, credit cards, and the addresses and phone numbers of the people I would be visiting once I got there. It also had a wonky latch that allowed it to fall onto the ground in the parking lot as I was putting my suitcase into the trunk of my car. This was pre–cell phones and pre-9/11, so I got to the airport and made it through security. It was only once I got to the gate that the crew told me I couldn't get on the plane without ID. "Oh, shit!" I cried. They didn't budge. I missed my friend's wedding.

Two years later, I missed another flight from Denver, this one to San Antonio, because I'd been under the impression you could arrive for a 2:00 p.m. flight at 1:50 p.m. I missed my flight. Oh, shit!

A year later, I had to take a flight from Denver to New York City. I had found a tiny table on the street and thought to myself, *I could use that table as a place to put my keys and wallet so I won't forget them on the way out of my apartment!* I was religious about immediately putting my wallet and keys on that tiny table by the front door. Unfortunately, the cab pulled up in the back alley, so I went out the back door, forgetting my wallet on the tiny table by the front door. Oh, shit! The cab ride was twice as expensive going from the airport back to my apartment, and then back to the airport, but I did get on that plane.

The first fight I had with my husband was because of an "Oh, shit" moment. He and his friends had rented a house in the Pines on Fire Island. I was more of a Cherry Grove girl myself, but I wanted to meet Neil's friends and continue to nurture our relationship. We had been dating only a few months at this point.

Neil and his crew went out for a whole week, but I could only come for the weekend because I had some temp job or an audition or maybe an improv class to teach? I am not organized enough to remember. So I went out the following Friday via the Long Island Rail Road. Once you get off the train in Sayville, you have to take a cab to the ferry and then a ferry to the actual island. It's a pain in the ass, but once you get to the island, it is a Shangri-La with no cars, wooden boardwalks, and beaches stacked three high with homosexuals.

Neil wanted me there for lunch so that we could sit and have a get-to-know-you meal with his nearest and dearest beach buddies. I knew this would be complicated, so I told myself, *Self, you have to figure out how to get there on your own. You have to plan for travel time and make sure you get on the subway to Penn Station early enough to make the train out to Long Island.* I did the math, people! I got to Penn Station in time to catch the train to Sayville. I was in Sayville a full hour before lunch! I figured out how to get a cab to the ferry station (this was before Uber and Lyft!). I got to the dock and was surprised to see that no one was waiting for the ferry. The waiting area for the Pines ferry was empty. I walked up to the ticket booth and saw that the next ferry wasn't leaving for three hours. That would be two hours after I was supposed to be there.

This was before smartphones but not before cell phones. I called Neil. I explained the situation. He was unimpressed. "Take a ferry to another town on Fire Island, then get a water taxi to take you to the Pines. You need to be here by lunch."

Oh, shit!

I want to impress my new boyfriend and his friends! I want to be on the gay beach! I want to eat Greek salad with huge chunks of feta and have mimosas! So even though I was completely out of my depth, I got on a ferry that was going to another town on Fire Island. This ferry was not going to either the Pines or Cherry Grove, the two gay enclaves. This ferry was going to a town called Sailors Haven, which sounds gay but is in fact very straight. Straight towns on Fire Island are terrifying. The whole point of going to Fire Island is to be in a community where you are accepted, and here I was, getting on a ferry with families carrying coolers full of Budweiser. They stared at me, probably because I was wearing my short-short bathing suit and a headband with rainbows on it. Fair.

I made it across the bay without any incident (unless you count slack-jawed stares as an incident), but I somehow got mixed up and found myself at a place called Sunken Forest. I swear I *would* have asked someone how I could get a water taxi, but I never saw anyone. I was on some sort of nature trail and there were zero people anywhere. I just kept walking and walking and finally I reached the beach, which is on the other side of the island (the ferries drop you off on the bay side). I knew you had to get a water taxi from the bay side 'cause the beach side had waves and shit. I also knew that there was no way I was getting back through that park again, so there was only one option. I needed to walk down the beach and keep walking until I got to the Pines. Then I would meet Neil.

I started walking.

I kept walking.

There was so much walking.

I had a rolling suitcase. On the beach. Wheels do not roll on sand. So I had to carry it.

I had remembered to check train times but hadn't thought to bring sunscreen. Or water.

I kept walking.

It was ninety-five degrees.

I kept walking.

It took me two hours to get to the Pines. I arrived at roughly the same time as the ferry I hadn't had time to wait for.

I had been calling Neil, keeping him up to date on my progress. He met me on the beach. His first words were "Hey, if we're going to keep dating, you need to get it together."

Reader, I fucking *lost it*!

"Oh, really? *Really*? I need to get it together? The only way you will date me is if I completely change my inner being? You think my entire life I haven't been told I need to get it together? My mother has been trying for thirty years to have me get it together and it *has not worked*! But somehow a few months with you and I will just be able to change 'cause it annoys you that I missed lunch even though I rode on a straight-person ferry in gay drag and walked miles and miles and carted this wheeled suitcase through the sand for the past two hours! Even though I am dying of thirst and I am arriving at the gay mecca drenched in sweat with a nose that is so burned, it is already peeling! If you want me to get it together, then you need to just get someone else who knows how to check the ferry schedule *and* the train schedule 'cause that seems to be more important to you than the fact that I tried very hard to get here! If you don't like this, then let's break the fuck up 'cause it ain't gonna change anytime soon!"

Oh, *shit*!

Neil was taken aback. I hadn't so much as expressed a preference for a type of cuisine up to this point, and now I was fully *screaming* in his face that we should break up. I'm not proud of it, but, honey, I had been pushed to the brink.

He calmly said, "I'm sorry," which sucked 'cause then I looked like a really overdramatic bitch, which I guess I was at that moment. We went inside. I met his friends. They were nice. We stayed together, but that trip to Fire Island was a turning point for me.

I still have lots of "Oh, shit" moments. In fact, just yesterday, I took the menorah and Christmas decorations down to our storage unit on the first floor of our apartment building, and while I was stacking the boxes, my phone rang. It was a radio station in Chicago calling me for a previously scheduled interview. This interview was live. On the air. They were doing me a huge favor so I could promote an upcoming stand-up show I had there. I had put the interview in my calendar and confirmed that morning, but I *still* forgot about it. I did the interview on my phone in a storage unit while holding a wooden manger scene to my chest. Thanks for the good reception, T-Mobile!

That moment on Fire Island wasn't a turning point that made me more together, it was one where I stopped ragging on myself for being myself. You know that story about the lady who helps the scorpion and then the scorpion stings her? And the scorpion says, "It is my nature"? Well, being a sweaty mess is my nature. I try really hard to be there on time and figure out logistics, but it isn't who I am. If I have to show up somewhere now, I ask for a detailed plan from the organizer.

"I'm not good with logistics. Can you spell it out for me?" I say to them.

"Will you be in charge of buying tickets and I'll Venmo you?" I say to friends who want to go to a show together.

I am traveling internationally, so I am going to pack my passport first, I say to myself.

I can't say that I am proud of this personality trait. I wish I were more organized, but I've spent so much of my life hating my— *Oh, shit! I forgot I had brunch plans and my friend is already at the restaurant! Gotta go!*

A Very Punchable Face

by COLIN JOST*

A friend of mine was very worried that Google provided predictive text as he typed his name into the search box. These are words based on common searches people enter with his name. My friend is a somewhat well-known Broadway actor, and he was disturbed that the predictive text after his name was the title of an out-of-town show he had been fired from.

"Now anyone who googles me will know this show didn't bring me with it when it came to New York!" he lamented. "Why is Google so mean?"

I didn't have the heart to tell him that Google wasn't being mean; Google was being honest. He *had* been in that show and that show had *not* taken him to Broadway. I was in an early version of the musical *Bright Star* by Steve Martin and Edie Brickell, but I was not in it when it went to Broadway. This was not my choice, and it stung to get left

---

*Colin Jost was hired as a writer for *Saturday Night Live* at twenty-three and made his on-air debut at age thirty-two.

behind when the show went on to the Great White Way, but it was the truth. Google wasn't being mean; my poor friend just couldn't handle the truth.

"Type in your name," he said. "Let's see what it says about you."

I wasn't worried. I assumed it would say *gay* or *height* or, worst-case scenario, *Bright Star*. I could handle it because I can handle the truth.

I typed in *Jeff Hiller*, and the following phrases came up in the predictive-text menu:

Jeff Hiller . . . age (*Can't help it if I look young.*)

Jeff Hiller . . . husband (*Can't help it if people need to know I'm taken.*)

Jeff Hiller . . . appearance (*Huh. Maybe they're searching for places I will be appearing?*)

Jeff Hiller . . . cancer (*I'm a Sagittarius.*)

Jeff Hiller . . . disease (*They think I have a disease? Or that I am one?*)

Jeff Hiller . . . plastic surgery (*What the . . .*)

As it turns out, people on Google really have only one question about me, which is this: "Why do you look like that?" Okay. My Broadway friend was right, Google *is* mean.

I shouldn't have been surprised. I spent years hoping that my face would be the first one to pop up when you googled my name. Up until very recently, the Jeff Hiller on the first page of results was a guy who bred betta fish in California. Frankly, it felt homophobic! Of course they gave pride of place to the Jeff Hiller who was a breeder.

Still, Google is only reporting what people search about me. So let me fill you in so you don't have to google for the answers anymore. Ask me anything in these pages and then never ask me these things in person 'cause I am not strong enough to handle it. Here is the FAQ that Google honestly revealed to me.

How old are you, exactly?

Let's get this easy one out of the way first. As I vulnerably declared earlier in this book, I was born on December 7, 1975, so you can do the math based on the year you are reading this, but I really do want to stress again that it is a December birthday. It can cause a *lot* of confusion depending on what month you're in when you're subtracting.

There is another reason for confusion about my age. Right now, the internet thinks I am thirty-five. I do not know why. I did not ask it to tell people I was born in 1988, but it tells people I was born in 1988. I admit to lying about my age over the years, but when I did, I shaved off only one or maybe two years. I've never shaved off thirteen years. That's practically a different generation. I wouldn't even know what my cultural touchstones were supposed to be! *No, En Vogue wasn't my favorite band in high school, it was . . . Ke$ha? I loved her song about . . . parties?*

This is not to say I wasn't flattered that the internet thought I was thirty-five. I am not above feeling good when people tell me I look young for my age. I have decent skin, and the roundness of my face telegraphs youth. I own these good things about my appearance. I also have good legs and straight teeth.

I have no idea how to change my age when people google it, and I had no desire to do that until recently when a writer who was developing a show wanted me to play the high-school best friend of the lead woman. The woman was in her late forties, the writer said. Her best friend would have to be in his late forties too. She told me I was too young for the role.

"But I'm forty-eight. There isn't much later one can get and still be in one's forties," I told her.

"We googled you and it said you were thirty-five."

The one time my advanced age would have helped! Thanks a lot, Google!

Who is your husband?

Another easy question. His name is Neil Goldberg and he is a successful visual artist. We are raising two beautiful pets together, a cat named Beverly and a dog named Yvonne De Carlo. Beverly was named by Animal Haven, the shelter we adopted her from. I thought there was nothing better than a tiny black kitten named Beverly, but then we saw the adoption form the shelter had filled out and they gave her adopted name as Beverly Goldberg-Hiller and there *was* something better. A tiny kitten with the name of a society woman on Manhattan's Upper West Side who married well and divorced better.

We didn't want to use our dog's shelter name, so we brainstormed and landed on Yvonne De Carlo (aka Lily on *The Munsters*). It's a long, rather boring story as to how we got there, but the short version is: We are gay.

If I sound like one of those people who treat their pets as if they're human children, that's because I am the kind of person who treats his pets as if they are human children. But who cares? I vote, I pay taxes—I even volunteer. What do you care if I also sing Coldplay in my dog's face to lull her to sleep at night? It's not like I push her around in a stroller. Primarily because she won't stay in it.

So . . . can we ask about your appearance?

Okay, let's talk about my face. (The Body Electric cliché!)

It's a weird face. I gotta give you that. The mouth is huge and the nose and eyes are tiny, as if a theme-park caricature artist crafted one of his drawings in human flesh.

You aren't weird-looking! Don't say that!

That is sweet of you, thanks. You are saying that because I am telling you I know that I am not hot. That makes people uncomfortable, and I apologize, but think about it. If I started this book saying, "I am so fucking hot! Look at this hot body," you would spend a lot of time yelling, "This conceited mofo! He isn't even *cute!*" It's okay, though. I do not hold my self-esteem in my beauty, and I know I am unusual-looking because people have told me so.

Journalists have asked me, "Is it important that you are a lead on a television show but not conventionally attractive?"

I suppose that representation matters.

Once while I was talking to a journalist from a very fancy outlet about season one of *Somebody Somewhere,* she asked about my on-screen boyfriend.

"Oh! That's Jon Hudson Odom, isn't he great?" I responded.

"He's so cute! I love that you two are together on TV 'cause that guy would never be with you in real life." She laughed.

Look, that is 100 percent true, but it feels like something *I* should say, not something someone should say to me.

About a year ago, I was on the subway and I recognized someone recognizing me. He was pretty obvious. He looked me up and down and then took out his phone and began furiously googling, which you can do on subways now. It happens so rarely that I find being recognized flattering—the price of semi-fame!

Right after I recognized him recognizing me, the doors opened and I was shoved to the other side of the train. Now I was no longer in front of the man but standing behind him, looking down, as he sat in the seat typing on his phone. He was searching *Actor with weird-looking face.*

I know that sounds like a joke, but that story is 100 percent true.

Julia Roberts has a big mouth and she isn't weird-looking!
Yeah, it works for Julia. However, it isn't just my mouth that makes me look weird. I think the strangest thing about my face is that I have no eyebrows. I'm pretty sure this is why people find my face—uh, let's go with *disarming.*

I used to have eyebrows. They were blond, but they were there on my face. I lost them after a stressful time in 2016 when my parents

were sick, I was turning forty, I was moving back to New York
from Los Angeles, and I hadn't worked for almost a year. Plus, that
presidential election took a lot out of me.

The official diagnosis was frontal fibrosing alopecia, which is
slightly different than the alopecia areata that I think Jada Pinkett
Smith has (obvs, I read her memoir, *Worthy*). Frontal fibrosing
alopecia is scarring, which caused all the hair on my face to fall out.
My eyebrows, some of my hairline, and my beard. I only have to shave
about once a month, and that's just to clean up some fine, fair hairs
that grow sporadically around my face, making me look like a Nordic
witch.

I'm told that the hair loss will eventually stop, but the hair will
never grow back.

I ordered eyebrow wigs from the internet. They were so cute!
Just two tiny strips of wig! I put them on immediately, but there was
something off about them. They were too small and not the right
shape. I looked as if I'd stood under a tree and two symmetrically
trained caterpillars fell onto my face.

Why don't you draw your eyebrows on?

Several makeup artists have painted on my eyebrows to varying effects
and I try to do it for big events. Unfortunately, I sweat a lot and on
more than one occasion I have sweated off both eyebrows, which is
bad, but once I sweated off just one of them, which was worse.

For now, I wear my glasses. If you ever see me without my glasses,
something really wonky has happened. Once on a red carpet, I wore
my transition glasses that have a green tint because in the sunlight,
they turn into sunglasses. They make me look like a pornographer in
the seventies. I can't explain why, but I like that the glasses make me
look like a chic dirtbag. Unfortunately, at that event I made two rookie
mistakes.

The first was that when the makeup artist that HBO had hired to
make me look good at this event was having a difficult time getting the

right shape and symmetry drawing on my eyebrows, I told her not to worry about them. I would be wearing glasses the entire time, so no one would see the empty spaces on my head where eyebrows should go. She thanked me, relieved she could stop trying.

The second mistake was not arriving hours early. This particular red-carpet event had some very big names. We are talking Cate Blanchett and Michelle Yeoh, people whose publicists don't have to beg photographers to take their pictures. I am not one of these people. I need to beg. So in order to get my picture taken, I had to wait for a lull between famous people. I waited just outside the tented carpet in the direct sun. My glasses lost their green tint and turned dark black from all the UV rays.

When I finally got on the carpet, the photographers shouted at me, but it wasn't my name. They yelled, "Take off your sunglasses." I took them off, eager to please these people who were tolerating me until Joel Kim Booster arrived. As soon as I did it, I realized: *Crap! I have no eyebrows on!*

So now there are lots of photos of me on Getty Images with a completely bare face. Always tell the makeup person to paint it all on, just in case.

Have you thought about microblading?

I have thought about microblading, which for those of you not in the know is eyebrow tattooing.

Friends told me I had to get a good microblader or I would regret it, so I spent several hours on Yelp! finding someone who didn't have reviews that said, "I look like Joan Crawford now!" I scheduled a free consultation where my eyebrows would be painted on to show how they would look.

As the woman was doing it, I heard her tut several times. She was really annoyed. Finally, she grabbed three paper towels and told me to wipe my face because "you sweat. A *lot*."

"Oh, yeah, sorry," I said. "I walked from the subway and it's humid out."

"Well, *if* I do this, you can't sweat for ten days or it will ruin the microblading," she admonished.

"I should go," I said, grabbing my bag.

"Maybe you could do it in the winter?" she offered.

"Nope," I said and left. Ten days without me sweating would require a medically induced coma and a heavily air-conditioned hospital room.

Actually, I didn't mean your face when I asked if we could talk about your appearance. I was talking about your hair. What is up with your hair?

Oh, sorry. The hair, yes. You really go there, don't you, FAQ? The hair is bad. I want it to be better. I researched getting a toupee, but it costs roughly ten thousand dollars, plus when I wore the sample rug at the wig studio, I looked like Rip Taylor. Only less masc. I love a lot about madcap 1960s comedian Rip Taylor, but his "lewk" isn't the main thing.

Why is your hair so bad?

Remember that stressful time in my life that caused my immune system to attack me with frontal fibrosing alopecia? In addition to that, I also had a recurrence of an autoimmune disorder I had in high school. It was a *really* rough time.

The second autoimmune disorder is called generalized morphea or localized scleroderma. As I understand from my rheumatologist, this autoimmune condition happens when my body attacks the good layer of fat underneath my skin, which causes that skin to scar and the hair to fall out.

My first occurrence was when I was in tenth grade. I had done something very stupid. I called a gay male sex line I found in the back pages of *Interview* magazine. My sister had a subscription. One night when my parents were sleeping, I took my dad's credit card out of his wallet and punched in 1-800-CALL-HIM. I spent a long time listening to different voicemails from men all over the country. I was afraid of how expensive this call was getting, so I decided I would leave my number in a recorded message so that others could call me and my dad's card wouldn't be charged by the sex line in the future. A smart idea to avoid the credit card charges, but a very stupid idea when you consider I did not have a cell phone. This was before cell phones. I didn't even have a private line in my bedroom. I gave out our family's *home phone number*—the same number listed in our church directory—so that gay men in their thirties would call and chat up my fifteen-year-old ass!

Men called our house for weeks. Then the credit card bill arrived. My phone call cost almost $70, or about $168 in today's money, according to an online inflation calculator I just checked. My parents were confused about why their phone line had turned into a community-theater production of *The Boys in the Band*, but they were livid when they got a credit card bill showing that they had been charged $1.99 a minute for the privilege.

"What is this line you are calling?" they asked me.

I told them it was a party line for teens. My mom stopped. I saw her thinking.

"Is this connected to all those men that are calling?" she asked.

"No," I said, figuring being vague was my best course of action.

They bought it. Or maybe they pretended to buy it in a futile hope that I wouldn't be gay if they didn't know about it. *Clearly*, I imagine they said to themselves, *someone wrote our phone number on a men's room wall and* also *our son called a sex line to meet hot, age-appropriate chicks.*

I was so stressed at the possibility of being outed, not to mention getting arrested for credit card fraud, that I took to my bed for a week, claiming mono. I didn't go to school, and I unplugged the phone so I wouldn't be reminded of my sins. I felt guilt and stress and self-hatred.

When I finally recovered from the "mono," I noticed a red rash on my legs. For months my parents tried new detergents and bath soaps, assuming I was allergic to something, but nothing helped. Finally, I went to a dermatologist, who took a biopsy and diagnosed me with morphea. I took some huge pills to suppress my immune system and eventually the episode ended, but it left scars on my legs, chest, and back. Those are the scars that the makeup artist had to paint over when I shot *Ghost Town*. They look less like scars and more like brown splotches. You can still sort of see them.

Can you show us a picture?

Sure. There is a photo from the set of *Ghost Town* in the photo section. Even after the makeup artist sprayed me down with her airbrush cannon, you can still see it around my rib cage.

The photo from that movie was in my college alumni magazine. I guess if I can show everyone who went to my college this bodacious bod, I can show it to people who bought my book. I do ask you to turn your eyes away if you checked this out from the library or borrowed it from a friend. Isn't it brave of me to show you?

Uh-huh, you were saying about your hair?

Oh, right. So, when I turned forty and had that next crippling amount of stress—you know, the one that I thought I could solve by getting thin? Well, the morphea came back and it brought its friend Al—Al O'Pecia—that I described above.

The morphea attacked my forehead and a large portion of scalp in the center of my head, and now there is this big chunk of my skull that is bare. So, to recap, I have no hair on my legs, my face, my chest, or the top of my head. It is as if God wants me to be a drag queen.

Is that why Joel's hair looks so . . . uh . . . what's the word . . .

Bad? Is that the word you are looking for?

We shot the pilot for *Somebody Somewhere* in October of 2019. The bare spot from the morphea was already there but not as advanced as it later became during the stress of the pandemic. I thought a perfect way to address it was to give Joel a comb-over. I told the hair person to make the part especially low on the left side of my noggin and dramatically comb it up onto my head.

Then eighteen months passed before we shot episode two, and the morphea got worse.

We block-shoot the show, which means that we do not shoot in order. We film all the scenes that take place in Sam's house in a couple of days, no matter what episode the scene falls in. This is cheaper for production because you don't have to move the trucks repeatedly and you have to rent the house from the homeowners for only three or so concentrated days rather than repeatedly over the course of two months.

While it's less expensive for production, it's harder for the actors and directors, who have to consider what is happening in the script at that time. It is also very difficult for the hair and makeup team. Your character might walk out of one room and into another in an episode, but in real life those two scenes were shot weeks apart. In season one, the first location we used was the office where Sam and Joel work. Those first three days of shooting the rest of season one were so incredibly exciting for me as an actor! I was in heaven! I loved everything . . . except for my hair. The hair team had been caught off guard when I showed up with significantly less hair than I'd had in the pilot. After those first three days, they put in some fake hair—not really a toupee, more like hair extensions—to mask the problem. I named the little strip of hair Jeanette because she reminded me of that girl chipmunk from *Alvin and the Chipmunks*.

You might notice that Joel has a completely different hairstyle after season one. That's because I *am* wearing a toupee in those subsequent seasons. In season two, I named her Gladys, but it never felt like the right name. In season three, I realized it was because her name was really Julie McCoy. That wig was just like *The Love Boat*'s cruise director. She wanted you to have a good time, but she didn't want to make herself the center of attention. Also, the wig had a raging cocaine addiction.

So what was so stressful about turning forty?
I turned forty in 2016. Okay, I turned forty in December of 2015, but that wasn't the hardest year. It was 2016 that was really bad for me. I had been living a sort of bicoastal life with an apartment in Los Angeles and my husband and home in New York City. I had gone to LA to make it because I believed that stupid song about New York City. Those liars said, "If you can make it here, you'll make it anywhere." I had been doing a show called *Bloody Bloody Andrew Jackson* at the Public Theater for almost five months, and then it transferred to Broadway for another four. I had spent the better part of 2010 as a working actor. I had "made it" in New York! So I went to LA to book a TV show in 2011 and then didn't work for four years. In 2015, I had no money left and my husband made the very good point that we were sacrificing quite a bit so that I could go hiking in Griffith Park every day. So I moved back to New York with my tail between my legs and, apparently, a very pissed-off immune system.

At the same time, my mom was diagnosed with pulmonary fibrosis, which affects the lungs, and by 2016 it was so bad that she couldn't walk from her bedroom to the kitchen without stopping to catch her breath several times. Her bedroom was six feet from the kitchen.

Before her diagnosis, my mom had been a bit of a caregiver to my dad, who had sustained a serious injury in college that left him with a severely weakened leg. He hadn't let it stop him in his life, but after thirty-five years of favoring his good leg, it had given out as well and now he was using a walker. It took him forty-five minutes to get from the front door to his car. The front door was ten feet from his car.

My mom died in October of 2016. We began researching assisted-living facilities for my dad. My sister went through a divorce. I went back to temping, now that my Snickers commercial money was gone. I tried to figure out how to live with Neil again. I was forty and all the students I had taught improv to seemed to have television jobs, while I was calling up my old catering company to see if they needed any waiters.

I hadn't started therapy yet, and my body went bonkers and ate all my hair.

You should shave your head. The Rock does that.
Thank you so much for the advice—that is so nice of you to offer that knowledge. I have considered it. My husband shaves his head and looks very handsome. I would argue he has a narrow face, which makes him angular even without hair. I have a very round head, so without hair I look like the Headless Horseman when he has that pumpkin on his shoulders.

I also think a gay couple with the same haircut is a bit twee, but that's not the primary issue.

The primary issue is those brown splotches that are on my chest are also on my scalp. The morphea also caused a significant dent on the left side of my head. So if I shaved my head, I wouldn't look like the Rock. I would look like *The Hills Have Eyes.*

So are you trying to say that you are bald but it isn't about aging?
I guess I *do* want people to know that the hair loss is primarily from an autoimmune condition, yes. I guess that is sort of a way to manipulate people into not judging me for rivaling Donald Trump for "most obvious comb-over." Let me be completely honest. I have a bald spot in the back of my head that is from age. I've taken Propecia for years to address it. Well, I've taken finasteride, the generic for Propecia, for years. This is because I am aging and balding and also cheap.

Isn't it weird that we as a society see baldness as some sort of failure or fault? We think of the lack of hair as something people should be ashamed of. We also think if you have *too* much hair, you should be ashamed about that. But if you are a man and you wear wigs or take drugs to fight baldness, you should feel shame because you are a prissy little vanity queen.

I'm heartened that women these days are more easily able to admit they wear wigs, extensions, and falls. I remember in the early 2000s a woman was so ashamed to admit to me she was wearing hair extensions that it seemed like she was telling me she had recently defrauded senior citizens. I think this female embrace of fake hair, makeup, and owning their vanity comes from *The Real Housewives*, *The Kardashians*, and, maybe, Wendy Williams. Thanks, ladies? It hasn't crossed the gender line, though. So I have a lot of embarrassment about wearing the wigs and having the big hole in my head and being vain enough to try to look like I have actual hair. I wish I could do something more permanent to address it or just embrace my bald, lumpy, scarred head, but I'm not there yet.

What are you going to do about it?

Not sure. For the time being, I am using wigs, extensions, and dark powder that is helpfully called "filling fiber." After season one of *Somebody Somewhere*, the hair team gave me a tiny version of Jeanette, and I cried because I would be able to go to auditions and red-carpet events even with the big chunk gone from the pandemic. The two women on the team, Lo and Emily, were clearly uncomfortable with my tears, but they were so sweet to know I needed a wiglet. Bobby, the head of the hair department on *American Horror Story: NYC*, gave me a brown lace-front toupee that I wore to a wedding. Josh, Ashley, and Kevin, the hair team on *American Horror Stories*, found a wig that perfectly matched my hair color. Ashley retied it, Josh shaped it, and Kevin taught me how to put it on and provided me with glue, alcohol, and hair spray. I wore that piece on *Jimmy Kimmel Live*.

I suppose I would like to find a more permanent solution. I asked my dermatologist if it was possible to get some sort of procedure to replace the hair. I wasn't sure what that would be exactly, but I thought maybe he could take some of my pubes and stick them on my head?

He looked at me and said, "There is nothing I can do, but you should feel grateful for this disease. Having morphea means you do not have lupus."

Did that make you realize anything?
Yes. I realized I needed a new dermatologist. That type of response is exactly why I hate gratitude journals.

I have researched hair transplants. The most common place to get them is Turkey, but the current political climate there seems rather extreme. Am I really so vain as to overlook the fact that it's a totalitarian regime?

I found a doctor I trust on the Upper East Side but he charges twenty-five thousand dollars for the amount of transplanted hair I need, and he isn't sure the alopecia won't make it all fall out again. If it weren't for the possibility of the transplant not taking, I would pay the twenty-five K and get the transplant. I have no qualms about plastic surgery. If you want Botox, you do you. If you want your age lines to show all your life experiences, you do you. Your body, your choice.

Are you equating abortion and plastic surgery?
Not intentionally, but I guess either way, it isn't for me to decide about you and your body.

Wait, weren't you saying earlier that you realized when you were trying to lose weight that it wouldn't make you any happier? Are you now implying that a hair transplant *would* make you happy?
You've done your research, and you are really nailing me to the wall right now.

Thanks. I minored in journalism in college.

That sounds fascinating. What was your major?

This isn't about me; please answer the question.

Okay, wow, these FAQs are *mad*-specific.

You are right. Thin won't make me happy, and neither will a luscious head of thick curls and swirls. I am working on the being-happy part, but I think it might be fun to be happy and also slay the red carpet.

Have you ever said *slay* in that context before?

I have not. Did I say it right?

I think so. But something troubles me.

It does?

You said earlier that you do not hold your self-esteem in the way you look, and yet you want to look good on the red carpet?

Oh. I guess you're right. Maybe my self-esteem isn't tied up in how gorgeous I am, but I still don't want people to think I look shitty. I know I am not hideous, and I guess I am looking for that one makeup designer or hair person who can take me from a lewk that is a C minus to a B plus?

I wonder if I would be so vain if I didn't have to worry about getting work based on the way I look. That isn't to say I use my beauty to book jobs. I think sometimes looking a little weird can help you land a role. A little weird is good, but I also know that if an actor looks *too* weird, like, say, they're missing a front tooth or have a large boil on the side of their face, that severely limits the amount of work they can get.

Also, I want to think that my looks are not being talked about behind my back. In your personal life, no one would ever say anything about your looks being strange right to your face, but after I've seen how makeup artists, directors, journalists, and randos on the subway address my face, I realize people I love might be doing it too. That makes me nervous. I know that no one cares if I look bad in a picture except me. I know that because I've never cared once that someone else looked bad in a picture. But that doesn't mean they aren't whispering behind my back about why my hair looks the way it does.

The thing that makes me nervous is that someone might wonder why Neil would want to be with me. Might wonder how I "trapped" him. It feels like I am being disrespectful to Neil in that sense. Like I need to look good as a reflection of him.

I also want to look better so that fans of *American Horror Story: NYC* don't comment on my Instagram that I am disgusting-looking. I know you shouldn't read the comments, I *know*! But I would still really love to post a pic on there where everyone says, "Daaaayuuuum! Fire emoji, fire emoji!" instead of "Jump scare when that weird-ass face is in my timeline!"

So, despite the platitudes of loving yourself and the ad nauseam self-help language you've slathered across the pages of this tedious book, you are just a basic vain bitch?
I mean . . . yeah, probably.

Same, girl, same. I hope you can learn to love yourself just as you are.
I hope the same for you.

I said I was vain, not that I didn't love myself! Honey, I am *fabulous*.
Yes, you are, FAQ. You really are. Thanks for talking to me.

You're welcome. And for the record, my major was English literature.

Cool! Do you think this book counts as English literature?

No. It is fluff semi-celeb memoir.

Joke's on you, FAQ! That's my favorite genre. Look who's loving themselves now!

Every Day I'm Hustling

by VIVICA A. FOX[*]

O nce I moved to New York, I was always cooking up a scheme, trying to somehow make my dreams come true. After all, I had left
social work to do this. If you are going to stop helping people in
order to perform, you should commit. So I hustled. I took improv and
acting classes. I put up sketch shows and did improv shows wherever
and whenever I could, never stooping for less than my required rate of
zero dollars and zero cents. More like zero sense! That joke won't make
sense in the audiobook, but you and I have it sweet, reader of the page!

I also spent a lot of time trying to find a job that allowed me
to make enough money to live in New York City but also gave me
enough free time to continue to audition and do shows so that
someone would notice me and give me money to act, write, or strip
(I would use the money to pay for college, I swear). Here are some
stories about day jobs that allowed me to pay my rent so I could

---

[*]Vivica A. Fox worked a lot in her twenties but reached international fame at thirty-two
when she starred in *Independence Day*.

afford to live in New York City and become a star, or at least an actor with health insurance.

I answered an ad sent out by the UCB Theatre to do "crowd work" in Union Square. I scored a telephone interview!

"We are a pest-control company and we want an improviser to dress up as a cockroach and taunt passersby by saying you're having a raucous party in the walls of their house."

I knew right away this was a firm no for me. I have enough class not to spend six hours humiliating myself in a ridiculous costume. It isn't as if a pest-control company would be hiring actors all that often, so there wasn't even any hope of future work for such debasement.

Just as I was about to demur, the woman said, "We will pay you five hundred dollars and you will get a free lunch."

"I'll need an extra-large roach suit," I replied.

There was a time when I taught CPR. I had done it during college because my mom's friend had a contract with the local school district. So I knew there was a business model that catered to people who needed to update their CPR certifications for professional reasons. Babysitters, dental hygienists, lifeguards, and more are required to be informed when the American Heart Association changes its rules about how to open someone's airway.

I actually loved this job. It was flexible and you kind of got to perform while you were teaching the class. The only reason I didn't do it more was that I didn't have seniority at the company and couldn't get enough classes to support myself. I thought about striking out on my own, but I would have had to buy a mannequin and that was both a financial burden and a storage conundrum. Where does one store half a human inside a tiny New York City apartment?

There were some interesting things about being a CPR instructor. For instance, while there was only one mannequin, each student received their own face and plastic lung for hygienic reasons. The "face" was just the nose and mouth, which could be inserted into the gaping hole on the mannequin's head. Consequently, I would sometimes be carrying a large mannequin and a big bag full of lungs and faces. The lungs just looked like plastic bags, but the faces looked like . . . well, there's no euphemism for it—they looked like sex toys. Just a mouth and nose waiting to be defiled by a person shoving their junk in them. (They didn't actually function that way; they just *looked* like they functioned that way.) Once when I was riding the subway to a job, about nine faces rolled out onto the floor of the 7 train and people looked at me like I was a sex fiend. The nice part was that while there was some judgment, some looks offered encouragement too.

Another time while I was teaching, I asked a woman in her twenties to narrate what she was doing while performing CPR, and she complied.

"Okay, I check the airway," she tentatively began, crouching over the mannequin, who had been named Ernie by the group.

"I confirm he isn't breathing and there is no pulse," she continued. "Then I give two large breaths." She breathed hard into the sex-doll face attached to Ernie's head, filling the plastic lungs with air. "And then I start compressions."

"Great job," I said. "How do you do that?"

She nodded and said, "I place my hands over his scrotum and push down."

The American Heart Association recommends placing your hands over the *sternum*, but who knows? Pushing down on a scrotum like it's a diving board might wake Ernie up too.

A terrible blizzard blew in on a Thursday morning at a day job where I had been working a few years.

"Looks bad out there," I said, glancing through my boss's office window at the snow whipping around outside.

"Yes, it is," my boss said. "I'm going to have you go out to pick up salads from the deli for the team."

"Okay, I'll get my coat."

"Thanks," she said. "Sorry to make you do this, but no human should go out in weather like this."

I worked on and off at one company for about ten years. I would work there for two years, then get an acting job, leave, and come back as a temp for two weeks here and six months there. It wasn't a very fun place to work, but at least there was a single-stall bathroom on the third floor if I needed to poop.

During one of my stints, I had a boss who didn't understand computers. I don't mean he couldn't code—I mean he couldn't email. He didn't understand how to look up flights to plan travel, and his concept of our interoffice shared drive was comical.

"Is it on the P drive? How do you get to the P drive? Where *is* the P drive exactly? *How do I get to the P drive?*"

On more than one occasion, he called me at home and asked me to google something for him. I could understand this if he was traveling, but he was calling from his desk, right next to his computer.

I was part-time, so I came in at noon. Immediately upon my arrival, he would beckon me over to help him with whatever technological paradox had been confounding him for the previous three hours. He was always nice about it and usually told me that he would not be able to function without me. That seemed true.

One day, he asked me to get him to the P drive. I did. Then he asked me to get him to the HR folder. I did. Then he asked me to leave his office. I did, but I could tell something was weird.

I guess he needs some privacy, I thought, then went to the third-floor single-stall bathroom for a bit of my own.

When I got back to my desk, I opened my email and saw one from the HR department announcing a new internal job opening at the company. It was a job posting for the position of an assistant. For my boss.

I was confused. *I* was the assistant to my boss. I went into his office and told him I had just gotten the email that went out.

"How did you get that? Did you go into my email?"

This was ridiculous on two counts. First, I had access to his email because that was literally my job. Second, this email was sent to the *entire* company, which happened anytime a new job was posted. I explained the latter to him and asked, "Am I being fired?"

"Not fired, it's just I need more help, and . . . I, uh, see . . ."

I let him off the hook. "Sure, no problem," I said.

I grabbed my coat and bag and went down to HR. When I discovered I would be eligible for six months of unemployment, I headed right out the door without going back upstairs.

I was almost to the subway before I realized how ridiculous this was. I had been at this company on and off for ten years. I needed to say goodbye.

So I went back inside and up to the third floor to say goodbye . . . to the single-stall bathroom. "Thanks for everything, baby," I whispered, and that was the last time we saw each other.

Dispatch from a temp job.

A company-wide email went out from an assistant asking, "Has anyone seen my boss, Elaine? I have an urgent phone call for her but she left her office about a half hour ago and I can't find her anywhere."

Thirty seconds later, in another company-wide email, someone responded.

"I saw Elaine going into the women's bathroom about a half hour ago."

I have saved the worst day job of all for last. I worked at Olive Garden.

When I was first hired, I was excited. I had heard that they added a 15 percent gratuity to every check in the New York City locations. I was also starting at the restaurant from the moment it opened, so everyone was new. It made it so much easier to get to know your coworkers. We spent two weeks training as new hires. Our manager talked us through the history of the company and listened to why we had chosen Olive

Garden "to serve." He had a paternal air that made you feel comfortable, and he was always pushing food those first two weeks. We tasted every single entrée on the menu and learned about wine pairings and how to suggest different bottles for specific dishes. We even got to practice being waiters on each other in the brand-new space. We got to know each other well and became friends. Sometimes we would go out after our shift and get drinks at a bar where one waitress's boyfriend worked. It was true—when you were there, you were family!

I knew what to say to all my colleagues as they pretended to be patrons. I excelled in all of the role-play thanks to my improv training. "I love the mussels. You might think of pairing that with a buttery chardonnay, like the Kendall-Jackson?" I would say as if I were at Le Cirque.

After two weeks, we opened. The first bummer was when our manager told us that this branch would not be adding an automatic 15 percent gratuity. "The Times Square location deals with many tourists from Europe and outside of the country who are unaware of American tipping customs, but our branch will be for New Yorkers. They are aware."

They were not aware.

First, no New Yorker goes to Olive Garden. Why would they? There are other Italian restaurants here. Better ones. The only people who came to a Manhattan Olive Garden were tourists from places like Connecticut and New Jersey. They would be very angry that the price for the Italian sampler in Manhattan was five dollars more than at home and to show their displeasure, they wouldn't tip. That'll show 'em!

The second and worse bummer was all the people who came in and ordered the unlimited soup, salad, and breadsticks. I understood why people ordered it. The sign outside the restaurant declared the incredible deal! *Only $7.99 for all-you-can-eat salad, soup, and breadsticks!* was prominently featured on triangular placards on every table. Of course they ordered it—who wouldn't love such a great deal?

The waiters, that's who. It was triple the work for a third of the tips.

I was a terrible waiter. I would get overwhelmed with running food for another server and then realize I hadn't poured water for table 407 for ages! I would delay half the order input so the appetizers would get there before the main course but then forget to put in the main course altogether, which meant I had to rush back to the chefs (who were an angry people) and beg them to rush a chicken parm. They screamed at me to follow protocol. *Totally, but also could you just rush the parm?*

We had to sing a song for people celebrating birthdays. Waiters had to round up other servers who could spare forty-five seconds to gather around a person on their special day and clap while singing "Buona festa, what a joyous day . . ." When I first started, I found it charming, but three shifts in, it became an incredible burden. I did not have time to sing an Italian-themed birthday song! I had three apple martinis to run from the bar, which took forever because you had to walk really slow so as not to spill.

I still have nightmares about waiting tables. My mind is filled with the din of conversation and the sound of forks scraping plates. In the dream, I realize I didn't bring a spoon with the pasta fagioli to the woman in the corner who was already sniffy! I run around and around and the sound never stops, the breadsticks are never delivered, and the people are never satisfied enough with my service to offer more than a 10 percent gratuity!

I haven't waited any sort of tables in seventeen years and I still have waiting-tables dreams.

I remember the night I left Olive Garden. I was closing and had a matinee in the Fringe Festival the next day. A man in his early sixties sat in my section. He came in at 10:50 p.m., which was always a nightmare since we closed at 11:00 p.m. That meant I would be staying there long past closing as he finished his meal. My sibling waiters looked at me with sympathy as they took off their aprons and packed their bags.

The man ordered a Caesar salad—that was it! I was thrilled! A salad wouldn't take long at all! I could get out in time to get a good night's rest before my matinee the next day.

I brought him his salad and asked if I could get him anything else. He said no, but as I was walking away, he grabbed my wrist.

"What is this?" he asked.

"Didn't you order a Caesar salad?" I asked, fearful I might have gotten his order wrong. It wouldn't have been the first time.

"This is not a Caesar salad," he said, shaking his head in confusion.

For the next twenty-four minutes, he lectured me on the proper way to make a Caesar salad. "You need anchovies! The dressing should be made table-side with a raw egg! The Parmesan should not be grated but chopped!" *Blah-blah-blah!*

He talked and talked. I couldn't say I needed to check on my other tables because he was the only table in the restaurant. I told him I could get him another salad. I told him I could refund his order. I even offered to get the chef out on the floor so that he could listen to this lecture instead of me, but nothing worked. He just really wanted to let me in on his knowledge of Caesar and his salad. I had to keep listening because that is part of "hospitaliano."

Finally, my manager approached. *Thank God! I am finally being rescued!* I thought.

"Jeff, I need to talk to you," he said.

I made my excuses to the customer and went over to my manager with gratitude in my eyes. "Thank you! He won't stop lecturing me on the proper way to—"

My manager cut me off. "You have to work lunch tomorrow," he said.

"I can't. I have a matinee. I got Sherry to cover my shift," I told him.

"Even with Sherry, we need people tomorrow. I only have two people on."

"But I can't."

"If you can't, don't bother coming back at all," he said with faux bravado in his voice.

I knew he was bluffing. He couldn't make me work a shift when I had found someone to cover for me, and I knew he needed all the waiters he could get, so firing me would only give him a bigger head-ache. I knew I could talk my way out of this and still get to my mati-nee, but I couldn't stand one more person telling me that their chicken wasn't hot enough or thinking they were the first person not to say "when" for a really long time while I was grating cheese onto their plate. I could not take one more person telling me how to make a Cae-sar salad.

"Okay. Um, I quit," I said and walked away quickly before he could talk me out of it. I tipped out the bartender and the busboy and avoided my manager.

"You can just mail my last check," I said on my way out.

He looked at me with a face that said *I'm not mad, I'm disappointed.*

It was a look that my dad would have given me, and if my dad had given me that look, I probably would have worked the shift the next day, but my manager wasn't my dad. He was my manager. And as it turns out, even when you are there, you aren't necessarily family.

My Life So Far

by JANE FONDA[*]

O n September 3, 2019, I got an email from Bridget Everett. I'm going to quote it here, but before you think I'm some sort of oversentimental person or that I have the memory of Marilu Henner, let me admit that I just never clean out my Gmail inbox, so I was able to look this up.

hey Jeff!

I'm not sure you're avail or interested but there's a part in a new pilot I'm doing that I think you would be great for. you should be hearing from casting soon.

let me know if you have any questions. the vibe of the pilot is super-grounded. the character is gay, funny, someone you might have missed in high school, sweet.

[*]Jane Fonda's breakthrough came with *Cat Ballou* when she was twenty-eight years old.

anyway–happy to help in any way if you decide you're interested in
reading for it!

x,

b

The idea that I might *not* be interested in reading for *anything*
is hilarious. There are some actors who are considered offer-only—
meaning that they won't read, or audition. These are people with huge
credits and awards. In theory, you wouldn't need to ask them to read
because they have such a deep well of roles in their careers. Nicole Kidman is one of these people. I am not.

Besides, I like auditioning. It's just acting but without the hair
and makeup. I would have auditioned for an unscripted podcast about
candle-making. I don't have kids. What else am I doing with my time?

The show was created especially for Bridget by playwrights Paul
Thureen and Hannah Bos. I knew of them from their theater company,
the Debate Society. It was being produced by indie-film-world wunder-
kinds the Duplass brothers and also by Carolyn Strauss, who had produced tiny li'l shows like *Game of Thrones* and *The Last of Us*. I knew
who Carolyn was because she had shown up in at least three celebrity
memoirs that I had read. She appears in *Hello, Molly!* by Molly Shannon,
Comedy Comedy Comedy Drama by Bob Odenkirk, and *Find Me* by Rosie
O'Donnell. I was impressed by this show's fancy pedigree.

I wrote back to Bridget a full day later, on September 4. I guess I
wanted to play hard to get.

Oh my gosh, Bridget, that script is so gooooooood. I love that you
are doing this show. I want it to run forever. It is so funny but tender,
sweet but not sappy. The family stuff is so real and lived-in and the
role of Joel is so unlike other gay characters. He's not some super-
power gay who turns you gorgeous or bitchy and nasty. It's so great.

I sent my tape in. I love the part where they are crying and then laughing about the fact that they are crying.

Anyway, I love the show, thank you SO MUCH for recommending me. And in the very likely outcome that I don't get this role and we run into each other at a party in two months, don't worry. I am really good at auditioning for my friends' stuff and not getting it. It happens a lot!

Seriously, though, thank you for the recommendation and congratulations on this amazing script and show.

xoxo,
Jeff

Well, so much for playing hard to get.

What I said wasn't a lie. I was used to auditioning for my friends' stuff and not getting it. Earlier that year I had screen-tested for a close friend's pilot and not only did I not get the role, neither did the other guy who was screen-testing with me. In fact, they reopened auditions after they'd narrowed it down to just the two of us. That role was created by a friend who I hung out with much more than Bridget, and we got through it just fine, so I wasn't worried about this.

I get a lot of questions about how well I knew Bridget before the show. The answer is—not very well. I definitely knew her. She had my email address, obviously, but we didn't have each other's phone numbers. Bridget was really famous in my corner of the world. Her cabaret shows at Joe's Pub in downtown New York were very well known. She had A-list fans like Patti LuPone, Sarah Jessica Parker, and Jerry Seinfeld.

If you know Bridget only from *Somebody Somewhere*, you cannot fathom what her cabaret shows are like. I was a fan of Bridget, but I was also sort of afraid of her. Her shows are wild, and I mean that not in a euphemistic sense but in the sense that when she is onstage, she *is* a wild animal. You cannot predict what she will do, and if you make a false move, she might rip your face off. She's so entertaining, it's worth the risk.

Something Bridget often says in her live shows has stuck with me. I wrote about it in my journal as far back as 2015. There was an episode of *Oprah's Master Class* where LL Cool J discussed his life and goals for the future. He said, "Dreams don't have deadlines." Bridget adopted the phrase for herself and uses it all the time, shortening it to DDHD. It's a fun phrase but also a profound one. It's saying: Do not give up on yourself. It's saying: You deserve hope too. It was incredibly helpful to me when I had that midlife crisis at forty. In fact, I would have called this book *DDHD* if the phrase didn't belong so strongly to Bridget and . . . LL? Mr. Cool J?

DDHD definitely summarizes my getting an HBO show at forty-five years old. Sometimes it feels like Joel was written for me. He wasn't. I have spoken to at least a dozen actors who told me they auditioned for the role too. It makes me anxious when I think that someone else might have gotten to play him, but then I remember all the roles I auditioned for and didn't get, and my life was fine, so I'm being dramatic.

It's bizarre how many things I have in common with Joel. Here is an incomplete list:

We are both gay.
We both grew up in the church.
Faith has played an important role in both our lives.
Joel drives a Buick LeSabre. I drove a Buick LeSabre when I lived in Denver.
We both find volunteering to be fulfilling and necessary.
We both love music.
We have both created vision boards. (I swear to you, I put a Vitamix on my vision board in 2012. My mom got me one for my

birthday in 2013. It was the one that goes fast enough to heat
soup.)

We both had difficulty moving in with our partners, feeling like it
was *his* place, not *ours*.

Both of us have differing views on how to load the dishwasher
than our partner does.

We were both picked on by other kids while growing up.

We both had rashes caused by stress in our adolescence.

We both wanted children.

Neither of us got them.

We both still have hope even in middle age.

There are other things too, but I don't count them because they
were put in by the writers once they saw them in my life. Joel loves
getting steps in, but only because the writers saw how much I loved
getting them in. Joel puts Mentholatum in his nose every night, but
only because Jeff and Bridget were already doing that. The giggle and
the hair and the way he looks are all there simply because I'm the actor
who plays him. The list above, however, came from the writers' minds
first and I was gobsmacked by how similar to me he was.

Here is how we are different, though:

I can't look at you and realize that your life would change for the
better if you just sang a song at my party.

I am not a good party host—I get overwhelmed and forget
important details like to buy ice and send invitations.

I can play the piano, but I need to practice a piece for a couple of
weeks before I play it well enough for someone to sing along.
Sam will just state the song she wants to sing, and Joel knows
every chord perfectly. If I tried that, there would be really big
pauses and several attempts at chords before finding the correct
ones.

Joel has real hair; I wear wigs. In fact, it takes me sixty minutes of

hair and makeup and then when it is over, I look like Joel. An
hour to look like . . . that.

The day after I sent my tape to my agent, I got an email from
Bridget that I remember warming my heart from how special it made
me feel.

I loved your read, Jeff!

xx

I guess that email was shorter than I remembered. In fact, it
doesn't really require quoting, does it? It didn't matter how short it was
because *I loved your read, Jeff!* is way more of a response than I usually
get to an audition.

We shot the pilot in October 2019. I thought it went well. I loved
how the director, Jay Duplass, actually asked me my opinions on the
character. Directors don't usually ask people with small roles their
opinions.

Five months went by with no word. That's normal. I taught improv.
I did one or two temping gigs. I wrote another solo show. I waited to
hear if we would get picked up.

Bridget called me and told me we got the green light! I couldn't
wait to be a member of the HBO family with Tony Soprano, Carrie
Bradshaw, and Arliss! We would start shooting in two months. Nothing
could go wrong now! I was on a TV show! It was March 3, 2020. (Hidden
Importance cliché!)

I spent the whole lockdown waiting. I guess we all did, but I finally
had something lined up. I just needed to shoot it! We started filming
season one in June of 2021, a short nineteen months after we'd shot the
pilot. I had waited twenty-five years; what was another one and a half?
Patience is a virtue.

We shot the show in Lockport, Illinois, a rural town south of Chicago. We didn't shoot in Kansas because . . . I don't really know why,

to be honest. Here is my guess: There are film crews in Chicago. There are lots of talented actors who can be guest stars in Chicago. And I bet there is some tax thing, but I couldn't explain it to you if you held a gun to my husband's head.

Just before the cast and crew arrived in Chicago, COVID's delta variant swept through the lungs of eight-hundred-something gay guys in Provincetown. It was in places other than P-Town, but I distinctly remember a huge outbreak during "bear week" because it was such a hilarious specific to hear newscasters report.

This new variant understandably scared production, so we were on strict lockdown, wearing masks, testing daily, and keeping six feet apart whenever possible. We were told to go home at the end of the day and not interact with anyone outside of our filming bubble.

That's when Bridget got creative. If we could interact with only each other, why not live together? It would allow some built-in social time. Bridget, Murray Hill (who plays Fred Rococo), and I moved into a ridiculously large Airbnb not too far from Lockport. It was one of those McMansions built in the early 2000s that a Real Housewife would live in. There were two spiral staircases framing a fireplace as you walked into the house. We all had our own bedrooms, of course, but we also all got our own bathrooms. I suppose that's not too shocking, but you know what is? This house was so big that we all had our own kitchens. Bridget used the main kitchen on the first floor, Murray was staying in what must have been a maid's room that had a kitchenette, and I had access to a kitchen just as large as Bridget's that was bizarrely located in the basement. The second kitchen was bigger than my primary residence. There was even room for executive producer Carolyn Strauss to have *her* own room and bathroom when she was in town. She didn't get her own kitchen, though. Sometimes sacrifices must be made. Rob Cohen, one of the directors on the show, dubbed the house "the Ding-Dong Dorm."

The owners of the Airbnb were new and hadn't properly furnished the house. They'd bought new beds for each room but everything else seemed like stuff they had lying around and didn't want anymore.

A papasan chair was the only comfy place to sit. There were six dining tables. We had only four drinking glasses but two pizza cutters. The refrigerator in the main kitchen was a smart fridge that played music, but we had to buy a frying pan.

Every night we ordered food. The people of Lemont, Illinois, found DoorDash to be a profitable side hustle in the summer of 2021. As we ate, we would go over what we were shooting the next day. This is always a good idea for an actor, but since we were block-shooting, we might film a scene from episode six in the morning and reshoot a scene from the pilot in the afternoon.

Murray appointed himself to the role of coach. He would gather us at one of the many tables and have us run our lines for the next day. If we missed even one word, he would yell, "From the top!" Then we had to start the scene all over again. This wasn't necessary. Our show isn't an Aaron Sorkin joint where you are expected to be precise and speak it exactly as written. In fact, the writers want the words to feel authentic above all else, so we were encouraged to speak in a way that felt natural.

Murray didn't care. He wanted the delivery word-perfect, so we knew those scenes word-perfect.

This was very helpful when I shot a scene where my character had spontaneously purchased a dog. During a tornado, the dog gets away from Joel, and after he chases the dog down, they must find shelter in a metal tube thingy in the middle of a field.

The night before we shot that tornado scene, there was an actual tornado.

We could hear sirens at the Ding-Dong Dorm and our phones flashed warnings from the National Weather Service. It was late at night and we had an early call, so we were already in bed when the commotion happened. I was worried, so I texted Bridget and Murray, who were several miles away in their respective bedrooms at this ridiculous mansion.

Do you hear the sirens? Should we go down to the basement in case there is a tornado?

Bridget responded as only a person who grew up in Kansas could. *The basement is sort of cold. We'll be fine.*

We were fine, though a tornado did touch down less than five miles from our house.

More than one person has told me that if you are in a tornado, you should never hide in a metal tube thingy in the middle of a field. This is good advice. Joel was originally meant to hide in a drainage ditch, but the previous night brought several inches of rain, flooding the intended set. So the incredibly talented crew quickly set up a metal tube thingy in the middle of a field.

I prepared to shoot my full-page monologue (the dog didn't have any lines, so I had to do the heavy lifting). Jay Duplass, the director of that episode, came over to me and said, "The weather isn't looking good, but we have a little time. We want to try and get this scene quickly."

I got one take in before we had to wrap for the night. There was lightning coming and another (actual, not TV) tornado warning. It was not safe to continue shooting. I thought of that monologue as the peak of Joel's season one arc, so I would have loved to get in at least two versions of it. The good news is, I knew my monologue backward and forward thanks to Coach Hill and his draconian line drills. We got the shot.

The show is complimented for the chemistry of the characters. I think our time living together fostered this chemistry. We laughed so much at night after days on the set. We masked up and took group trips to Target. On the nights that Mary Catherine Garrison (who plays Tricia) came over, we watched HGTV while eating salsa made by Bridget. Murray tried to teach me about the NBA, but the only thing I learned was that Giannis Antetokounmpo is very handsome.

We also spent a ton of time staring at the beauty of Poppy, Bridget's unbelievably sweet Pomeranian. She would gaze at us with what can only be described as a smile, looking both elegant and goofy. She was our mascot. Our collective baby. We all loved her, but of course no one loved her more than Bridget.

She got sick that season. Very sick. She had been to the vet several times, had lost an eye, gotten a new tumor diagnosed, and even fainted. It was so sad, and we were terrified. If you aren't a dog person, you might think, *It's just a dog.* You can't really understand how sad it is to know this sweet animal who you love is in pain. If you are a dog person, you understand completely.

After many vet visits, one Sunday afternoon, Bridget told us she needed to go to the animal hospital. "I think it's time," she said. We knew what she meant, but we all still hoped for a miracle. Murray, Carolyn, and I volunteered to take Bridget and Poppy to an animal hospital a half hour away. I drove.

When we got to the vet, only the animal and one human could go inside the facility due to COVID restrictions. Bridget went in with Poppy while Murray, Carolyn, and I sat in the car listening to Joan Armatrading.

Then a truck pulled up, one of those trucks that have wheels that are five feet tall. It had a flag on the back that read *Don't Tread on Me* with a snake coiled and ready to strike. The man inside the truck looked tough, with tattoo sleeves. He ran inside the vet office holding a bundle in his arms.

It was such an odd sight. I broke the silence and said, "Don't tread on me, but also save my wittle kitty cat!"

We laughed, which felt good, but also wrong.

Bridget called us and told us to meet her around back. The vet was allowing these sad moments to be performed outdoors so that more than one person could be present. We stood under a large tree and watched Poppy pass away. We cried so hard. We hugged each other. We cried more.

That night we went back to the Ding-Dong Dorm and ate some unsatisfying takeout dinner in silence. I cleaned up the cardboard boxes and took them outside to the recycling containers. When I turned around, I gasped. The sun was setting, and the clouds were the hottest pink, the sky a brilliant orange that became fiery red on the horizon.

I ran back inside and announced that everyone needed to take in the sunset. We went out to the large deck, which had a brilliant view of nature's stunning painting. It felt spiritual to me, but I was embarrassed to say anything. The Ding-Dong Dorm was full of acerbic wit, not spiritual goop.

I looked at Bridget. She said, "That's from Poppy."

"Yes!" I said with absolutely no chill whatsoever. "I thought so too!"

I could cry right now. It was as if Poppy were saying, *I love you. Thank you.* We love you, Poppy.

Anyway, I think that shit bonded us too. Intense feelings of sadness, creating art, and no contact with anyone else for eight weeks? You get acquainted.

We finished filming season one and decided to be a little dangerous. We had a mini wrap party at the Ding-Dong Dorm, where we ate without masks. I didn't recognize some of the crew when I saw their noses and mouths.

We played music on the smart fridge. The co-showrunner Hannah kept yelling, "Hey, man! Turn that fridge *up!*" She and Paul were so taken with the silliness of a smart fridge that they added it into a Tricia plotline for season two.

The next day it was time to leave. Both Murray and Bridget had earlier flights than I did. That left me alone in the big house for an hour as I waited for my ride to O'Hare. I had already packed but thought I should walk through the house just in case I missed anything. I went from room to room looking at the vast empty spaces where furniture should be but wasn't, and I started to cry.

It wasn't a single beautiful tear like Ingrid Bergman in *Casablanca*. It was loud, filled with snot and convulsions and cartoonish gasps for air. I was sad because the adventure was over. Working as an actor in any capacity is rare, but working on a TV show that you love with a lead character you delight in playing— that almost never happens (in my experience). As I walked around the Ding-Dong Dorm I mourned that it might never happen again. It didn't seem likely.

I was wrong. We got a second season. We weren't a ratings juggernaut, but our fans loved our show passionately.

I was reminded of a lyric from a Broadway musical (no surprise there) called *Title of Show*. It's a meta piece—a musical about writing a musical. At one point, the two writer characters, Hunter and Jeff, reveal their wish for the audience's reaction to their musical. They say, "I'd rather be nine people's favorite thing than a hundred people's ninth-favorite thing." In other words, I would rather be the small show that people love passionately than a mainstream hit that everyone knows but no one thinks of as special.

That is *Somebody Somewhere*. We are nine people's favorite thing, and a hundred people have never heard of us.

We tried to have a premiere party for season one, but by that point, the omicron variant was raging. The premiere was canceled, but HBO surprised us by throwing a finale party on the roof of a building in Los Angeles. We could celebrate a job well done in season one and look forward to the excitement of season two! The party would be COVID-safe because we would be outdoors. It was in the last week of February, but Los Angeles is a city that is mild and temperate. It was the perfect solution.

On the night of the party, LA was hit by a record cold front. It was twenty-two degrees. I spoke to an incredibly kind woman who complimented the show for several minutes before I realized she was Rosie O'Donnell. She was so wrapped up in blankets, coats, and masks that I didn't recognize her until the conversation was over.

We celebrated as we shivered. We were proud.

That night was the last time I saw Mike Hagerty, who played Ed, Sam and Tricia's father. I loved Mike. I remember meeting him at the table read and thinking that his presence made the pilot feel legitimate. He was in *Overboard*! An actor in one of my favorite movies of all time was in this TV show! This was real!

The night of the coldest party in history, Mike laughed and joked with us. He said, "I've never heard those words strung together before.

I've heard the word *second* and the word *season*, but never in the same sentence."

We roared!

Mike and I huddled under a heating lamp, fantasizing about season two. He said, "I told the writers we gotta have a scene together. Ed needs to meet Joel. He'd like him." I agreed.

When we got the scripts for season two, we did have a scene together. It was small, but I was excited about it.

The week before we were scheduled to shoot season two, Bridget called to tell me that Mike had died suddenly in a hospital in Los Angeles. He'd gone to take care of an infection in his leg before heading to work in Illinois but had an allergic reaction to the antibiotics.

To say it was sad is not enough. It was tragic. It was painful. I felt guilty. Why did the rest of us get to move on to season two and not sweet Mike?

Production was halted for two weeks, but our budget was so small that we couldn't hold off any more than that. Hannah, Paul, Bridget, and the other writers, including Lisa Kron and Rachel Axler, had to rewrite the entire season around losing him. They did this while they were mourning.

The writers decided that the character of Ed would not die. I think they were missing Mike so much and somehow, if Ed was still around in the world of *Somebody Somewhere*, then we could hold on to a piece of Mike too.

There was a memorial service in Los Angeles for Mike, but none of us could attend because we had to be on set in Chicago. Someone kindly sent us a video of the memorial. I watched it on my laptop, laughing and crying at all the beautiful things that people said about Mike.

At the end of the memorial, there was a reel with clips from Mike's amazing acting career. They showed scenes from our show but also from many of the other projects Mike had done during his long career. There he was in *Wayne's World*, on *Friends*, and onstage at Second City.

At the end of the video, there was a scene from what I have since identified as *Austin Powers: The Spy Who Shagged Me*. You see only flashes of people saying lines out of context that sound sort of dirty. Mike, dressed as a snack vendor, is yelling, "Nuts!" and then the camera moves on to the next person—a young father. Out of all the actors in the world to appear next in this ridiculous montage, the camera lands on a young Tim Bagley. Tim had just been hired to play Joel's love interest Brad on *Somebody Somewhere*.

I know, I know. Don't go to some woo-woo place! I'm not. Well, maybe I am because it felt so nice. Like Mike was giving us his blessing to go on.

I love that Mike had season one of our show on his résumé. He had shown for decades how capable and nimble he was around comedy, but as Ed, he was able to show his incredible dramatic talent as well. He was so tender with the character, allowing only a little bit of the turmoil going on inside to show through that stoic farmer demeanor. I am so sad he didn't get more seasons to shine. We love you, Mike.

Coincidentally, Bridget, Mary Catherine, Murray, and I have mutual friends—Jim Andralis and Larry Krone—who throw legendary dinner parties. Jim is the kind of cook who effortlessly throws several disparate things into a pan and then presents you with an unfussy and delicious meal. Larry is also an amazing chef, but his sense of camp sometimes creeps its way into his culinary treats, like appetizers made from Wonder Bread and artichoke hearts, and he isn't afraid of mayonnaise, but it is always delicious.

"Why are you talking about these guys, Jeff? I don't care about how your friends cook their food," you are probably saying.

Here's why I'm telling you this. One of Larry's signature dishes involves wrapping ham around a pickle and cream cheese. He calls it St. Louis Sushi.

Let me set the record straight here. None of Larry's food has ever made me have crippling diarrhea. However, the writers wanted Sam and Joel to bond over such an affliction and they needed a food to pin it on. How can you *not* use St. Louis Sushi? It just has such obvious brand-ing opportunities.

Bridget told Larry that St. Louis Sushi would be a plot point in the season, but he was such a fan of the show that he didn't want to hear any spoilers. When I first read the diarrhea scene, I thought, *Hilarious. What a great way to show that these two have zero boundaries at this point in their relationship.* When I spoke to the intimacy coordinator, they asked if I was comfortable wearing a thong and having my bare legs seen while I sat on the toilet. I said, "Of course! It will be hilarious to see Joel and Sam in such a vulnerable state." When I got on set, several people asked me if I felt strange or odd, and I said, "Nah, this is just funny! It's not embarrassing!"

Then I saw the final scene on television. The sound effects were added after they edited the episode. When it aired and I saw myself writhing, pants around my ankles, and heard those horrific and gnarly sounds, I thought, *Sweet Lord, this is the most vulnerable I have ever felt in my entire life!*

Can you imagine how strange it was to watch that episode with Larry on a night that he served St. Louis Sushi? He was a wonderful sport about the whole thing.

When the second season ended, we learned we would shoot a third. I was so happy to get to go back! We were scheduled to start shooting in the summer of 2023. Then the writers' and actors' strikes happened. It lasted six months. I'm pro-labor, so I showed up on the picket line. I mean, I did go to the picket line that was closest to the Union Square farmers' market so I could get produce after, but what's wrong with doing the right thing and also getting fresh tomatoes?

It was important to fight for our rights as actors and writers, but it was difficult to be out of work that long and I was eager to get back to the show. The strikes pushed production of season three to February of 2024, seventeen months after we'd wrapped season two. I always thought I would be rich if I could just get on a TV show, but when you film seven episodes every year and a half, it's difficult to build up a nest egg.

Shooting season three was dreamy. The scripts were challenging, which was exciting for me as an actor, but what made it great was the community on set. So many crew members returned each year. I loved the camaraderie that comes from working on a TV show for an entire season instead of just a few days. I loved making fun of my friend Gina who did my makeup every morning as she closed one eye and held out a thumb, trying to get my painted-on eyebrows symmetrical. I loved hanging out with Kim, Bridget's driver, a secretly trained chef who would bring us incredible food. I loved meeting Iris, the truly adorable brand-new baby of our director of photography, Shana. I loved having a moment at the beginning and end of each shoot day with Victoria as she gave me and then collected my prop glasses. Perhaps best of all was that one of my best friends, Lennon Parham, was hired to direct three episodes of season three. Not only did I get to work with my pal, but we got to hang out on the weekends too. I know it's a cliché, but we felt like a chosen family as we shot this show about chosen family.

As I am writing this, season three hasn't aired yet. I just saw the screeners yesterday, though, and I think it is really good. If you haven't watched the show yet—well, first of all, thanks for reading this book and especially this chapter! It must have been boring and confusing for you. And second of all, I hope you do watch the show. It is surprisingly short. It isn't like *Grey's Anatomy*, where you really have to commit your life to watch it all. You can watch an entire season in less time than it takes to watch one *Avatar* movie. Also, people often say to me, "I don't know if I can watch your show—I don't want to cry." The thing is, the show doesn't make you cry because it makes you sad. It makes you cry because it recognizes your humanity.

Bridget Everett could have made some wild show and called it *Tits a-Flyin'!* and Lord knows, I would have watched it. Instead, she made this beautiful show about found family, connection, and grief. She allowed other actors to shine in it. Mary Catherine had been a very successful stage actor but moved to Virginia after having her son. Murray had been making a very modest living performing in nightclubs for thirty years. Tim Bagley and Mike Hagerty hadn't had a chance to show off the breadth of their talent. I've spent hundreds of pages telling you about my pitiful attempts to be a full-time performer. Many actors would be too selfish and insecure to let other people shine the way Bridget has.

So let me thank the person who made that possible. Please indulge me, because we never won any awards that would allow me to do this at a podium: Thank you, Bridget Everett, for sharing your success with others. Thank you for doing a show that highlights the importance of friendship and found family. And, with proper respect to LL Cool J, thank you for teaching us that dreams don't have deadlines.

The Bedwetter

by SARAH SILVERMAN*

T he pandemic was hard for all of us, and I am no exception. That said, I feel like everyone I speak to about that time tells me they learned something special about themselves. A beautiful silver lining came out of that long lockdown. "I learned nature is important to me," they say, or "I learned to bake bread and now that's my career!"

You know what I learned about myself in the pandemic? That I am a liar. I have told myself for decades that I would get so much done if I just had the time. Then I had fourteen months inside my apartment. I could have written a novel. I didn't even read one. I was too busy reading celebrity memoirs.

I wasted my global pandemic. What did I do with all that time? I know I spent a lot of it watching people from old musicals reunite on Zoom and sing songs in their bathrooms. They were always in their bathrooms—I guess for acoustics, or maybe a nervous tummy?

---

*Sarah Silverman was twenty-three when her stand-up career landed her a spot on *Saturday Night Live*. She was fired after one season and went back to stand-up, honing her craft.

My husband watched all this with me. One day, he asked me why their eyes looked so strange, and I realized he didn't know what a ring light was! Can you imagine such an innocent time? I had to explain that a ring light is a ring-shaped light that illuminates your face fully without shadows to highlight your wrinkles. Of course, it also makes you look possessed by the devil, but better that than admit you've aged, I guess.

The next day, one arrived for me in the mail. My husband had ordered it for me while we were talking about them! It was very sweet and also slightly insulting to my aging face.

The only other thing I can remember doing during the pandemic was getting an anal fissure. It's time for asshole story number 3, and this time, it's personal!

Do you know what an anal fissure is? It is when the skin of your rectum tears. I bet you just had a frisson of pain, didn't you? You should have had one. It hurts like hell.

I would love to tell you that I got this fissure from getting railed three ways to Saturday, but the truth is that I just ate too many carbs and didn't drink enough water. If you get nothing else from reading my book, let it be this: Never push.

I was in extreme pain in October of 2020. So much so that I told my husband I couldn't go with him to a planned event. This was still pre-vaccine pandemic, so events were difficult to come by. You can imagine how much my butt must have hurt for me to turn down a social gathering on a beautiful autumn day.

A group of friends were going to a park down by the Statue of Liberty to write postcards for the upcoming election encouraging people to vote. We had done it once before, and it was lovely to sit on a bench six feet away from friends and have some social time while also being politically active.

As Neil was leaving, I shouted out, "Don't tell anyone why I can't be there!" but I got the vibe the door had shut before he could hear.

Sure enough, my friend Steven called me up. "Hey, gurl, I heard you blew out your hole."

I was embarrassed but then relieved when Steven told me that I should call the butthole specialist. He informed me that there is a medical practice that specializes in helping wrecked rectums. It is located in the heart of Chelsea, which is, not for nothing, Manhattan's gayborhood.

This is why we live in cities. People who write comments online in the Real Estate section of the *New York Times* are always saying things like "Two million dollars for a thousand square feet? I'll stay here in Michigan, thank you very much!" They don't get it. Yes, cities are expensive and loud and sometimes people cut in line at Chekhov in the Park, but do you think there is a butthole specialist in Ludington, MI?

I called the doctor's office and spoke with the receptionist.

"We're not seeing patients right now," she said.

"Oh, right," I said.

"It's the pandemic and all," she said.

"No, totally."

"The doctor is over sixty-five years old," she said.

"Mmm-hmm, of course," I said.

"So the doctor will see you on telemedicine," she said.

This surprised me. The butthole doctor was going to examine me on Zoom?

"Yep, Tuesday at three thirty," she said.

I know what you're thinking! You hear *butthole doctor* and *Zoom*, and your mind goes to one place! Well, guess what—you are right. I had to show my hole on cam.

Okay, the truth is, it wasn't the first time, but it was the first time in a clinical setting. Plus, I had been in a long-term monogamous relationship for twelve years at that point. I had forgotten my angles!

The doctor told me to show him my problem area and I was overwhelmed at how to do it. I set up my laptop, turned around, and pulled down my pants. Then I bent over and aimed my ass at my MacBook Air, hoping for the best.

"Can you see it?" I asked.

"No. You need to get higher!" he shouted.

Hoo, boy. What to do?

I have a chair in my bedroom. It's from IKEA, but it's sturdy. It has these padded arms that are about desk height. I decided I could place my knees on the arms of the chair, which put me at about the same height as the table where my laptop rested. I arched my back to create a good line for the camera. I'd learned that from Tyra Banks, who I remember called it a "booty tooch." I thought back to the actor who made fifty dollars on that pilot presentation and the patient who had been a landlord to three cotton balls for a day or more and thought, *This is karma. You deserve this.*

"Can you see it now?" I asked again.

"*No!* It's too dark!" the doctor shouted.

Of course it was dark; I had my blinds closed, for goodness' sake. My neighbors weren't paying me to do a show, and seeing as they have children, they probably didn't want to see it.

How could I find light in the darkness? What was my great hope? It was the ring light my husband bought me. I turned on that ring light and lit up my ring.

The doctor said, "Wow. This is the youngest-looking asshole I've ever seen."

Okay, he didn't actually say that, but when he referred me to a doctor who I could see masked and in person he added, "You'll like this guy. He has really small fingers."

He really did say that.

The House of Hidden Meanings

by RuPAUL*

There is a great scene in season one of *Somebody Somewhere* in which Sam discovers Joel's vision board. So much of Joel is revealed in that scene. He wants a husband and a family and a Vitamix that heats up so you can make soup. I myself have always been the type of person to enjoy a vision board. It just feels like a great way to map out your life goals. I guess I am a Joel (I am also a Miranda; go figure). Here are the items on my personal vision board:

My dog and cat snuggling consensually
Instagrammable photos of said snuggling
A country house set in the middle of a hundred acres so that I
    can take my shirt off in our private pool with no neighbors ever
    seeing me

*RuPaul was thirty-three when he released *Supermodel*.

Becoming close enough friends with Oprah that we regularly
    brunch at her Santa Barbara home

Becoming close enough friends with Adele that we do Carpool
    Karaoke with me in the James Corden seat

Becoming close enough friends with Barbra Streisand that we . . .
    actually, no. I just want to continue admiring her from afar. No
    Barbra, no Judy, no Branigan.

A gorgeous pair of shoes that conveys fashion, youth, and sex but
    also doesn't aggravate my plantar fasciitis

Cum gutters on my body. And what the hell, on my husband's
    body too.

A couch long enough for me to take a nap on

Eyebrows

Playing a character who doesn't wear pleated khaki pants

A camel-colored cloak with a shocking graphic lining

Being a judge on RuPaul's *Drag Race* 'cause I do it on my couch all
    the time

Becoming an Auntie Mame figure to one of my friends' kids where
    the relationship is so special that my friend becomes jealous of
    my bond with their child

Somehow finally getting into yoga

A high, firm ass. For me, and what the hell, for my husband too.

Playing one of the rich people on *White Lotus 7*, *Knives Out 6*, or a
    Hunger Games prequel

The courage not to clean up for my house cleaner

Turning my journals into a book so I don't have to write another book

Abdominal muscles above my cum gutters. And what the hell, for
    my husband too.

Having a paradigm shift in my internal cravings so that I am
    repulsed by refined sugars and crave broccoli

Not getting wretched farts from eating broccoli

A perfectly symmetrical face without anyone noticing I didn't have
    one previously

A yellow sheet cake with vanilla frosting that you could buy at a
supermarket. Actually, this one feels attainable. I'm gonna start
here.

That was a cheeky look at a vision board, but I have done several
sincere versions over the years. I have read books on how to "mani-
fest," read my horoscope for clues about auditions, and set goals while
lighting a candle with Annie Potts's face on it (she is the hardest-
working character actor in Hollywood). I am not afraid to go woo-woo.
Woo-woo stuff is fun and offers security for one's future. It scratches
the same itch that religion did when I was growing up. There has to be
something bigger than us that makes sense of this world.

For the first twenty years of my acting career, I would look at my
friends who were successful performers and think, *Why them and not
me? I'm just as talented as they are.* Now that I am having a tiny bit of
success, I look at my friends who are incredible performers but are
having trouble making ends meet and I think, *Why me and not them?
They're just as talented as I am.*

I want some sort of explanation for the randomness of life. How
did I get lucky enough to be born in the country I was born in and to
loving parents? How did I *not* get lucky enough to be born a hot nepo
baby? What force in the universe governs our destinies and how do we
make that force be nice to us?

I have tried personal manifestations. Mine used to be too grand:
"This year I want to book five Broadway shows and have grandchildren
even though I have no children." I figured if you were manifesting anyway, go big. Unfortunately, I must have overwhelmed the universe. Or
maybe it thought I was too greedy? What are the universe's pronouns?
Is *it* insulting?

For the past seven Januarys, I have picked a word to represent my
upcoming year. In 2017, my word was *create*, and that was the year I did
my first solo show. It worked! In 2020, I knew I wanted to set boundaries. I wanted to value my time as an artist, which meant things like

turning down auditions for jobs I did not want and not getting coffee with people I didn't really want to see. So my word for 2020 was *no*. I chose the word *no* in 2020! I know there is a debate about whether it was an animal at a food market or a lab leak, but I have to let you know that *I* caused the pandemic with my personal manifestations. Sorry 'bout that.

These things work! I'm not the only person to believe in this stuff either. An actor friend of mine told me, "I know why you got your TV show. It's because your mother died."

As you can imagine, I had some follow-up questions.

This person explained to me that my mother was good, and when she died all her energy went out into the universe and circled the people she loved the most, bringing them good things. Sort of like a karmic inherited 401(k) account, I guess? I had been incredibly depressed since my mother died, but when I stopped to think about it, I did book a lot.

I told my friend Pam this story and she said, "How come your mom's spirit got you an HBO show but when my dad died, I just got an internet-only commercial?" I guess my mother had a bigger spiritual estate.

It's beautiful to believe that your parents are still caring for you from beyond the grave, but I do worry some actor might read this and murder their mom to get a sitcom.

My sister is into the woo-woo stuff too. She often sees signs from our dead mother. She's seen more signs than Ace of Base. My sister says my mom has come to her in dreams to give her information on friendships and romantic relationships. She has found lost items after asking my mom aloud for help. My mom has consoled her in times of stress and worry. She sees signs from our mom almost every day, though occasionally, I've noted some mistakes. A week after my mother died, my dad, sister, nephews, and I went to my mom's favorite restaurant. My sister and I ordered margaritas, my mom's favorite drink, and toasted her memory. When we returned to my parents' house, we noticed the lamp on the piano was on, and we all knew it had been off when we left to go to dinner.

"Look!" my sister whispered. "Mama left a light on for us!"

I didn't have the heart to tell her that just two days before she died, my mom told me on the phone that the piano lamp had a short and kept turning on in the middle of the night. "That stupid lamp is bugging the s-h-i-t out of me!" my mom whisper-shouted, never connecting the letters to actually say the word.

My sister almost always has an empty seat in her row when she flies. When she and my mom flew together from Texas to visit me in New York, they always booked the window and aisle seat and hoped that no one would take the middle. They took a gamble that they might not sit next to each other in the hope that they might get extra space. Now that she is flying alone, my sister attributes those empty seats on the plane to my mother. Every time my sister flies, she texts me a picture of the empty seat next to her. *Sitting next to Mama on the plane*, she will say, adding heart emojis. It has been surprisingly consistent.

It's heartwarming right up to the moment I realize that my mother doesn't save *me* a seat on my flights. I was her child too and I'm much taller than my sister, so I need that extra space more than she does. Did I waste all my mom magic on getting a TV show?

I started looking for signs myself but, disappointingly, couldn't find any. About six months after my mom died, I was walking down Delancey Street. There was a lot of litter on that block, which was not uncommon, but I noticed that there was an empty box of L'Oréal hair dye next to the trash can. That's a rather uncommon piece of trash to see next to a public trash can, don't you think? Oh, you don't? Well, I was really looking for a sign, so it felt unusual to me.

My mom had been dyeing her hair since I was an infant. Apparently, being pregnant with me made her light blond hair turn to dishwater blond, so she liked to brighten it. She used L'Oréal light ash blond 9½A. I knew because she sent me to buy it at the drugstore on more than a few occasions. I always wondered if people thought I was buying it for my own hair. Part of me wanted them to think I was adventurous enough to do such a thing and part of me feared they thought I was gay enough to do such a thing. Errands were complicated for me.

Could this box be my sign from my mother? As I approached the box, I thought, *Please be light ash blond 9½A. Please be light ash blond 9½A.* I looked down at the box. It wasn't light ash blond 9½A. It was some different color with the word *auburn* in it. Was this my sign? If so, what did it mean? Was my mom trying to tell me to get lowlights?

I needed to see a sign like my sister got because I'd felt a lot of guilt after my mother's passing. The deep pit of emotions stemmed from the Bucks County Playhouse in New Hope, Pennsylvania, as emotions often do. I had been asked to play the narrator and Eddie in a production of *The Rocky Horror Show* there in October of 2016. The show was a fall tradition and starred some pretty impressive Broadway vets. I was set to start rehearsals on a Tuesday. My mom called the Friday before to tell me she was being put in hospice.

"I guess I should drop out of this play," I said to her. "Shouldn't I?"

"*No!*" my mother said. "Do *not* change your life over my illness. Go do the play!"

I wish I had said, *No. You are the most important person in my life. I am coming down to Texas immediately.*

Instead, I said, "Okay, I'll go do this job in Pennsylvania."

I had chosen my career over my mother. My regional-theater career. It was ridiculous. This wasn't some life-changing job. This was a fine job. A job you took to get weeks toward your health insurance. A job you took so you could pick apples on your day off. A job you took when there was nothing better going on in your life. This was not a job you took while your mother was dying of pulmonary fibrosis several states away.

I called my agent and told her my mom was in hospice, but I would still be doing *Rocky Horror*.

"No," she said. "Don't do this job. Go home and be with your mother."

So *that* was why I didn't do the job. Because my agent told me not to. My *agent*. Her entire profession was notorious for caring more about making a dime than about a human life and even she was like, *Sweet Lord, go be with your mother, you monster!*

I was surprised when my mother died. I don't know why. She was on oxygen. She had a terminal illness. She was in hospice care. None of those warnings got it through my thick skull that she could possibly leave us. She was too much of a force not to be present anymore. I purchased a ticket to San Antonio for Wednesday, but she died on Monday. I wasn't in Bucks County, but I wasn't with my mom either.

I think a part of me believed that if I did *Rocky Horror*, my mom wouldn't die. Some sort of "the show must go on" twisted logic? Maybe my mom felt that too. No, she didn't. I know what she was thinking. She was thinking what she always thought: *What is best for my kids?*

I actually did *Rocky Horror* at Bucks County the next year. Wow. That show has not aged well in terms of consent, trans issues, or disability rights. We were doing this in October of 2017, right around the time the Ronan Farrow article about Harvey Weinstein came out. It's hard not to feel a little creepy when it's the dawn of the #MeToo era and you're watching a scene where Frank-N-Furter pretends to be Brad to fool Janet into having sex with him. That said, I did get to go apple picking.

I finally got a sign from my mom. In the spring of 2019, two and a half years after my mom died, my sister and I went to my parents' house because my father had been in a rehab facility for several months. We were letting a family friend stay in the house so that it didn't sit empty because—and this feels like an important metaphor—without anyone living there to scare them off, vultures had roosted on the roof. Vultures. You know, the birds associated with death? Is it still a metaphor when it's so blatantly obvious?

We were cleaning things out of cupboards and cabinets to make room for our family friend and I found something I had never seen before: a Ziploc bag full of brochures from sites we'd visited on our family vacation to Washington, DC, and New York City in June 1989. On the very top were two mementos from New York. One was a *Playbill* from the Broadway show we saw—the first show I ever saw on Broadway! It was called *Metamorphosis*, based on the Franz Kafka novella, and starred Mikhail Baryshnikov as Gregor. It was a modern ballet . . . I think? Misha was swinging and climbing around the set while talking about being a roach. Let's just say you can understand how the tickets were at the discounted ticket booth.

Just beneath the *Playbill* was a newspaper. I don't remember my mom grabbing it on our trip, but there it was: the *West Village Observer: The New York Gay Monthly*. The cover displayed a huge banner celebrating the twentieth anniversary of Stonewall; I found it a few months before the fiftieth anniversary of Stonewall.

I remember our family being in New York City on gay pride weekend in 1989. We were on the subway heading downtown from our Times Square hotel. A group of men wearing all white got on the train. Some had white coveralls, others white overalls with no shirt on. Many of them wore white high-top sneakers with bunched-up white socks. I associated that particular shoe/sock combo with women teaching aerobics classes, but here were a group of men wearing it.

I was filled with self-hating revulsion. If I was too close to them, would they recognize me, just like I had recognized my health teacher? I pretended not to see them. I silently prayed my parents didn't see them either, but my mom excitedly said, "Oh! They must be going to the gay pride parade!" I remember that so clearly. She sounded happy for them. There was no judgment in her voice.

The gay guys didn't think there was no judgment, unfortunately. They shouted, "Yeah, *bitch*! We are! Get used to it!"

That didn't stop her from loving that trip to New York, though. Their taunts didn't stop her from being accepting of LGBTQ people. And it didn't stop her from taking souvenirs for her kids to find thirty years later, including this gay paper celebrating pride. There was no arguing about it. This was a sign from my mom just for me. A bag full of Broadway and New York gay stuff? It was almost as obvious as the vultures on the roof.

I got a little weepy.

Only that sign didn't change anything for me. I was still sad my mom was dead. I was still sad my dad couldn't walk anymore. I still felt guilty that I hadn't come to Texas right away. I was still in debt. I still wasn't skinny. I still didn't have a full-time job performing.

The only difference was that I was . . . oh, crap, I was grateful. That's what the sign gave me. Gratitude to have had a mom who loved me unconditionally, especially because nobody else in the world had wanted to for quite some time. In that moment, I had enough gratitude to fill up multiple gratitude journals.

Ugh, I guess all those self-help books were right. I guess gratitude is important. So start a gratitude journal and write, *I'm thankful I have an autoimmune disorder that isn't lupus* at the top. Or don't start one—this isn't a self-help book. I guess my point is just that I miss my mom because she was a really great mom. I read *I'm Glad My Mom Died* by Jennette McCurdy and *Mommie Dearest* by Christina Crawford. A good mom is not guaranteed. I grieve because I lost someone who loved me. I am so grateful I had her. So I guess in the end, my mom sent me a sign to remind me of her silly song: "An attitude of gratitude will get you through the day."

I suppose that is a lesson I need to hear again. I just found out that *Somebody Somewhere* will not be coming back for a fourth season. We don't get to return to Manhattan, Kansas, and find out what is going on with Sam, Joel, and Fred Rococo. I'm sad about it, but I can't say I'm surprised. Frankly, the surprise is that the show was made at all, much less that we had three seasons. It is a quiet show that isn't focused on plot. It stars middle-aged, nonfamous people in boring clothes. It's a huge accomplishment that HBO let us make this tiny show.

So I guess I need to be reminded that, while I am grieving the end of the show, I should be grateful to have had it at all.

Still, I'm scared. I've done the math to see when famous people got their break and compared it to my age when I got mine, but what if *Somebody Somewhere* isn't my break? What if the show was just a weird, wonderful anomaly where I actually got to play a character who had a rich interior life? What if that never comes my way again? What if I have to go back to guest-star roles playing the bitchy customer-service representative? What if I have to go back to teaching improv? Or, worse, waiting tables?

Comparison is the thief of joy. I've highlighted my ability to compare and then despair in the pages of this book. Julie Andrews was how old when she got *My Fair Lady*? How is that helpful? We are completely different actors in different times and with different circumstances. I have to focus on my own life.

And is there even such thing as a break? When I looked up Sarah Silverman's break, I noted that she landed *Saturday Night Live* at twenty-three but was fired one season later. After that, her Wikipedia page shows a lot of hard work that she mostly created herself. Careers are about longevity, not bright flashes of promise in our youth. I cried in the Ding-Dong Dorm to mourn the loss of the show after season one, and I was wrong about that. More good things can happen.

I am clearly career obsessed and I should focus on my personal life a little more. But, like, I don't have kids. And having kids so I can *not* think about work doesn't seem like a healthy reason to have kids. I do have pets and spend a lot of time showering them with intense affection that my dog tolerates and my cat does not.

I sometimes take my dog to the dog park so she can have fun and let out her energy. The ten-minute walk to the park, however, takes us twenty-five minutes because she is constantly sniffing other dogs' piss along the way. I used to keep saying to her, "Come *on*, Yvonne De Carlo! We have to get to the dog park for your enrichment!" But then I watched a video on Instagram that said dogs *need* to smell other dogs' urine because they communicate through it. My dog can tell the other dogs' genders, ages, everything they ate that day, and even what kind of mood they were in! It's dog social media. So the long walk to the dog run to give my dog enrichment *is* enrichment for my dog.

In my own life, I am constantly focused on reaching the destination, but *life* is the journey. If I am not paying attention to the journey, I am not living life. There is no job, no person, no piece of real estate or perfect family that will make someone happy forever. I set a goal to get a boyfriend by the time I turned thirty-two. I found one. I even married him. But I still have to work at the marriage. I have to check in with him and make sure we are connecting and prioritize the relationship. It felt so good seeing Renée Zellweger and Colin Firth kissing at the end of *Bridget Jones's Diary* as snow fell around them, but did you see the sequels? It's not a happily-ever-after situation, because there is no such thing. Life is a series of peaks and valleys. My HBO show was certainly a peak, and knowing it is over is absolutely a valley, but just like Bridget Jones, I'm going to keep going. Also, I'll probably eat some Tate's cookies and drink some wine to mourn it like Ms. Jones would.

The universe said, "Don't give up," when I turned forty, and now on the brink of fifty (December birthday), I need to listen to that again. I don't know if things that I believe are signs are actually signs. After all, life is pretty messy. Sometimes a cigar is just a cigar. So let me just say that I am grateful for my messy life. I am grateful to you for letting me talk about mine. If we ever run into each other, feel free to tell me stories about your life—it's only fair. And if you really want a moral from this book, let it be this: If you show your butthole on camera, ask for more than fifty dollars (unless it's for a doctor).

Acknowledgments

I can't believe I wrote a book. It's shocking, no? Obviously, it took a village, and I have to thank my editor, Mindy Marqués, for taking a chance on me and for not judging my poor grammar, spelling, and vocabulary (I could have sworn *themic* was a word). Thank you to Simon & Schuster, specifically to Johanna Li and Hana Park, for reading and holding my hand through this process. Thank you to my agent, Robert Guinsler, who believed I had a book in me, and then I did!

Thank you to my beautiful friend Sue Simon for letting me write much of this book at her house outside of the city—it was invaluable. Thank you, Laurie Woolery, the director of three of my solo shows, who focused the content that made it into this book. Thanks to the members of my writers' group, Anything But Poetry, who have read versions of this non-poetic book since the proposal: Mark Sam Rosenthal, Peter Grosz, Kathy Fusco, Sid Karger, Brian Sloan, Sabrina Martin, Irina Arnaut, Chris Kipiniak, and Panio Gianopoulos. Eric Bernat, Katie Dippold, Brian Gallivan, John Flynn, Bobby Moynihan, and Chris Kula brainstormed great cover ideas for me (sorry we didn't use any of them), and Colleen McHugh brainstormed hundreds of subtitles, one of which we used!

My bro Murray Hill wrote his book in tandem with me in the middle of Naperville, Illinois, and Amy Heidt, Sarah Gunderson, Tara Copeland, Nadia Quinn, and Jenn Harris let me talk through chapters in this book via Marco Polo. Thank you to Ryan Donovan and Erik Gensler for Deb, and thank you to Larry Krone and Jim Andralis for T and C. Huge, never-ending attitude of gratitude to Melissa Callaway, not only for finding most of the photos in this book and scanning them in but also for being a wonderful friend and sister to me my entire life, and of course thank you to Neil, Beverly, and Vonnie, my family. I love you very much for making my life so rich (and thank you, Neil, for telling me how to make photos into TIFF, whatever the hell that means).

Thank you to all of the people who let me tell my side of our stories, and thank you to you for reading this book!